The Java™ Application Programming Interface, Volume 2

The Java™ Series

Lisa Friendly, Series Editor
Bill Joy, Technical Advisor

The Java™ Programming Language
Ken Arnold and James Gosling

The Java™ Application Programming Interface, Volume 1
Core Packages
James Gosling, Frank Yellin, and the Java Team

The Java™ Application Programming Interface, Volume 2
Window Toolkit and Applets
James Gosling, Frank Yellin, and the Java Team

The Java™ Language Specification
James Gosling, Bill Joy, and Guy Steele

The Java™ Virtual Machine Specification
Tim Lindholm and Frank Yellin

The Java™ Tutorial
Object-Oriented Programming for the Internet
Mary Campione and Kathy Walrath

The Java™ Class Libraries
An Annotated Reference
Patrick Chan and Rosanna Lee

The Java™ FAQ
Frequently Asked Questions
Jonni Kanerva

The Java™ Application Programming Interface, Volume 2

Window Toolkit and Applets

James Gosling
Frank Yellin
The Java Team

Addison-Wesley Publishing Company
Reading, Massachusetts • Menlo Park, California • New York
Don Mills, Ontario • Harlow, England • Amsterdam • Bonn
Sydney • Singapore • Tokyo • Madrid • San Juan
Seoul • Milan • Mexico City • Tiapei

THE PUBLISHER OFFERS DISCOUNTS ON THIS BOOK WHEN ORDERED IN QUANTITY FOR SPECIAL SALES. FOR MORE INFORMATION, PLEASE CONTACT:

CORPORATE AND PROFESSIONAL PUBLISHING GROUP

ADDISON-WESLEY PUBLISHING COMPANY

ONE JACOB WAY

READING, MASSACHUSETTS 01867

ISBN: 0-201-63459-7

Text printed on recycled and acid-free paper.

12345678910 - MA -99989796

First Printing, May 1996

In memory of FirstPerson, Inc.
To the Java Team, past and present

Volume II

Contents

Volume I

Contents

Exceptions

Errors

Package java.io 187

Classes

Interfaces

Exceptions

Preface

A Bit of History

JAVA is a general-purpose object-oriented programming language. Its syntax is similar to C and C++, but it omits semantic features that make C and C++ complex, confusing, and insecure. Java was initially developed to address the problems of building software for small distributed systems to embed in consumer devices. As such it was designed for heterogeneous networks, multiple host architectures, and secure delivery. To meet these requirements, compiled Java code had to survive transport across networks, operate on any client, and assure the client that it was safe to run.

The popularization of the World Wide Web helped catapult these attributes of Java into the limelight. The Internet demonstrated how interesting, media-rich content could be made accessible in simple ways. Web browsers like Mosaic enabled millions of people to roam the Net and made Web surfing part of popular culture. At last there was a medium where what you saw and heard was essentially the same whether you were using a Mac, PC, or UNIX machine, connected to a high-speed network or a modem.

With popularity comes scrutiny, however, and soon Web enthusiasts felt that the content supported by the Web's HTML document format was too limited. HTML extensions, such as forms, only highlighted those limitations while making it clear that no browser could include all the features users wanted. Extensibility was the answer. At just this time the Java programming language found itself looking for another application.

Sun's HotJava browser was developed to showcase Java's interesting properties by making it possible to embed Java programs inside Web pages. These Java programs, known as *applets*, are transparently downloaded into the HotJava browser along with the HTML pages in which they appear. Before being accepted by the browser, applets are carefully checked to make sure they are safe. Like HTML pages, compiled Java programs are network- and platform-independent. Applets behave the same regardless of where they come from or what kind of machine they are being loaded into.

The Web community quickly noticed that Java was something new and important. With Java as the extension language, a Web browser could have limitless capabilities. Programmers could write an applet once and it would then run on any machine, anywhere. Visitors to Java-powered Web pages could use the content found there with confidence that nothing would damage their machine.

With applets as the initial focus, Java has demonstrated a new way to make use of the Internet to distribute software. This new paradigm goes beyond browsers. We believe it is an innovation with the potential to change the course of computing.

Tim Lindholm
Senior Staff Engineer
JavaSoft
April 1996

About the Java Series

THE Java Series provides definitive reference documentation for Java programmers and end users. These books are written by members of the Java Team and published under the auspices of JavaSoft, a Sun Microsystems business. The World Wide Web allows Java documentation to be made available over the Internet, either by downloading or as hypertext. Nevertheless, the world wide interest in Java led us to write these books.

To learn the latest about Java or to download the latest Java release, visit our World Wide Web site at `http://java.sun.com`. For updated information about the Java Series, including sample code, errata, and previews of forthcoming books, visit `http://java.sun.com/books/Series`.

We would like to thank the Corporate and Professional Publishing Group at Addison-Wesley for their partnership in putting together the Series. Our editor, Mike Hendrickson, and his team have done a superb job of navigating us through the world of publishing. The support of James Gosling, Ruth Hennigar, and Bill Joy of Sun Microsystems ensured that this series would have the resources it needed to be successful. A personal note of thanks to my children, Christopher and James, for putting a positive spin on the many trips to my office during the development of the Series.

Lisa Friendly
Series Editor

Contributors to the API

Designers of Classes and Interfaces

Tom Ball

Lee Boynton

Patrick Chan

David Connelly

Pavani Diwanji

Amy Fowler

James Gosling

Jim Graham

Herb Jellinek

Bill Joy

Tim Lindholm

Jonathan Payne

Sami Shaio

Doug Stein

Arthur van Hoff

Chris Warth

Frank Yellin

Testers

Carla Schroer

Kevin Smith

Vijay Srinivasan

Headley Williamson

Layout and Supplemental Documentation

Lisa Friendly

James Gosling

Jonni Kanerva

Guy Steele

Annette Wagner

Kathy Walrath

Frank Yellin

About the Java Packages

These two volumes describe the Java Application Programming Interface (API), a standard set of libraries for writing Java programs. The libraries evolved over several years of writing Java code to implement a variety of systems, ranging from consumer device networks to animated user interfaces to operating systems to compilers. In 1995, the libraries were reorganized to support Internet programming, and thus the Java API was created. Many people, both from inside and outside Sun, have been involved in the design of the API.

Although the API has not reached perfection yet, we believe it is useful and hope to make it a ubiquitous layer, available to all Internet applications.

Have fun.

Arthur van Hoff

Introduction

These books are reference manuals for Java application and applet programmers. To make full use of them you should be familiar with the Java programming language and its core concepts such as object orientation, garbage collection, and multithreading.

The extent of the API and the choice of functionality have been driven by several factors. First and foremost, the API should be simple and easy to use. Parts of the API, such as the support for multithreading, might introduce functionality that is new to you, but we think you will find these new concepts simpler and easier to use than in most other programming environments.

The libraries in these books are the first generation of an API for writing Internet programs. A simple form of an Internet program is an *applet*—a small Java program that can be embedded in an HTML page.

The API has been designed with the Java language in mind. Important Java features such as object orientation, garbage collection, and multithreading played an important role in the API design. Instead of taking existing libraries and simply rewriting them in Java, we designed and implemented the API with full use of the Java language.

For Java 1.0, we have tried to stay away from certain complex functionality, such as video and 3D, so that library implementations can be ported easily. We can include only functionality that is not proprietary and that is easily implemented on many platforms.

We expect to add to the API, but not to subtract from it or change its behavior. The API documented in this book will remain available to all Java programs through future releases.

If you have ideas about how the API could be improved or how to implement some of the missing functionality, we would like to hear from you. Please send your ideas and implementations to java@java.sun.com.

Using These API Books

Do not get overwhelmed by the multitude of classes documented in these two books. The structure of the Java language encourages the programmer to break up libraries into many classes, each describing a small part of the functionality. The class diagrams in the following section are a good starting point for getting an impression of the relationships among classes.

As you design and implement Java programs, you should write short test programs to verify your understanding of the classes. When in doubt, try it out!

The Java web site, `http://java.sun.com/`, contains many excellent and sometimes interactive explanations that can help you along. Another good source of information is the newsgroup `comp.lang.java`.

Package Overview

This overview describes each package in the Java API, starting with the most general-purpose package (`java.lang`) and ending with one of the most specialized packages (`java.applet`). Each package groups classes and interfaces that have similar functionality. The API contains the following packages:

- ◆ Volume I: Core Packages
  - ◆ java.lang: The Java Language Package
  - ◆ java.io: The Java I/O Package
  - ◆ java.util: The Java Utility Package
  - ◆ java.net: The Java Networking Package
- ◆ Volume II: Window Toolkit and Applets
  - ◆ java.awt: The Abstract Window Toolkit (AWT) Package
  - ◆ java.awt.image: The AWT Image Package
  - ◆ java.awt.peer: The AWT Peer Package
  - ◆ java.applet: The Java Applet Package

java.lang: THE JAVA LANGUAGE PACKAGE

The `java.lang` package provides the classes and interfaces that form the core of the Java language and the Java Virtual Machine. For example, the classes `Object`, `String`, and `Thread` are used by almost every program and are closely intertwined with the Java language definition. Other `java.lang` classes define the exceptions and errors that the Java Virtual Machine can throw.

Another set of `java.lang` classes provide wrappers for primitive types. For example, the `Integer` class provides objects to contain `int` values.

Still other classes, such as `ClassLoader`, `Process`, `Runtime`, `Security-Manager`, and `System`, provide access to system resources. For other generally useful classes, see the `java.util` package.

The `java.lang` package is imported automatically into every Java program.

`java.io`: THE JAVA I/O PACKAGE

The `java.io` package provides a set of input and output (I/O) streams used to read and write data to files or other I/O sources. Java streams are byte oriented and the classes defined here can be chained to implement more sophisticated stream functionality.

`java.util`: THE JAVA UTILITY PACKAGE

The `java.util` package contains a collection of utility classes and related interfaces. It includes classes that provide generic data structures (`Dictionary`, `Hashtable`, `Stack`, `Vector`), string manipulation (`StringTokenizer`), and calendar and date utilities (`Date`).

　　　The `java.util` package also contains the `Observer` interface and `Observable` class, which allow objects to notify one another when they change.

`java.net`: THE JAVA NETWORKING PACKAGE

The `java.net` package contains networking classes and interfaces, including classes that represent a URL and a URL connection, classes that implement a socket connection, and a class that represents an Internet address.

`java.awt`: THE ABSTRACT WINDOW TOOLKIT (AWT) PACKAGE

The `java.awt` package provides the standard graphical user interface (GUI) elements such as buttons, lists, menus, and text areas. It also includes containers (such as windows and menu bars) and higher-level components (such as dialogs for opening and saving files). The AWT contains two more packages: `java.awt.image` and `java.awt.peer`.

`java.awt.image`: THE AWT IMAGE PACKAGE

The `java.awt.image` package contains classes and interfaces for performing sophisticated image processing. These classes and interfaces can be used by applications that need to create or manipulate images and colors.

`java.awt.peer`: THE AWT PEER PACKAGE

The `java.awt.peer` package contains interfaces used to connect AWT components to their window system–specific implementations (such as Motif widgets).

　　　Unless you are creating a window system–specific implementation of the AWT, you should not need to use the interfaces in the `java.awt.peer` package.

`java.applet`: THE APPLET PACKAGE

The `java.applet` package contains classes and interfaces for creating applets.

References

IEEE Standard for Binary Floating-Point Arithmetic, ANSI/IEEE Std. 754-1985. Available from Global Engineering Documents, 15 Inverness Way East, Englewood, Colorado 80112-5704 USA, 303-792-2181 or 800-854-7179.

The Unicode Standard: Worldwide Character Encoding, Version 1.0, Volume 1 ISBN 0-201-56788-1 and Volume 2 ISBN 0-201-60845-6. Additional information about Unicode 1.1 may be found at `ftp://unicode.org`.

Class Hierarchy Diagrams

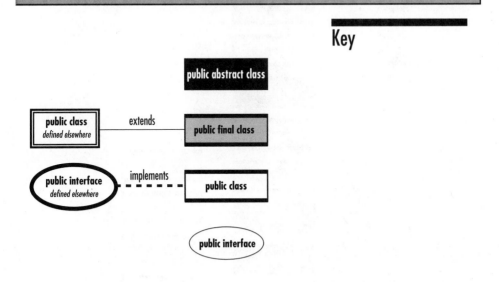

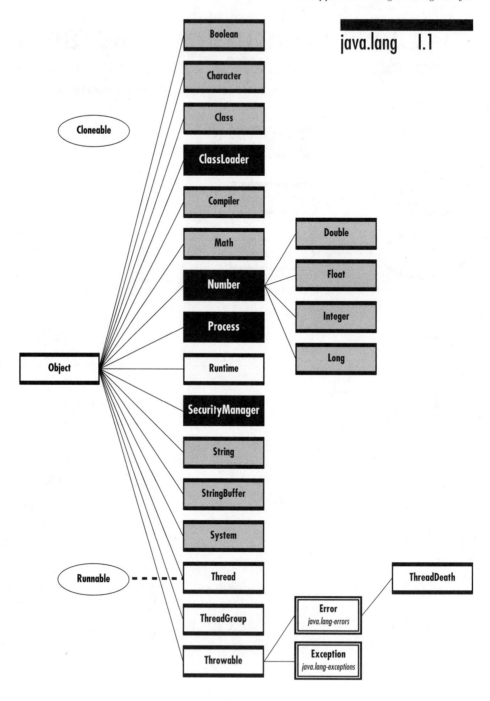

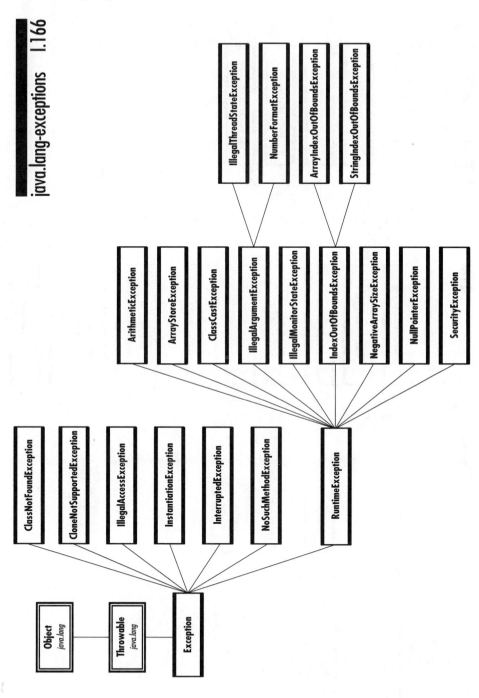

java.lang-exceptions   I.166

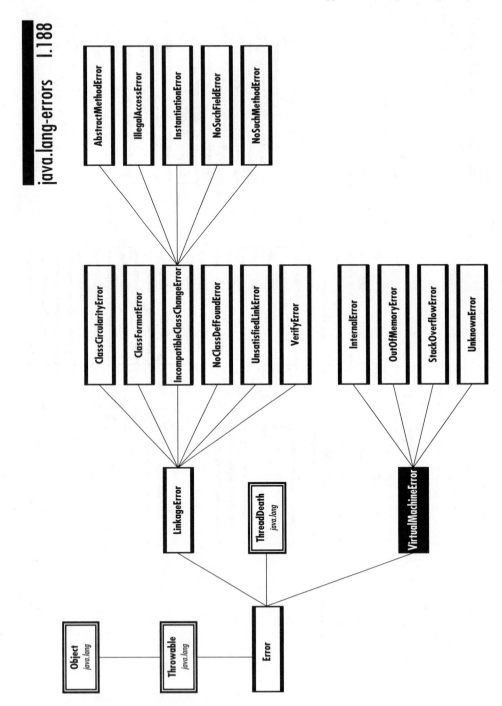

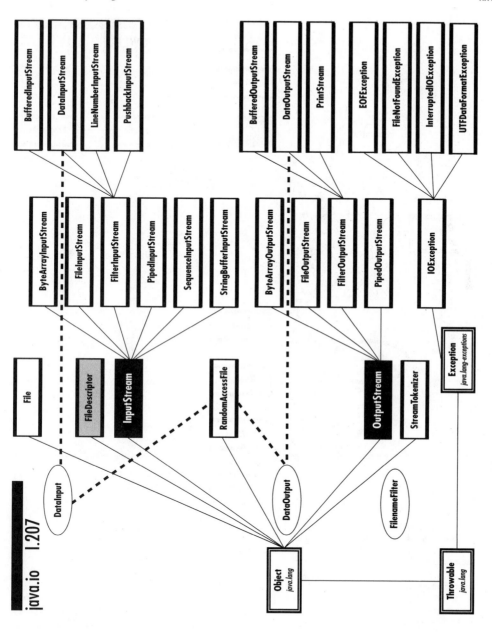

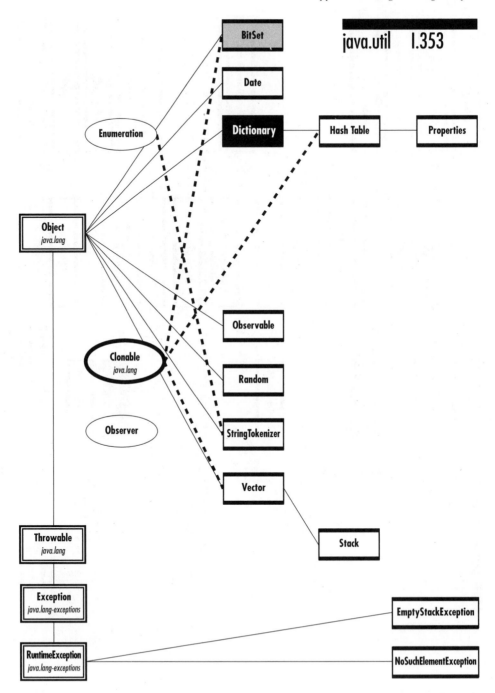

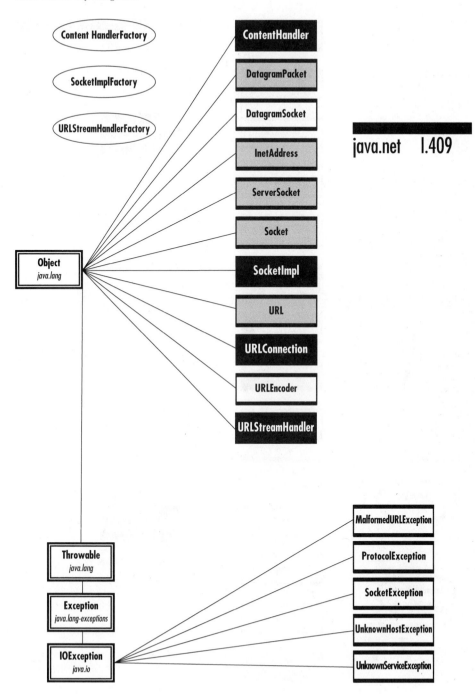

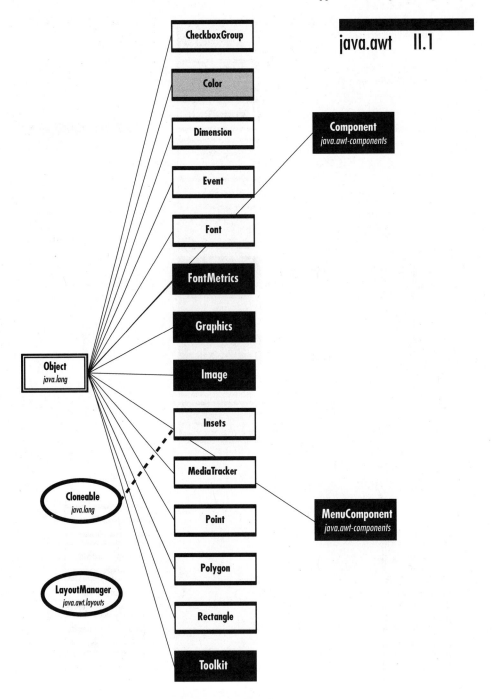

java.awt   II.1

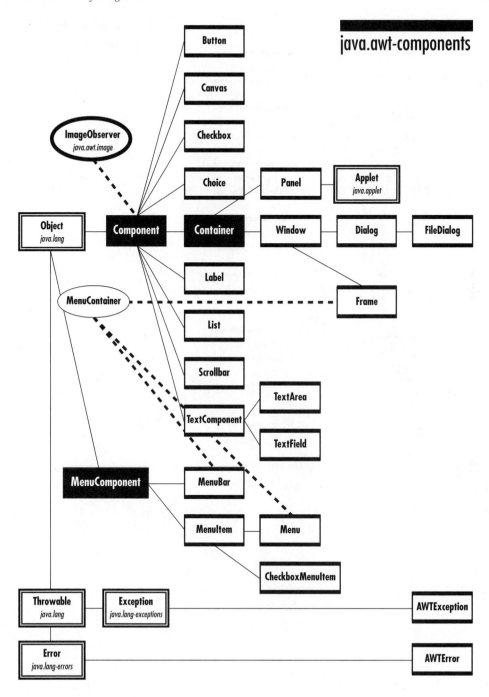

java.awt-layouts

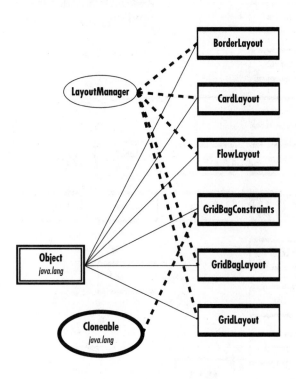

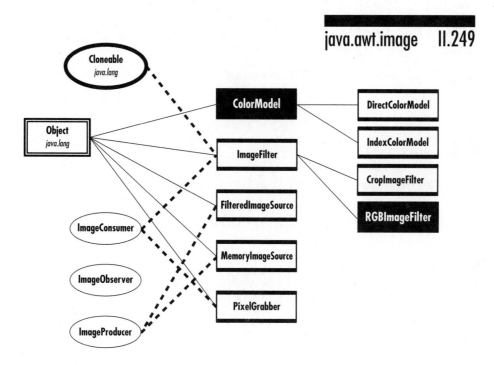

java.awt.image   II.249

java.awt.peer   II.311

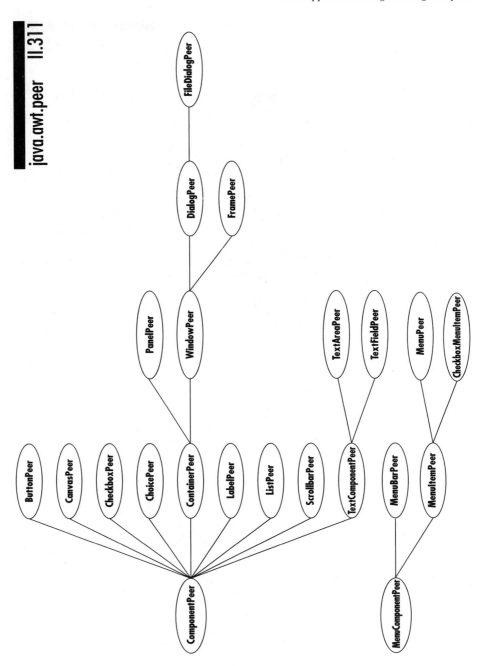

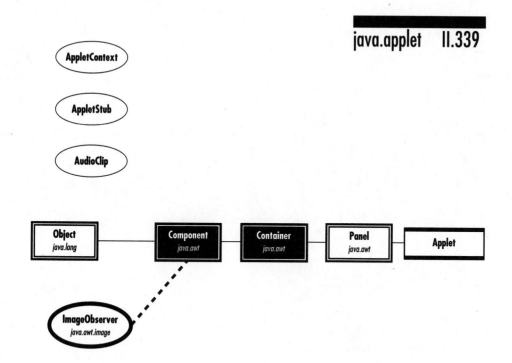

CHAPTER 1

Package java.awt

THE java.awt package provides an easy-to-use set of standard graphical user interface (GUI) elements. It includes both basic components and higher-level interfaces. In addition, applications can build their own custom components.

The classes and interfaces in this package can be divided into several groups:

- **Basic Graphical Elements:** These are the classes that provide the basic components of a user interface. The classes in this group include `Button` **(II-§1.2)**, `List` **(II-§1.27)**, `TextArea` **(II-§1.38)**, `TextField` **(II-§1.40)**, `Label` **(II-§1.26)**, `Checkbox` **(II-§1.5)**, and `CheckboxGroup` **(II-§1.6)**. All graphical elements are a subclass of `Component` **(II-§1.10)**.

- **Advanced Graphical Elements:** These classes provide even more sophisticated graphical elements in a user interface, though they are somewhat more complex to set up and use. These classes include `Canvas` **(II-§1.3)**, `Scrollbar` **(II-§1.37)**, `Choice` **(II-§1.8)**, and `FileDialog` **(II-§1.15)**.

- **Menu Bars:** These classes let applications create menu bars that provide easy access to frequently used commands. These classes include `Menu` **(II-§1.29)**, `MenuBar` **(II-§1.30)**, `MenuItem` **(II-§1.32)**, and `CheckboxMenuItem` **(II-§1.6)**. Each of these is a subclass of `MenuComponent` **(II-§1.31)**. `Menu` and `MenuBar` implement the `MenuContainer` **(II-§1.44)** interface.

- **Text Input:** The `TextArea` **(II-§1.38)** and `TextField` **(II-§1.40)** classes provide an easy means for the user to input textual information. Both of these are subclasses of `TextComponent` **(II-§1.39)**.

- **Basic Graphics Concepts:** These classes encapsulate basic graphical descriptions of objects. These classes include `Point` **(II-§1.34)**, `Dimension` **(II-§1.13)**, `Font` **(II-§1.17)**, `Rectangle` **(II-§1.36)**, `Polygon` **(II-§1.35)**, `Color` **(II-§1.9)**, `Insets` **(II-§1.25)**, and `FontMetrics` **(II-§1.18)**.

  The `Graphics` **(II-§1.20)** object abstracts a graphics context for drawing and writing text to components in a machine-independent way.

1

♦ **Images:** The Image **(II-§1.24)** class provides for the asynchronous drawing of images. Applications that need further control over the drawing of images can use the MediaTracker **(II-§1.28)**.

♦ **Containers:** Certain graphical elements are not interesting in themselves, but can contain other components. The most simple such container is Panel **(II-§1.33)**. Other containers supported by the AWT are Frame **(II-§1.19)**, Dialog **(II-§1.12)** and Window **(II-§1.42)**. All containers are subclasses of Container **(II-§1.11)**.

♦ **Layout Managers:** Layout managers allow an application to control the way in which components are arranged within a container, even if the container is resized. The simplest layout managers are FlowLayout **(II-§1.16)** and GridLayout **(II-§1.23)**. Slightly more complicated are BorderLayout **(II-§1.1)** and CardLayout **(II-§1.4)**.

The GridBagLayout **(II-§1.22)** is the most flexible and complicated layout manager. It uses constraints encapsulated in objects called GridBagConstraints **(II-§1.21)** to give the application almost complete control over the layout of the components.

All layout managers must implement the LayoutManager **(II-§1.43)** interface.

♦ **Events:** All external events, such as keyboard input and mouse movements, are presented to an application via Event **(II-§1.14)** instances.

♦ **The Toolkit:** Rather than defining what buttons, check boxes, and other graphical components look like, the Abstract Window Toolkit uses a special Toolkit **(II-§1.41)** class to define the components' look and feel. Applications can modify the underlying component implementations without having to change the functionality presented by the AWT.

♦ **Exceptions and Errors:** The exception AWTException **(II-§1.45)** indicates that the AWT has encountered a problem. The more serious AWTError **(II-§1.46)** indicates a serious, irrecoverable error.

Applications that need to perform more sophisticated image processing or color processing can also use the routines found in the java.awt.image package **(II-§1)**. Applications that want to redefine components to have a different appearance or behavior can use the Toolkit class **(II-§1.41)** together with the interfaces defined in the package java.awt.peer **(II-§3)**.

1.1 Class BorderLayout

```
public class java.awt.BorderLayout
    extends java.lang.Object (I-§1.12)
    implements java.awt.LayoutManager (II-§1.43)
{
    // Constructors
    public BorderLayout();                              §1.1.1
    public BorderLayout(int hgap, int vgap);            §1.1.2

    // Methods
    public void addLayoutComponent(String name,         §1.1.3
                              Component comp);
    public void layoutContainer(Container target);      §1.1.4
    public Dimension minimumLayoutSize(Container target);  §1.1.5
    public Dimension preferredLayoutSize(Container target); §1.1.6
    public void removeLayoutComponent(Component comp);  §1.1.7
    public String toString();                           §1.1.8
}
```

A border layout lays out a container using members named "North", "South", "East", "West", and "Center". The components are laid out according to their preferred sizes and the constraints of the container's size. The "North" and "South" components may be stretched horizontally; the "East" and "West" components may be stretched vertically; the "Center" component may stretch both horizontally and vertically to fill any space left over.

Here is an example of five buttons in an applet laid out using the BorderLayout layout manager:

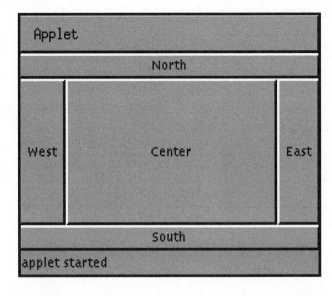

The code for this applet is the following:

```java
import java.awt.*;
import java.applet.Applet;

public class buttonDir extends Applet {
  public void init() {
    setLayout(new BorderLayout());
    add("North", new Button("North"));
    add("South", new Button("South"));
    add("East", new Button("East"));
    add("West", new Button("West"));
    add("Center", new Button("Center"));
  }
}
```

Constructors

BorderLayout   §1.1.1

    public BorderLayout()

Constructs a new border layout.

BorderLayout   §1.1.2

    public BorderLayout(int hgap, int vgap)

Creates a new border layout with the specified horizontal and vertical gaps.
The horizontal and vertical gaps specify the space between the components.

PARAMETERS:

hgap: the horizontal gap.
vgap: the vertical gap.

Methods

addLayoutComponent §1.1.3

```
public void addLayoutComponent(String name, Component comp)
```

Adds the specified component to this border layout using the indicated tag.

For border layouts, the tag should be one of "North", "South", "East", "West", or "Center". Any other tag is ignored.

Most applications do not call this method directly. This method is called when a component is added to a container using the two-argument add method (**II-§1.11.3**).

PARAMETERS:

name: a tag understood by the layout manager.
comp: the component to be added.

layoutContainer §1.1.4

```
public void layoutContainer(Container target)
```

Lays out the container argument using this border layout.

This method reshapes the components in the specified container in order to satisfy the constraints of this BorderLayout object. The "North" and "South" components, if any, are placed at the top and bottom of the container, respectively. The "West" and "East" components are then placed on the left and right, respectively. Finally, the "Center" object is placed in any remaining space in the middle.

Most applications do not call this method directly. This method is called when a container calls its layout method (**II-§1.11.11**).

PARAMETERS:

target: the container in which to do the layout.

SEE ALSO:

Container (**II-§1.11**).

minimumLayoutSize §1.1.5

```
public Dimension minimumLayoutSize(Container target)
```

Determines the minimum size of the `target` container using this layout manager.

This method is called when a container calls its `minimumSize` method (**II-§1.11.14**). Most applications do not call this method directly.

PARAMETERS:

`target`: the container in which to do the layout.

RETURNS:

the minimum dimensions needed to lay out the subcomponents of the specified container.

SEE ALSO:

`Container` (**II-§1.11**).
`preferredLayoutSize` (**II-§1.1.6**).

preferredLayoutSize §1.1.6

```
public Dimension preferredLayoutSize(Container target)
```

Determines the preferred size of the `target` container using this layout manager.

This method is called when a container calls its `preferredSize` method (**II-§1.11.17**). Most applications do not call this method directly.

PARAMETERS:

`target`: the container in which to do the layout.

RETURNS:

the preferred dimensions to lay out the subcomponents of the specified container.

SEE ALSO:

`Container` (**II-§1.11**).
`minimumLayoutSize` (**II-§1.1.5**).

removeLayoutComponent §1.1.7

```
public void removeLayoutComponent(Component comp)
```

Removes the specified component from this border layout. This method is called when a container calls its `remove` (**II-§1.11.19**) or `removeAll` (**II-§1.11.20**) methods. Most applications do not call this method directly.

PARAMETERS:

`comp`: the component to be removed.

toString §1.1.8

    `public String toString()`

    RETURNS:

    a string representation of this border layout.

    OVERRIDES:

    `toString` in class `Object` **(I-§1.12.9)**.

1.2 Class Button

```
public class java.awt.Button
    extends java.awt.Component (II-§1.10)
{
    // Constructors
    public Button();                              §1.2.1
    public Button(String label);                  §1.2.2

    // Methods
    public void addNotify();                      §1.2.3
    public String getLabel();                     §1.2.4
    protected String paramString();               §1.2.5
    public void setLabel(String label);           §1.2.6
}
```

This class creates a labeled button. The application can cause some action to happen when the button is pushed. Below are three views of a "`Quit`" button in Solaris:

The first shows the button normally. The second shows the button when it has the input focus: the darkening of the outline lets the user know that this is an active object. The third shows the button when the user clicks the mouse over the button, and thus requests that the mouse's action(s) be performed.

When a button is pushed and released,[1] AWT sends an action event (**II-§1.14.11**) to the button. This event's target is the button, and its object is the string label of the button. An application should override the `action` method (**II-§1.10.1**) of the button or of one of its containing windows in order to cause some action to occur.

Constructors

Button   §1.2.1

    `public Button()`

      Creates a button with no label.

Button   §1.2.2

    `public Button(String label)`

      Creates a button with the indicated label.

    PARAMETERS:

    `label`: a string label for the button.

Methods

addNotify   §1.2.3

    `public void addNotify()`

      This method calls the `createButton` method (**II-§1.41.3**) of the button's toolkit (**II-§1.10.20**) in order to create a `ButtonPeer` (**II-§3.1**) for this button. This peer allows the application to change the look of a button without changing its functionality.

      Most applications do not call this method directly.

    OVERRIDES:

    `addNotify` in class `Component` (**II-§1.10.2**).

getLabel   §1.2.4

    `public String getLabel()`

    RETURNS:

    the label of this button, or `null` if this button has no label.

    SEE ALSO:

    `setLabel` (**II-§1.2.6**).

---

[1] In Java 1.0, the AWT does not send mouse or focus events to a button. In Java 1.1, the AWT sends the button all mouse, keyboard, and focus events that occur over it.

paramString §1.2.5

 `protected String paramString()`

  Returns the parameter string representing the state of this button. This string is useful for debugging.

 RETURNS:

 the parameter string of this button.

 OVERRIDES:

 paramString in class Component **(II-§1.10.51)**.

setLabel §1.2.6

 `public void setLabel(String label)`

  Changes this button's label to be the `String` argument.

 PARAMETERS:

 label: the new label, or null for no label.

 SEE ALSO:

 getLabel **(II-§1.2.4)**.

1.3 Class Canvas

```
public class java.awt.Canvas
    extends java.awt.Component (II-§1.10)
{
    // Constructors
    public Canvas();                            §1.3.1

    // Methods
    public void addNotify();                    §1.3.2
    public void paint(Graphics g);              §1.3.3
}
```

 A Canvas component represents a blank rectangular area of the screen onto which the application can draw or from which the application can trap input events from the user.

 An application must subclass the Canvas class in order to get useful functionality such as creating a custom component. The paint method **(II-§1.3.3)** must be overridden in order to perform custom graphics on the canvas.

 The AWT sends the canvas all mouse, keyboard, and focus events that occur over it. The gotFocus **(II-§1.10.21)**, lostFocus **(II-§1.10.39)**, keyDown **(II-§1.10.31)**, keyUp **(II-§1.10.32)**, mouseEnter **(II-§1.10.43)**, mouseExit **(II-§1.10.44)**, mouseMove **(II-§1.10.45)**, mouseDrag **(II-§1.10.42)**, mouseDown **(II-§1.10.41)**, and mouseUp **(II-§1.10.46)** methods may be overridden in order to catch user events.

Constructors

Canvas   §1.3.1

```
public Canvas()
```
Creates a canvas.

Methods

addNotify   §1.3.2

```
public void addNotify()
```
This method calls the `createCanvas` method (**II-§1.41.4**) of the canvas's toolkit (**II-§1.10.20**) in order to create a `CanvasPeer` (**II-§3.2**) for this canvas. This peer allows the application to change the look of a canvas without changing its functionality.

Most applications do not call this method directly.

OVERRIDES:

addNotify in class Component (**II-§1.10.2**).

paint   §1.3.3

```
public void paint(Graphics g)
```
This method is called to repaint this canvas. Most applications that subclass `Canvas` should override this method in order to perform some useful operation.

The `paint` method provided by `Canvas` redraws this canvas's rectangle in the background color.

The graphics context's $\langle 0, 0 \rangle$ point is the top-left corner of this canvas. Its clipping region is the area of the context.

PARAMETERS:

g: the graphics context.

OVERRIDES:

paint in class Component (**II-§1.10.49**).

1.4 Class CardLayout

```
public class java.awt.CardLayout
    extends java.lang.Object (I-§1.12)
    implements java.awt.LayoutManager (II-§1.43)
{
    // Constructors
    public CardLayout();                                    §1.4.1
    public CardLayout(int hgap, int vgap);                  §1.4.2

    // Methods
    public void addLayoutComponent(String name,            §1.4.3
                                Component comp);
    public void first(Container target);                   §1.4.4
    public void last(Container target);                    §1.4.5
    public void layoutContainer(Container target);         §1.4.6
    public Dimension minimumLayoutSize(Container target);  §1.4.7
    public void next(Container target);                    §1.4.8
    public Dimension preferredLayoutSize(Container target);§1.4.9
    public void previous(Container target);                §1.4.10
    public void removeLayoutComponent(Component comp);     §1.4.11
    public void show(Container target, String name);       §1.4.12
    public String toString();                              §1.4.13
}
```

A layout manager for a container that contains several "cards." Only one card is visible at a time, allowing the application to flip through the cards.

Constructors

CardLayout   §1.4.1

```
public CardLayout()
```

Creates a new card layout.

CardLayout   §1.4.2

```
public CardLayout(int hgap, int vgap)
```

Creates a new card layout with the specified horizontal and vertical gaps. The horizontal gaps are placed at the left and right edges. The vertical gaps are placed at the top and bottom edges.

PARAMETERS:

hgap: the horizontal gap.
vgap: the vertical gap.

Methods

---

addLayoutComponent   §1.4.3

```
public void addLayoutComponent(String name, Component comp)
```
  Adds the specified component to the card layout using the indicated name tag. The show method (**II-§1.4.12**) can be used to display the component with the specified tag.

PARAMETERS:

name: a tag understood by the layout manager.
comp: the component to be added.

first   §1.4.4

```
public void first(Container target)
```
  Flips to the first card of the container.

PARAMETERS:

target: the container in which to do the layout.

last   §1.4.5

```
public void last(Container target)
```
  Flips to the last card of the container.

PARAMETERS:

target: the container in which to do the layout.

layoutContainer   §1.4.6

```
public void layoutContainer(Container target)
```
  Lays out the container argument using this card layout.
  Each component in the target container is reshaped to be the size of the container minus space for surrounding insets, horizontal gaps, and vertical gaps.
  Most applications do not call this method directly. This method is called when a container calls its layout method (**II-§1.11.11**).

PARAMETERS:

target: the container in which to do the layout.

minimumLayoutSize   §1.4.7

> `public Dimension minimumLayoutSize(Container target)`

Determines the minimum size of the container argument using this card layout.

The minimum width of a card layout is the largest minimum width of the cards in the container, plus twice the horizontal gap, plus the left and right insets.

The minimum height of a card layout is the largest minimum height of the cards in the container, plus twice the vertical gap, plus the top and bottom insets.

Most applications do not call this method directly. This method is called when a container calls its `layout` method (**II-§1.11.11**).

PARAMETERS:

`target`: the container in which to do the layout.

RETURNS:

the minimum dimensions needed to lay out the subcomponents of the specified container.

SEE ALSO:

`preferredLayoutSize` (**II-§1.4.9**).

next   §1.4.8

> `public void next(Container target)`

Flips to the next card of the specified container. If the currently visible card is the last one, this method flips to the first card in the layout.

PARAMETERS:

`target`: the container in which to do the layout.

preferredLayoutSize   §1.4.9

`public Dimension preferredLayoutSize(Container target)`

Determines the preferred size of the container argument using this card layout.

The preferred width of a card layout is the largest preferred width of the cards in the container, plus twice the horizontal gap, plus the left and right insets.

The preferred height of a card layout is the largest preferred height of the cards in the container, plus twice the vertical gap, plus the top and bottom insets.

Most applications do not call this method directly. This method is called when a container calls its `preferredSize` method **(II-§1.11.17)**.

PARAMETERS:

`target`: the container in which to do the layout.

RETURNS:

the preferred dimensions to lay out the subcomponents of the specified container.

SEE ALSO:

`minimumLayoutSize` **(II-§1.4.7)**.

previous   §1.4.10

`public void previous(Container target)`

Flips to the previous card of the specified container. If the currently visible card is the first one, this method flips to the last card in the layout.

PARAMETERS:

`target`: the container in which to do the layout.

removeLayoutComponent   §1.4.11

`public void removeLayoutComponent(Component comp)`

Removes the specified component from the layout.

This method is called when a container calls its `remove` **(II-§1.11.19)** or `removeAll` **(II-§1.11.20)** methods. Most applications do not call this method directly.

PARAMETERS:

`comp`: the component to be removed.

show §1.4.12

```
public void show(Container target, String name)
```

Flips to the component that was added to this layout (**II-§1.4.3**) with the specified name tag. If no such component exists, then nothing happens.

PARAMETERS:

`target`: the container in which to do the layout.

`name`: a tag.

toString §1.4.13

```
public String toString()
```

RETURNS:

a `String` representation of this card layout.

OVERRIDES:

toString in class `Object` (**I-§1.12.9**).

1.5 Class Checkbox

```
public class java.awt.Checkbox
    extends java.awt.Component (II-§1.10)
{
    // Constructors
    public Checkbox();                                  §1.5.1
    public Checkbox(String label);                      §1.5.2
    public Checkbox(String label, CheckboxGroup group,  §1.5.3
                    boolean state);

    // Methods
    public void addNotify();                            §1.5.4
    public CheckboxGroup getCheckboxGroup();            §1.5.5
    public String getLabel();                           §1.5.6
    public boolean getState();                          §1.5.7
    protected String paramString();                     §1.5.8
    public void setCheckboxGroup(CheckboxGroup g);      §1.5.9
    public void setLabel(String label);                 §1.5.10
    public void setState(boolean state);                §1.5.11
}
```

A check box is a graphical component that has an "on" (`true`) and "off" (`false`) state. Clicking on the check box changes its state from "on" to "off" or from "off" to "on."

For example, the code:

```
setLayout(new GridLayout(3, 1));
add(new Checkbox("one", null, true));
add(new Checkbox("two"));
add(new Checkbox("three"));
```

produces the following three check boxes:

The button labeled one is "on." The other two are "off."

When the check box is clicked,[2] AWT sends an action event **(II-§1.14.11)** to the check box. This event's target is the check box, and its object is a `Boolean` **(I-§1.1)** giving the new state of the check box. An application should override the `action` method **(II-§1.10.1)** of the check box or of one of its containing windows in order to cause some action to occur.

Optionally, several check boxes can be grouped together into a `Checkbox-Group` **(II-§1.6)**. At most one button in a group can be in the "on" state at any given time. Pushing a check box to turn it "on" forces any other check box in the group that is "on" to become "off."

Constructors

Checkbox   §1.5.1

  `public Checkbox()`

  Creates a check box with no label. The check box is set to "off" and is not part of any check box group.

Checkbox   §1.5.2

  `public Checkbox(String label)`

  Creates a check box with the specified label. The check box is set to "off" and is not part of any check box group.

PARAMETERS:

`label`: a string label for the check box, or `null` for no label.

---

2. In Java 1.0, the AWT does not send mouse or focus events to a check box. In Java 1.1, the AWT sends the check box all mouse, keyboard, and focus events that occur over it.

Checkbox   §1.5.3

```
public Checkbox(String label, CheckboxGroup group,
                boolean state)
```

Creates a check box with the specified label, in the specified check box group, and set to the specified state.

PARAMETERS:

`label`: a string label for the check box, or `null` for no label.

`group`: this check box's check box group, or `null` for no group.

`state`: the initial state of the check box: `true` indicates "on"; `false` indicates "off."

Methods

addNotify   §1.5.4

```
public void addNotify()
```

This method calls the `createCheckbox` method **(II-§1.41.5)** of the check box's toolkit **(II-§1.10.20)** in order to create a CheckboxPeer **(II-§3.4)** for this button. This peer allows the application to change the look of a check box without changing its functionality.

Most applications do not call this method directly.

OVERRIDES:

`addNotify` in class Component **(II-§1.10.2)**.

getCheckboxGroup   §1.5.5

```
public CheckboxGroup getCheckboxGroup()
```

Determines this check box's group.

RETURNS:

this check box's group, or `null` if it is not part of a check box group.

SEE ALSO:

setCheckboxGroup **(II-§1.5.9)**.

getLabel   §1.5.6

```
public String getLabel()
```

RETURNS:

the label of this check box, or `null` if this check box has no label.

SEE ALSO:

setLabel **(II-§1.5.10)**.

getState   §1.5.7

```
public boolean getState()
```

Determines if this check box is "on" or "off."

RETURNS:

the state of this check box; the value `true` indicates "on," `false` indicates "off."

SEE ALSO:

setState (**II-§1.5.11**).

paramString   §1.5.8

```
protected String paramString()
```

Returns the parameter string representing the state of this check box. This string is useful for debugging.

RETURNS:

the parameter string of this check box.

OVERRIDES:

paramString in class Component (**II-§1.10.51**).

setCheckboxGroup   §1.5.9

```
public void setCheckboxGroup(CheckboxGroup g)
```

Sets the group of this check box to be the specified check box group. If this check box is already in a different check box group, it is first taken out of that group.

PARAMETERS:

g: the new check box group, or `null` to remove the check box from any check box group.

SEE ALSO:

getCheckboxGroup (**II-§1.5.5**).

setLabel   §1.5.10

```
public void setLabel(String label)
```

Sets this check box's label to be the string argument.

PARAMETERS:

label: the new label, or `null` for no label.

SEE ALSO:

getLabel (**II-§1.5.6**).

setState §1.5.11

```
public void setState(boolean state)
```

Sets this check box to the specified `boolean` state: `true` indicates "on"; `false` indicates "off."

PARAMETERS:

`state`: the boolean state of the check box.

SEE ALSO:

`getState` (II-§1.5.7).

1.6 Class CheckboxGroup

```
public class java.awt.CheckboxGroup
    extends java.lang.Object (I-§1.12)
{
    // Constructors
    public CheckboxGroup();                          §1.6.1

    // Methods
    public Checkbox getCurrent();                    §1.6.2
    public void setCurrent(Checkbox box);            §1.6.3
    public String toString();                        §1.6.4
}
```

This class is used to group together a set of `Checkbox` buttons.

Exactly one check box button in a `CheckboxGroup` can be in the "on" state at any given time. Pushing any button turns it "on" and forces any other button that is "on" to become "off."

For example, the code:

```
setLayout(new GridLayout(3, 1));
CheckboxGroup cbg = new CheckboxGroup();
add(new Checkbox("one",   cbg, true));
add(new Checkbox("two",   cbg, false));
add(new Checkbox("three", cbg, false));
```

produces the following three check boxes:

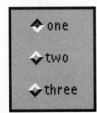

When a check box in a check box group is clicked, AWT sends an action event (**II-§1.14.11**) to that check box. This event's target is the check box, and its object is a value equal to `Boolean.TRUE` (**I-§1.1.2**). No action event is sent to a check box (if any) that is turned off. An application should override the `action` method (**II-§1.10.1**) of the check box or of one of its parent containers in order to cause some action to occur.

Constructors

CheckboxGroup   §1.6.1

    `public CheckboxGroup()`

        Creates a new `CheckboxGroup`.

Methods

getCurrent   §1.6.2

    `public Checkbox getCurrent()`

    RETURNS:

    the check box in this check box group that is currently "on," or `null` if all are "off."

setCurrent   §1.6.3

    `public void setCurrent(Checkbox box)`

        If the indicated check box argument belongs to this check box group, this method sets that check box to be "on," and all other checkboxes in this group to be "off."

        If the check box argument is `null` or belongs to a different check box group, then this method does nothing.

    PARAMETERS:

    box: the Checkbox to set "on."

toString   §1.6.4

    `public String toString()`

    RETURNS:

    a string representation of this check box group.

    OVERRIDES:

    `toString` in class `Object` (**I-§1.12.9**).

1.7 Class CheckboxMenuItem

```
public class java.awt.CheckboxMenuItem
    extends java.awt.MenuItem (II-§1.32)
{
    // Constructors
    public CheckboxMenuItem(String label);               §1.7.1

    // Methods
    public void addNotify();                             §1.7.2
    public boolean getState();                           §1.7.3
    public String paramString();                         §1.7.4
    public void setState(boolean state);                 §1.7.5
}
```

This class represents a check box that can be included in a menu. Clicking on the check box in the menu changes its state from "on" to "off" or from "off" to "on."

The picture of a menu bar (page II-181) shows a menu. The item labeled Check shows a check box menu item in its "off" state.

When a check box menu item is clicked, the AWT sends an action event (**II-§1.14.11**) to the check box menu item's containing frame. The event's target is the check box menu item, and its object is the string label of the check box.

Constructors

CheckboxMenuItem   §1.7.1

```
public CheckboxMenuItem(String label)
```

Creates a check box with the specified label. The check box is initially set to "off."

PARAMETERS:

label: a string label for the check box menu item, or null for an unlabeled menu item.

Methods

---

addNotify   §1.7.2

`public void addNotify()`

This method calls the `createCheckboxMenuItem` method **(II-§1.41.6)** of the check box's toolkit **(II-§1.10.20)** in order to create a `CheckboxMenuItemPeer` **(II-§3.3)** for this button. This peer allows the application to change the look of a check box menu item without changing its functionality.

Most applications do not call this method directly.

OVERRIDES:

`addNotify` in class `MenuItem` **(II-§1.32.2)**.

getState   §1.7.3

`public boolean getState()`

Determines whether this check box menu item is "on" or "off."

RETURNS:

the state of this check box menu item: `true` indicates "on," `false` indicates "off."

paramString   §1.7.4

`public String paramString()`

Returns the parameter string representing the state of this check box menu item. This string is useful for debugging.

RETURNS:

the parameter string of this check box menu item.

OVERRIDES:

`paramString` in class `MenuItem` **(II-§1.32.8)**.

setState   §1.7.5

`public void setState(boolean state)`

Sets this check box menu item to the specifed boolean state: `true` indicates "on"; `false` indicates "off."

PARAMETERS:

`state`: the boolean state of this check box menu item.

1.8 Class Choice

```
public class java.awt.Choice
    extends java.awt.Component (II-§1.10)
{
    // Constructors
    public Choice();                                    §1.8.1

    // Methods
    public void addItem(String item);                   §1.8.2
    public void addNotify();                            §1.8.3
    public int countItems();                            §1.8.4
    public String getItem(int index);                   §1.8.5
    public int getSelectedIndex();                      §1.8.6
    public String getSelectedItem();                    §1.8.7
    protected String paramString();                     §1.8.8
    public void select(int pos);                        §1.8.9
    public void select(String str);                     §1.8.10
}
```

The Choice class presents a pop-up menu of choices. The current choice is displayed as the title of the menu.

For example, the code:

```
Choice ColorChooser = new Choice();
ColorChooser.addItem("Green");
ColorChooser.addItem("Red");
ColorChooser.addItem("Blue");
```

produces the following pop-up menu, after it has been added to a panel:

In the picture, "Green" is the current choice. Pushing the mouse button down on it causes a menu to appear with the current choice highlighted.

After any choice is made,[3] AWT sends an action event (**II-§1.14.11**) to the choice menu. The event's target is the choice menu, and its object is the string label of the currently selected item. An application should override the `action` method (**II-§1.10.1**) of the choice menu or of one of its parent containers in order to cause some action to occur.

Constructors

Choice   §1.8.1

```
public Choice()
```

Creates a new choice menu. The menu initially has no items in it.

By default, the first item added to the choice menu becomes the selected item, until a different selection is made by the user or by calling one of the `select` methods (**II-§1.8.9, §1.8.10**).

Methods

addItem   §1.8.2

```
public void addItem(String item)
```

Adds an item to this choice menu.

PARAMETERS:

`item`: the item to be added.

THROWS:

`NullPointerException` (**I-§1.40**)
if the item's value is equal to null.

addNotify   §1.8.3

```
public void addNotify()
```

This method calls the `createChoice` method (**II-§1.41.7**) of this object's toolkit (**II-§1.10.20**) in order to create a `ChoicePeer` (**II-§3.5**) for this button. This peer allows the application to change the look of a choice menu without changing its functionality.

Most applications do not call this method directly.

OVERRIDES:

`addNotify` in class `Component` (**II-§1.10.2**).

[3.] In Java 1.0, the AWT does not send mouse or focus events to a choice menu. In Java 1.1, the AWT sends the choice menu all mouse, keyboard, and focus events that occur over it.

countItems §1.8.4

```
public int countItems()
```

RETURNS:

the number of menu items in this choice menu.

SEE ALSO:

getItem (**II-§1.8.5**).

getItem §1.8.5

```
public String getItem(int index)
```

PARAMETERS:

index: the index.

RETURNS:

the string at the specified index in this choice menu.

SEE ALSO:

countItems (**II-§1.8.4**).

getSelectedIndex §1.8.6

```
public int getSelectedIndex()
```

RETURNS:

the index of the currently selected item in this choice menu.

SEE ALSO:

getSelectedItem (**II-§1.8.7**).

getSelectedItem §1.8.7

```
public String getSelectedItem()
```

RETURNS:

a string representation of the currently selected item in this choice menu.

SEE ALSO:

getSelectedIndex (**II-§1.8.6**).

paramString §1.8.8

```
protected String paramString()
```

Returns the parameter string representing the state of this choice menu. This string is useful for debugging.

RETURNS:

the parameter string of this choice menu.

OVERRIDES:

paramString in class Component (**II-§1.10.51**).

select   §1.8.9

`public void select(int pos)`

Sets the selected item in this choice menu to be the item at the specified position.

PARAMETERS:

`pos`: the selected item position.

THROWS:

`IllegalArgumentException` (**I-§1.32**)
if the choice item position is invalid.

SEE ALSO:

`getSelectedItem` (**II-§1.8.7**).
`getSelectedIndex` (**II-§1.8.6**).

select   §1.8.10

`public void select(String str)`

Sets the selected item in this choice menu to be the choice whose name is equal (**I-§1.16.14**) to the specified string. If more than one choice is equal to the specified string, the one with the smallest index whose name matches is selected.

PARAMETERS:

`str`: the string to select.

SEE ALSO:

`getSelectedItem` (**II-§1.8.7**).
`getSelectedIndex` (**II-§1.8.6**).

1.9 Class Color

```
public final class java.awt.Color
    extends java.lang.Object (I-§1.12)
{
    // Fields
    public final static Color black;              §1.9.1
    public final static Color blue;               §1.9.2
    public final static Color cyan;               §1.9.3
    public final static Color darkGray;           §1.9.4
    public final static Color gray;               §1.9.5
    public final static Color green;              §1.9.6
    public final static Color lightGray;          §1.9.7
    public final static Color magenta;            §1.9.8
    public final static Color orange;             §1.9.9
    public final static Color pink;               §1.9.10
    public final static Color red;                §1.9.11
    public final static Color white;              §1.9.12
    public final static Color yellow;             §1.9.13

    // Constructors
    public Color(float r, float g, float b);      §1.9.14
    public Color(int rgb);                         §1.9.15
    public Color(int r, int g, int b);            §1.9.16

    // Methods
    public Color brighter();                       §1.9.17
    public Color darker();                         §1.9.18
    public boolean equals(Object obj);            §1.9.19
    public int getBlue();                          §1.9.20
    public static Color getColor(String nm);      §1.9.21
    public static Color getColor(String nm, Color v);  §1.9.22
    public static Color getColor(String nm, int v);    §1.9.23
    public int getGreen();                         §1.9.24
    public static Color                            §1.9.25
        getHSBColor(float h, float s, float b);
    public int getRed();                           §1.9.26
    public int getRGB();                           §1.9.27
    public int hashCode();                         §1.9.28
    public static int HSBtoRGB(float hue,          §1.9.29
                   float saturation, float brightness);
    public static float[] RGBtoHSB(int r, int g, int b,  §1.9.30
                            float hsbvals[]);
    public String toString();                      §1.9.31
}
```

This class encapsulates colors using the RGB format. In this format, the red, blue, and green components of a color are each represented by an integer in the range 0–255. The value 0 indicates no contribution from this primary color. The value 255 indicates the maximum intensity of this color component.

Fields

black   §1.9.1
```
public final static Color black = new Color(0, 0, 0)
```
The color black.

blue   §1.9.2
```
public final static Color blue = new Color(0, 0, 255)
```
The color blue.

cyan   §1.9.3
```
public final static Color cyan = new Color(0, 255, 255)
```
The color cyan.

darkGray   §1.9.4
```
public final static Color darkGray = new Color(64, 64, 64)
```
The color dark gray.

gray   §1.9.5
```
public final static Color gray = new Color(128, 128, 128)
```
The color gray.

green   §1.9.6
```
public final static Color green = new Color(0, 255, 0);
```
The color green.

lightGray   §1.9.7
```
public final static Color lightGray
    = new Color(192, 192, 192)
```
The color light gray.

magenta   §1.9.8
```
public final static Color magenta = new Color(255, 0, 255)
```
The color magenta.

orange   §1.9.9

    `public final static Color orange = new Color(255, 200, 0)`

      The color orange.

pink   §1.9.10

    `public final static Color pink = new Color(255, 175, 175)`

      The color pink.

red   §1.9.11

    `public final static Color red = new Color(255, 0, 0)`

      The color red.

white   §1.9.12

    `public final static Color white = new Color(255, 255, 255)`

      The color white.

yellow   §1.9.13

    `public final static Color yellow = new Color(255, 255, 0)`

      The color yellow.

Constructors

Color   §1.9.14

    `public Color(float r, float g, float b)`

Creates a color with the specified red, green, and blue values, where each of the values is in the range 0.0–1.0. The value 0.0 indicates no contribution from the primary color component. The value 1.0 indicates the maximum intensity of the primary color component.

The actual color used in rendering depends on finding the best match given the color space available for a given output device.

PARAMETERS:

r: the red component.

g: the green component.

b: the blue component.

Color   §1.9.15

```
public Color(int rgb)
```

Creates a color with the specified RGB value, where the red component is in bits 16–23 of the argument, the green component is in bits 8–15 of the argument, and the blue component is in bits 0–7. The value 0 indicates no contribution from the primary color component.

The actual color used in rendering depends on finding the best match given the color space available for a given output device.

PARAMETERS:

rgb: an integer giving the red, green, and blue components.

SEE ALSO:

getRGBdefault in class ColorModel (**II-§2.1.9**).

Color   §1.9.16

```
public Color(int r, int g, int b)
```

Creates a color with the specified red, green, and blue components. The three arguments must each be in the range 0–255.

The actual color used in rendering depends on finding the best match given the color space available for a given output device.

PARAMETERS:

r: the red component.
g: the green component.
b: the blue component.

Methods

brighter   §1.9.17

```
public Color brighter()
```

RETURNS:

a brighter version of this color.

darker   §1.9.18

```
public Color darker()
```

RETURNS:

a darker version of this color.

equals §1.9.19

    public boolean equals(Object obj)

The result is `true` if and only if the argument is not `null` and is a `Color` object that has the same red, green, and blue value as this object.

PARAMETERS:

`obj`: the object to compare with.

RETURNS:

`true` if the objects are the same; `false` otherwise.

OVERRIDES:

`equals` in class `Object` (I-§1.12.3).

getBlue §1.9.20

    public int getBlue()

Returns the blue component of this color. The result is in the range 0 to 255.

RETURNS:

the blue component of this color.

getColor §1.9.21

    public static Color getColor(String nm)

Finds a color in the system properties.

The first argument is treated as the name of a system property to be obtained as if by the method `System.getProperty` (I-§1.18.10). The string value of this property is then interpreted as an integer value [see `Integer.getInteger` (I-§1.8.10) for information on how the string value is interpreted as an integer]. This integer is then converted to a color by using the `Color` constructor that takes one integer argument (II-§1.9.15).

If the specified property is not found, or could not be parsed as an integer, then `null` is returned.

PARAMETERS:

`nm`: the property name.

RETURNS:

the color value of the property.

getColor   §1.9.22

```
public static Color getColor(String nm, Color v)
```

Finds a color in the system properties.

The first argument is treated as the name of a system property to be obtained as if by the method System.getProperty (**I-§1.18.10**). The string value of this property is then interpreted as an integer value [see Integer.getInteger (**I-§1.8.10**) for information on how the string value is interpreted as an integer]. This integer is then converted to a color by using the Color constructor that takes one integer argument (**II-§1.9.15**).

If the specified property is not found, or could not be parsed as an integer, then the color specified by the second argument is returned instead.

PARAMETERS:

nm: the property name.
v: default Color value.

RETURNS:

the Color value of the property.

getColor   §1.9.23

```
public static Color getColor(String nm, int v)
```

Finds a color in the system properties.

The first argument is treated as the name of a system property to be obtained as if by the method System.getProperty (**I-§1.18.10**). The string value of this property is then interpreted as an integer value [see Integer.getInteger (**I-§1.8.10**) for information on how the string value is interpreted as an integer].

If the specified property is not found, or could not be parsed as an integer, then the integer value v is used instead.

This integer is then converted to a color by using the Color constructor that takes one integer argument (**II-§1.9.15**).

PARAMETERS:

nm: the property name.
v: the default color value.

RETURNS:

the new color.

getGreen   §1.9.24

```
public int getGreen()
```

Returns the green component of this color. The result is in the range 0 to 255.

RETURNS:

the green component of this color.

getHSBColor

```
public static Color getHSBColor(float h, float s, float b)
```

Determines the hue, saturation, and brightness of a color. Each of the three components should be a floating-point number in the range $0.0 \le h, s, b \le 1.0$.

PARAMETERS:

h: the hue component.
s: the saturation of the color.
b: the brightness of the color.

RETURNS:

the color object with the specified hue, saturation, and brightness.

getRed

```
public int getRed()
```

Returns the red component of this color. The result is in the range 0 to 255.

RETURNS:

the red component of this color.

getRGB

```
public int getRGB()
```

Calculates a single integer representing the red, green, and blue components of this color. The red, green, and blue components of the color are each scaled to be a value between 0 (absence of the color) and 255 (complete saturation). The integer returned is the number between 0 and 0xFFFFFF such that bits 16–23 are the red value, bits 8–15 are the green value, and bits 0–7 are the blue value.

RETURNS:

an integer representing this color.

SEE ALSO:

getRGBdefault in class ColorModel (**II-§2.1.9**).

hashCode

```
public int hashCode()
```

RETURNS:

a hash code value for this object.

OVERRIDES:

hashCode in class Object (**I-§1.12.6**).

HSBtoRGB §1.9.29

```
public static int
HSBtoRGB(float hue, float saturation, float brightness)
```

Converts a color specified by hue, saturation, and brightness to a corresponding RGB value.

PARAMETERS:

hue: the hue component of the color.
saturation: the saturation of the color.
brightness: the brightness of the color.

RETURNS:

the RGB value (**II-§1.9.27**) of the color with the indicated hue, saturation, and brightness.

RGBtoHSB §1.9.30

```
public static float[]
RGBtoHSB(int r, int g, int b, float hsbvals[])
```

Converts a color specified by its red, green, and blue components to hue, saturation, and brightness.

If the hsbvals argument is null, then a new array is allocated to return the result. Otherwise, hsbvals is returned as the result, with the values put into that array.

PARAMETERS:

r: the red component of the color.
g: the green component of the color.
b: the blue component of the color.
hsbvals: the array to be used to return the three HSB values, or null.

RETURNS:

an array of three elements containing the hue, saturation, and brightness (in that order), of the color with the indicated red, green, and blue components.

SEE ALSO:

getRGBdefault in class ColorModel (**II-§2.1.9**).
getRGB (**II-§1.9.27**).

toString §1.9.31

```
public String toString()
```

RETURNS:

a string representation of this color.

OVERRIDES:

toString in class Object (**I-§1.12.9**).

1.10 Class Component

```
public abstract class java.awt.Component
    extends java.lang.Object (I-§1.12)
    implements java.awt.image.ImageObserver (II-§2.11)
{
    // Methods
    public boolean action(Event evt, Object what);           §1.10.1
    public void addNotify();                                 §1.10.2
    public Rectangle bounds();                               §1.10.3
    public int checkImage(Image image,                       §1.10.4
                    ImageObserver observer);
    public int checkImage(Image image,                       §1.10.5
                    int width, int height,
                    ImageObserver observer);
    public Image createImage(ImageProducer producer);        §1.10.6
    public Image createImage(int width, int height);         §1.10.7
    public void deliverEvent(Event evt);                     §1.10.8
    public void disable();                                   §1.10.9
    public void enable();                                    §1.10.10
    public void enable(boolean cond);                        §1.10.11
    public Color getBackground();                            §1.10.12
    public ColorModel getColorModel();                       §1.10.13
    public Font getFont();                                   §1.10.14
    public FontMetrics getFontMetrics(Font font);            §1.10.15
    public Color getForeground();                            §1.10.16
    public Graphics getGraphics();                           §1.10.17
    public Container getParent();                            §1.10.18
    public ComponentPeer getPeer();                          §1.10.19
    public Toolkit getToolkit();                             §1.10.20
    public boolean gotFocus(Event evt, Object what);         §1.10.21
    public boolean handleEvent(Event evt);                   §1.10.22
    public void hide();                                      §1.10.23
    public boolean imageUpdate(Image img, int flags,         §1.10.24
                        int x, int y,
                        int w, int h);

    public boolean inside(int x, int y);                     §1.10.25
    public void invalidate();                                §1.10.26
    public boolean isEnabled();                              §1.10.27
    public boolean isShowing();                              §1.10.28
    public boolean isValid();                                §1.10.29
    public boolean isVisible();                              §1.10.30
    public boolean keyDown(Event evt, int key);              §1.10.31
    public boolean keyUp(Event evt, int key);                §1.10.32
    public void layout();                                    §1.10.33
    public void list();                                      §1.10.34
    public void list(PrintStream out);                       §1.10.35
    public void list(PrintStream out, int indent);           §1.10.36
    public Component locate(int x, int y);                   §1.10.37
```

```
    public Point location();                                       §1.10.38
    public boolean lostFocus(Event evt, Object what);              §1.10.39
    public Dimension minimumSize();                                §1.10.40
    public boolean mouseDown(Event evt, int x, int y);             §1.10.41
    public boolean mouseDrag(Event evt, int x, int y);             §1.10.42
    public boolean mouseEnter(Event evt, int x, int y);            §1.10.43
    public boolean mouseExit(Event evt, int x, int y);             §1.10.44
    public boolean mouseMove(Event evt, int x, int y);             §1.10.45
    public boolean mouseUp(Event evt, int x, int y);               §1.10.46
    public void move(int x, int y);                                §1.10.47
    public void nextFocus();                                       §1.10.48
    public void paint(Graphics g);                                 §1.10.49
    public void paintAll(Graphics g);                              §1.10.50
    protected String paramString();                                §1.10.51
    public boolean postEvent(Event evt);                           §1.10.52
    public Dimension preferredSize();                              §1.10.53
    public boolean                                                 §1.10.54
        prepareImage(Image image, ImageObserver observer);
    public boolean                                                 §1.10.55
        prepareImage(Image image, int width, int height,
                     ImageObserver observer);
    public void print(Graphics g);                                 §1.10.56
    public void printAll(Graphics g);                              §1.10.57
    public void removeNotify();                                    §1.10.58
    public void repaint();                                         §1.10.59
    public void repaint(int x, int y,
                        int width, int height);                    §1.10.60
    public void repaint(long tm);                                  §1.10.61
    public void repaint(long tm, int x, int y,                     §1.10.62
                        int width, int height);
    public void requestFocus();                                    §1.10.63
    public void reshape(int x, int y,
                        int width, int height);                    §1.10.64
    public void resize(Dimension d);                               §1.10.65
    public void resize(int width, int height);                     §1.10.66
    public void setBackground(Color c);                            §1.10.67
    public void setFont(Font f);                                   §1.10.68
    public void setForeground(Color c);                            §1.10.69
    public void show();                                            §1.10.70
    public void show(boolean cond);                                §1.10.71
    public Dimension size();                                       §1.10.72
    public String toString();                                      §1.10.73
    public void update(Graphics g);                                §1.10.74
    public void validate();                                        §1.10.75
}
```

The Component class is the abstract superclass of many of the Abstract Window Toolkit classes. It represents something that has a position and a size, can be painted on the screen, and can receive input events.

Methods

action §1.10.1

    public boolean action(Event evt, Object what)

This method is called when an action occurs inside this component. This method is usually called by handleEvent (**II-§1.10.22**), in which case the what argument contains the arg field of the event argument. The specific value and type of the what argument depend on the component that originally triggered the action.

The method returns true to indicate that it has successfully handled the action, or false if the event that triggered the action should be passed up to the component's parent. Most applications should return either true or the value of super.handleEvent(evt).

The action method of Component simply returns false.

PARAMETERS:

evt: the event that caused the action.
what: the action.

RETURNS:

true if the event has been handled and no further action is necessary; false if the event is to be given to the component's parent.

addNotify §1.10.2

    public void addNotify()

This method notifies the Component to create a peer. This peer allows the application to change the look of a component without changing its functionality.

The addNotify method of Component sets a flag indicating that the component needs to be laid out again because its size has possibly changed.

Most applications do not call this method directly.

SEE ALSO:

getPeer (**II-§1.10.19**).
removeNotify (**II-§1.10.58**).

bounds §1.10.3

    public Rectangle bounds()

RETURNS:

the containing rectangle of this component.

SEE ALSO:

reshape (**II-§1.10.64**).

checkImage   §1.10.4

`public int checkImage(Image image, ImageObserver observer)`

Returns the status of the construction of a screen representation of the specified image.

This method does not cause the image to begin loading. An application must use the `prepareImage` method **(II-§1.10.55)** to force the loading of an image.

The `checkImage` method of `Component` calls its peer's `checkImage` method **(II-§3.6.1)** to calculate the flags. If this component does not yet have a peer, the component's toolkit's `checkImage` method **(II-§1.41.2)** is called instead.

Information on the flags returned by this method can be found in **II-§2.11**.

PARAMETERS:

`image`: the `Image` whose status is being checked.

`observer`: the `ImageObserver` object to be notified as the image is being prepared.

RETURNS:

the bitwise inclusive **OR** of `ImageObserver` **(II-§2.11)** flags indicating what information about the image is currently available.

checkImage §1.10.5

```
public int checkImage(Image image, int width, int height,
                      ImageObserver observer)
```

Returns the status of the construction of a scaled screen representation of the specified image.

This method does not cause the image to begin loading. An application must use the `prepareImage` **(II-§1.10.55)** method to force the loading of an image.

The `checkImage` method of `Component` calls its peer's `checkImage` method **(II-§3.6.1)** to calculate the flags. If this component does not yet have a peer, the component's toolkit's `checkImage` method **(II-§1.41.2)** is called instead.

Information on the flags returned by this method can be found in **II-§2.11**.

PARAMETERS:
`image`: the Image whose status is being checked.
`width`: the width of the scaled version whose status is to be checked.
`height`: the height of the scaled version whose status is to be checked.
`observer`: the ImageObserver object to be notified as the image is being prepared.

RETURNS:
the bitwise inclusive **OR** of the ImageObserver flags for the data that is currently available.

createImage §1.10.6

```
public Image createImage(ImageProducer producer)
```

Creates an image from the specified image producer.

PARAMETERS:
`producer`: the image producer.

RETURNS:
the image produced.

createImage §1.10.7

```
public Image createImage(int width, int height)
```

PARAMETERS:
`width`: the specified width.
`height`: the specified height.

RETURNS:
an off-screen drawable image, which can be used for double buffering.

deliverEvent   §1.10.8

    `public void deliverEvent(Event evt)`

    Delivers an event to this component or one of its subcomponents.

    The `deliverEvent` method of `Component` calls the component's `postEvent` method (**II-§1.10.52**) on the event.

PARAMETERS:

`evt`: the event.

SEE ALSO:

`handleEvent` (**II-§1.10.22**).

disable   §1.10.9

    `public void disable()`

    Makes this component insensitive to user input.

SEE ALSO:

`isEnabled` (**II-§1.10.27**).

`enable` (**II-§1.10.10**).

enable   §1.10.10

    `public void enable()`

    Makes this component sensitive to user input. This is the default.

SEE ALSO:

`isEnabled` (**II-§1.10.27**).

`disable` (**II-§1.10.9**).

enable   §1.10.11

    `public void enable(boolean cond)`

    If the `boolean` argument is `true`, enables this component. If `false`, disables it.

PARAMETERS:

`cond`: a `boolean` indicating whether to enable or disable this component.

getBackground   §1.10.12

    `public Color getBackground()`

    Determines the background color of this component. If this component has not specified a background color using the `setBackground` method (**II-§1.10.67**), the background color of its parent component is returned.

RETURNS:

the background color of this component.

getColorModel §1.10.13

    public ColorModel getColorModel()

Detetermines the color model of this component. The ColorModel (**II-§2.1**) is an abstract class that encapsulates how to translate between pixel values of an image and its red, green, blue, and alpha (transparency) components.

The getColorModel method of Component calls its peer's getColor-Model method (**II-§3.6.7**) to determine the component's color model. If this component does not yet have a peer, the component's toolkit's getColor-Model method (**II-§1.41.22**) is called instead.

RETURNS:

the color model of this component.

getFont §1.10.14

    public Font getFont()

Determines the font of this component. If this component has not yet specified a font using the setFont method (**II-§1.10.68**), the font of its parent component is returned.

RETURNS:

the font of this component.

getFontMetrics §1.10.15

    public FontMetrics getFontMetrics(Font font)

Determines the font metrics for the specified font when rendered by a platform-dependent toolkit.

The getFontMetrics method checks to see if this component has a peer (**II-§1.10.19**). If so, the peer's getFontMetrics method (**II-§3.6.8**) is called. Otherwise, the component's toolkit's getFontMetrics method (**II-§1.41.25**) is called.

PARAMETERS:

font: the font.

RETURNS:

the font metrics for the specified font.

SEE ALSO:

getFont (**II-§1.10.14**).

getForeground   §1.10.16

    `public Color getForeground()`

    Determines the foreground color of this component. If this component has not specified a forground color using the `setForeground` method (**II-§1.10.69**), the forground color of its parent component is returned.

    RETURNS:

    the foreground color of this component.

getGraphics   §1.10.17

    `public Graphics getGraphics()`

    RETURNS:

    the graphics context of this component; this method returns `null` if the component does not currently have a peer.

    SEE ALSO:

    `paint` (**II-§1.10.49**).

getParent   §1.10.18

    `public Container getParent()`

    RETURNS:

    the parent of this component.

getPeer   §1.10.19

    `public ComponentPeer getPeer()`

    RETURNS:

    the peer of this component.

getToolkit   §1.10.20

    `public Toolkit getToolkit()`

    The toolkit is used to create this component's peer when its `addNotify` method (**II-§1.10.2**) is called.

    A `Component`'s toolkit is determined by its containing `Frame` (**II-§1.19**).

    RETURNS:

    the toolkit of this component.

gotFocus

> `public boolean gotFocus(Event evt, Object what)`

This method is called when the component receives the input focus. This method is usually called by `handleEvent` (**II-§1.10.22**), in which case the `what` argument contains the `arg` field of the event argument.

The method returns `true` to indicate that it has successfully handled the action, or `false` if the event that triggered the action should be passed up to the component's parent. Most applications should return either `true` or the value of `super.handleEvent(evt)`.

The `getFocus` method of `Component` simply returns `false`.

The `what` argument is currently always `null`.

PARAMETERS:

`evt`: the event that caused the action.
`what`: the action.

RETURNS:

`true` if the event has been handled and no further action is necessary; `false` if the event is to be given to the component's parent.

SEE ALSO:

`requestFocus` (**II-§1.10.63**).
`lostFocus` (**II-§1.10.39**).

handleEvent

> `public boolean handleEvent(Event evt)`

This method is called when any event occurs inside this component.

The method returns `true` to indicate that it has successfully handled the action, or `false` if the event that triggered the action should be passed up to the component's parent.

The `handleEvent` method of `Component` determines the type of event, and calls one of the following methods, if appropriate:

`action` (**II-§1.10.1**)	
`gotFocus` (**II-§1.10.21**)	`lostFocus` (**II-§1.10.39**)
`keyDown` (**II-§1.10.31**)	`keyUp` (**II-§1.10.32**)

mouseEnter (**II-§1.10.43**)	mouseExit (**II-§1.10.44**)
mouseMove (**II-§1.10.45**)	mouseDrag (**II-§1.10.42**)
mouseDown (**II-§1.10.41**)	mouseUp (**II-§1.10.46**)

The handleEvent method returns whatever value the called method returns. If none of those methods is appropriate, then handleEvent returns false.

All the listed methods are called with the event as their first argument. The action method is called with the arg field of the event as its second argument. The keyUp and keyDown are passed the key field of the event as its second argument. The six mouse methods are passed the *x* and *y* fields of the event as their second and third argument, respectively.[4]

PARAMETERS:

nevt: the event.

RETURNS:

true if the event has been handled and no further action is necessary; false if the event is to be given to the component's parent.

hide   **§1.10.23**

public void hide()

Hides this component. The component continues to exist and be in its containing object, but it is not visible and does not have any space allocated for it.

SEE ALSO:

isVisible (**II-§1.10.30**).
show (**II-§1.10.70**).

imageUpdate   **§1.10.24**

```
public boolean
imageUpdate(Image img, int flags, int x, int y,
          int w, int h)
```

This imageUpdate method of an ImageObserver (such as Component) is called when more information about an image which had been previously requested using an asynchronous interface (such as drawImage) becomes available. See **II-§2.11.9** on page 293 for more information on this method and its arguments.

The imageUpdate method of Component incrementally draws an image on the component as more of the bits of the image are available.

---

[4] In Java 1.0, AWT does not send all components mouse, keyboard, and focus events. Each component documents the events that AWT sends it.

If the system property "awt.image.incrementalDraw" is missing or has the value "true", the image is incrementally drawn, If the system property has any other value, then the image is not drawn until it has been completely loaded.

Also, if incremental drawing is in effect, the value of the system property "awt.image.redrawrate" is interpreted as an integer to give the maximum redraw rate, in milliseconds. If the system property is missing or cannot be interpreted as an integer, the redraw rate is once every 100ms.

The interpretation of the x, y, width, and height arguments depends on the infoflags argument.

PARAMETERS:

img: the image being observed.
infoflags: see **II-§2.11.9** for more information.
x: an *x* coordinate.
y: a *y* coordinate.
width: the width.
height: the height.

RETURNS:

true if the flags have indicated that the image is completely loaded; false otherwise.

inside §1.10.25

```
public boolean inside(int x, int y)
```

Determines if the specified $\langle x, y \rangle$ location is inside this component.

The inside method of Component returns true if the $\langle x, y \rangle$ location is inside the bounding box **(II-§1.10.3)** of the component.

PARAMETERS:

x: the *x* coordinate.
y: the *y* coordinate.

RETURNS:

true if the specified $\langle x, y \rangle$ location lies within this component; false otherwise.

SEE ALSO:

locate **(II-§1.10.37)**.

invalidate   §1.10.26

```
public void invalidate()
```

Invalidates this component. This component is marked as having changed. The next call to the `validate` (**II-§1.10.75**) method on this component or its parent(s) causes the component to be laid out again.

SEE ALSO:

`layout` (**II-§1.10.33**).
`LayoutManager` (**II-§1.43**).

isEnabled   §1.10.27

```
public boolean isEnabled()
```

Indicates whether this component is enabled to receive events. By default, components are initially enabled.

A component is disabled by calling its `disable` method (**II-§1.10.9**). A component is enabled by calling its `enable` method (**II-§1.10.10**).

RETURNS:

`true` if this component is enabled; `false` otherwise.

isShowing   §1.10.28

```
public boolean isShowing()
```

Indicates whether this component is visible. A component is showing if it is visible (**II-§1.10.30**) and is inside a container that is both visible and showing.

A component is hidden by calling its `hide` method (**II-§1.10.23**). A component is made visible by calling its `show` method (**II-§1.10.70**).

RETURNS:

`true` if this component is showing; `false` otherwise.

isValid   §1.10.29

```
public boolean isValid()
```

Indicates whether this component is valid. A component is valid if it has a peer and it and its subcomponents have been properly laid out.

RETURNS:

`true` if this component is valid; `false` otherwise.

SEE ALSO:

`validate` (**II-§1.10.75**).
`invalidate` (**II-§1.10.26**).

isVisible §1.10.30

```
public boolean isVisible()
```

Indicates whether this component is visible. Except for top-level components such as frames, components are visible unless they have been specifically made invisible by a call to the hide method (**II-§1.10.23**).

RETURNS:

true if this component is showing; false otherwise.

SEE ALSO:

show (**II-§1.10.70**).

keyDown §1.10.31

```
public boolean keyDown(Event evt, int key)
```

This method is called when a key is pressed and this component has the focus. This method is usually called by handleEvent (**II-§1.10.22**), in which case the key argument contains the key field of the event argument.

This method returns true to indicate that it has successfully handled the action, or false if the event that triggered the action should be passed up to the component's parent. Most applications should return either true or the value of super.handleEvent(evt).

The keyDown method of Component simply returns false.

Note that the key argument is an int rather than a char.

PARAMETERS:

evt: the event that caused the action.
key: the key that has been pressed.

RETURNS:

true if the event has been handled and no further action is necessary; false
   if the event is to be given to the component's parent.

keyUp   §1.10.32

```
public boolean keyUp(Event evt, int key)
```

This method is called when a key is released and this component has the focus. This method is usually called by handleEvent (II-§1.10.22), in which case the key argument contains the key field of the event argument.

This method returns `true` to indicate that it has successfully handled the action, or `false` if the event that triggered the action should be passed up to this component's parent. Most applications should return either `true` or the value of `super.handleEvent(evt)`.

The keyUp method of Component simply returns `false`.

Note that the key argument is an `int` rather than a `char`.

PARAMETERS:

evt: the event that caused the action.
key: the key that has been pressed .

RETURNS:

true if the event has been handled and no further action is necessary; `false` if the event is to be given to the component's parent.

layout   §1.10.33

```
public void layout()
```

This method is called to lay out the subcomponents of this component so that they fit inside the borders of this component.

This method is called when this component is validated by a call to the validate method (II-§1.10.75). Most applications should not call this method directly.

The layout method of Component does nothing.

SEE ALSO:

LayoutManager (II-§1.43).

list   §1.10.34

```
public void list()
```

Prints a listing of this component to System.out (I-§1.18.3).

list   §1.10.35

```
public void list(PrintStream out)
```

Prints a listing of this component to the specified output stream.

PARAMETERS:

out: a print stream.

list   **§1.10.36**

> `public void list(PrintStream out, int indent)`

Prints a listing of this component to the specified output stream. The listing starts at the specified indentation.

The `list` method of `Component` calls the `println` method **(I-§2.18.23)** on the component after indenting by the specified amount.

PARAMETERS:

`out`: a print stream.
`indent`: number of spaces to indent.

locate   **§1.10.37**

> `public Component locate(int x, int y)`

Determines if this component or one of its immediate subcomponents contains the $\langle x, y \rangle$ coordinate, and if so, returns the containing component. This method only looks one level deep. If the point $\langle x, y \rangle$ is inside a subcomponent that itself has subcomponents, it does not go looking down the subcomponent tree.

The `locate` method of `Component` simply returns the component itself if the $\langle x, y \rangle$ coordinate is inside **(II-§1.10.25)** its bounding box, and `null` otherwise.

PARAMETERS:

`x`: the x coordinate.
`y`: the y coordinate.

RETURNS:

the component or subcomponent that contains the $\langle x, y \rangle$ coordinate; `null` if the coordinate is outside this component.

location   **§1.10.38**

> `public Point location()`

RETURNS:

the location of this component in its parent's coordinate space.

SEE ALSO:

move **(II-§1.10.47)**.

lostFocus   §1.10.39

```
public boolean lostFocus(Event evt, Object what)
```

This method is called when this component loses the input focus. This method is usually called by handleEvent (**II-§1.10.22**), in which case the what argument contains the arg field of the event argument.

This method returns true to indicate that it has successfully handled the action, or false if the event that triggered the action should be passed up to this component's parent. Most applications should return either true or the value of super.handleEvent(evt).

The getFocus method of Component simply returns false.

The what argument is currently always null.

PARAMETERS:

evt: the event that caused the action.
what: the action that is occurring.

RETURNS:

true if the event has been handled and no further action is necessary; false
    if the event is to be given to the component's parent.

SEE ALSO:

requestFocus (**II-§1.10.63**).
gotFocus (**II-§1.10.21**).

minimumSize   §1.10.40

```
public Dimension minimumSize()
```

Determines the minimum size of this component.

The minimumSize method of Component checks to see if the component has a peer (**II-§1.10.19**). If so, the minimumSize request is passed to the peer (**II-§3.6.13**). Otherwise, the minimum size is the width and height specified by the most recent reshape (**II-§1.10.64**) or resize (**II-§1.10.65**) method call.

RETURNS:

the minimum size of this component.

SEE ALSO:

preferredSize (**II-§1.10.53**).
LayoutManager (**II-§1.43**).

mouseDown §1.10.41

```
public boolean mouseDown(Event evt, int x, int y)
```

This method is called when the mouse button is pushed inside this component. This method is usually called by handleEvent (**II-§1.10.22**), in which case the x and y arguments contain the x and y fields of the event argument. The $\langle x, y \rangle$ coordinate is relative to the top-left corner of this component.

This method returns true to indicate that it has successfully handled the action, or false if the event that triggered the action should be passed up to this component's parent. Most applications should return either true or the value of super.handleEvent(evt).

The mouseDown method of Component simply returns false.

PARAMETERS:

evt: the event that caused the action.
x: the x coordinate.
y: the y coordinate.

RETURNS:

true if the event has been handled and no further action is necessary; false if the event is to be given to the component's parent

mouseDrag §1.10.42

```
public boolean mouseDrag(Event evt, int x, int y)
```

This method is called when the mouse button is moved inside this component with the button pushed. This method is usually called by handleEvent (**II-§1.10.22**), in which case the x and y arguments contain the x and y fields of the event argument. The $\langle x, y \rangle$ coordinate is relative to the top-left corner of this component.

Mouse-drag events continue to be sent to this component even when the mouse has left the bounds of the component. The drag events continue until a mouse-up event occurs.

This method returns true to indicate that it has successfully handled the action, or false if the event that triggered the action should be passed up to this component's parent. Most applications should return either true or the value of super.handleEvent(evt).

The mouseDrag method of Component simply returns false.

PARAMETERS:

evt: the event that caused the action.
x: the x coordinate.
y: the y coordinate.

RETURNS:

true if the event has been handled and no further action is necessary; false if the event is to be given to the component's parent.

mouseEnter   §1.10.43

```
public boolean mouseEnter(Event evt, int x, int y)
```

This method is called when the mouse first enters this component. This method is usually called by handleEvent (**II-§1.10.22**), in which case the x and y arguments contain the *x* and *y* fields of the event argument. The $\langle x, y \rangle$ coordinate is relative to the top-left corner of this component.

This method returns true to indicate that it has successfully handled the action, or false if the event that triggered the action should be passed up to this component's parent. Most applications should return either true or the value of super.handleEvent(evt).

The mouseEnter method of Component simply returns false.

PARAMETERS:

evt: the event that caused the action.
x: the *x* coordinate.
y: the *y* coordinate.

RETURNS:

true if the event has been handled and no further action is necessary; false if the event is to be given to the component's parent.

mouseExit   §1.10.44

```
public boolean mouseExit(Event evt, int x, int y)
```

This method is called when the mouse exits this component. This method is usually called by handleEvent (**II-§1.10.22**), in which case the x and y arguments contain the *x* and *y* fields of the event argument. The $\langle x, y \rangle$ coordinate is relative to the top-left corner of this component. Most applications should return either true or the value of super.handleEvent(evt).

This method returns true to indicate that it has successfully handled the action, or false if the event that triggered the action should be passed up to this component's parent. Most applications should return either true or the value of super.handleEvent(evt).

The mouseExit method of Component simply returns false.

PARAMETERS:

evt: the event that caused the action.
x: the *x* coordinate.
y: the *y* coordinate.

RETURNS:

true if the event has been handled and no further action is necessary; false if the event is to be given to the component's parent.

mouseMove §1.10.45

```
public boolean mouseMove(Event evt, int x, int y)
```

This method is called when the mouse is moved inside this component with the mouse button not pushed. This method is usually called by handleEvent (**II-§1.10.22**), in which case the x and y arguments contain the *x* and *y* fields of the event argument. The ⟨x, y⟩ coordinate is relative to the top-left corner of this component.

This method returns `true` to indicate that it has successfully handled the action, or `false` if the event that triggered the action should be passed up to this component's parent. Most applications should return either `true` or the value of `super.handleEvent(evt)`.

The mouseMove method of Component simply returns `false`.

PARAMETERS:

evt: the event that caused the action.
x: the *x* coordinate.
y: the *y* coordinate.

RETURNS:

true if the event has been handled and no further action is necessary; `false` if the event is to be given to the component's parent.

mouseUp §1.10.46

```
public boolean mouseUp(Event evt, int x, int y)
```

This method is called when the mouse button is released inside this component. This method is usually called by handleEvent (**II-§1.10.22**), in which case the x and y arguments contain the *x* and *y* fields of the event argument. The ⟨x, y⟩ coordinate is relative to the top-left corner of the component.

This method returns `true` to indicate that it has successfully handled the action, or `false` if the event that triggered the action should be passed up to this component's parent. Most applications should return either `true` or the value of `super.handleEvent(evt)`.

The mouseUp method of Component simply returns `false`.

PARAMETERS:

evt: the event that caused the action.
x: the *x* coordinate.
y: the *y* coordinate.

RETURNS:

true if the event has been handled and no further action is necessary; `false` if the event is to be given to the component's parent.

move   **§1.10.47**

```
public void move(int x, int y)
```

Moves this component to the coordinate $\langle x, y \rangle$ in the parent's coordinate space. The $\langle x, y \rangle$ coordinate is relative to the top-left corner of the parent component.

Components that are in a container with a layout manager should not call this method explicitly.

PARAMETERS:

x: the *x* coordinate.
y: the *y* coordinate.

SEE ALSO:

location **(II-§1.10.38)**.
reshape **(II-§1.10.64)**.

nextFocus   **§1.10.48**

```
public void nextFocus()
```

Moves the input focus to the next component, as determined by the component's peer **(II-§3.6.14)**.

SEE ALSO:

requestFocus **(II-§1.10.63)**.
gotFocus **(II-§1.10.21)**.

paint   **§1.10.49**

```
public void paint(Graphics g)
```

Paints this component. Most application components, including applets, override this method.

The $\langle 0, 0 \rangle$ coordinate of the graphics context is the top-left corner of this component. The clipping region of the graphics context is the bounding rectangle of this component.

The paint method of Component calls the repaint method **(II-§3.6.19)** of this component's peer.

PARAMETERS:

g: the graphics context to use for painting.

SEE ALSO:

update **(II-§1.10.74)**.

paintAll §1.10.50

```
public void paintAll(Graphics g)
```

Paints this component and all of its subcomponents.

The $\langle 0, 0 \rangle$ coordinate of the graphics context is the top-left corner of this component. The clipping region of the graphics context is the bounding rectangle of this component.

PARAMETERS:

g: the graphics context to use for painting.

SEE ALSO:

paint **(II-§1.10.49)**.

paramString §1.10.51

```
protected String paramString()
```

Returns the parameter string representing the state of this component. This string is useful for debugging.

RETURNS:

the parameter string of this component.

postEvent §1.10.52

```
public boolean postEvent(Event evt)
```

Posts an event to this component by calling its handleEvent method **(II-§1.10.22)**. If handleEvent returns false, the event is posted to this component's parent.

If this component and all of its parents return false, the event is passed to this component's peer object's handleEvent method **(II-§3.6.11)**.

PARAMETERS:

evt: the event.

RETURNS:

true if this component, one of its parents, or this component's peer handled the event; false otherwise.

SEE ALSO:

deliverEvent **(II-§1.10.8)**.

preferredSize   §1.10.53

    public Dimension preferredSize()

Determines the preferred size of the component.

The preferredSize method of Component checks to see if this component has a peer (**II-§1.10.19**). If so, the preferredSize request is passed to the peer (**II-§3.6.16**). Otherwise, the preferred size is the width and height specified by the most recent reshape (**II-§1.10.64**) or resize (**II-§1.10.65**) method call.

RETURNS:

the preferred size of this component.

SEE ALSO:

minimumSize (**II-§1.10.40**).
LayoutManager (**II-§1.43**).

prepareImage   §1.10.54

    public boolean
    prepareImage(Image image, ImageObserver observer)

Prepares an image for rendering on this component.

The image data is downloaded asynchronously in another thread, and the appropriate screen representation of the image is generated.

PARAMETERS:

image: the Image for which to prepare a screen representation.
observer: the ImageObserver (**II-§2.11**) object to be notified as the image is being prepared.

RETURNS:

true if the image has already been fully prepared; false otherwise.

prepareImage §1.10.55

```
public boolean
prepareImage(Image image, int width, int height,
            ImageObserver observer)
```

Prepares an image for rendering on this component at the specified width and height.

The image data is downloaded asynchronously in another thread, and an appropriately scaled screen representation of the image is generated.

PARAMETERS:

image: the Image for which to prepare a screen representation.
width: the width of the desired screen representation.
height: the height of the desired screen representation.
observer: the ImageObserver (**II-§2.11**) object to be notified as the image is being prepared.

RETURNS:

true if the image has already been fully prepared; false otherwise.

print §1.10.56

```
public void print(Graphics g)
```

Prints this component. Applications should override this method for components that must do special processing before being printed or should be printed differently than they are painted.

The print method of Component calls the paint method (**II-§1.10.49**).

The $\langle 0, 0 \rangle$ coordinate of the graphics context is the top-left corner of this component. The clipping region of the graphics context is the bounding rectangle of this component.

PARAMETERS:

g: the graphics context to use for printing.

SEE ALSO:

paint (**II-§1.10.49**).

printAll §1.10.57

```
public void printAll(Graphics g)
```

Paints this component and all of its subcomponents.

The $\langle 0, 0 \rangle$ coordinate of the graphics context is the top-left corner of this component. The clipping region of the graphics context is the bounding rectangle of this component.

PARAMETERS:

g: the graphics context to use for printing.

SEE ALSO:

print (**II-§1.10.56**).

removeNotify   §1.10.58

`public void removeNotify()`

Notifies this component and all its subcomponents to destroy their peers. Applications should not call this method directly. It is called when a component is removed (**II-§1.11.19, §1.11.20**) from its container.

The `removeNotify` method of `Component` removes the component's peer and has the peer clean up after itself by calling its `dispose` method (**II-§3.6.5**).

SEE ALSO:

getPeer (**II-§1.10.19**).
addNotify (**II-§1.10.2**).

repaint   §1.10.59

`public void repaint()`

Repaints this component.

This method causes a call to this component's `update` method (**II-§1.10.74**) as soon as possible.

repaint   §1.10.60

`public void`
`repaint(int x, int y, int width, int height)`

Repaints the specified rectangle of this component.

This method causes a call to this component's `update` method (**II-§1.10.74**) as soon as possible.

PARAMETERS:

`x`: the x coordinate.
`y`: the y coordinate.
`width`: the width.
`height`: the height.

repaint   §1.10.61

`public void repaint(long tm)`

Repaints this component within `tm` milliseconds.

This method causes a call to this component's `update` method (**II-§1.10.74**).

PARAMETERS:

`tm`: maximum time in milliseconds before update.

repaint §1.10.62

```
public void repaint(long tm, int x, int y,
                    int width, int height)
```

Repaints the specified rectangle of this component within tm milliseconds. This method causes a call to this component's update method (**II-§1.10.74**).

PARAMETERS:

tm: maximum time in milliseconds before update.
x: the *x* coordinate.
y: the *y* coordinate.
width: the width.
height: the height.

requestFocus §1.10.63

```
public void requestFocus()
```

Requests that this component get the input focus.

This component's gotFocus method (**II-§1.10.21**) is called when this method is successful.

The requestFocus method of Component calls the requestFocus method (**II-§3.6.21**) of the component's peer.

reshape §1.10.64

```
public void reshape(int x, int y, int width, int height)
```

Reshapes this component to the specified bounding box in its parent's coordinate space. Components that are in a container with a layout manager should not call this method explicitly.

PARAMETERS:

x: the *x* coordinate.
y: the *y* coordinate.
width: the width of this component.
height: the height of this component.

SEE ALSO:

bounds (**II-§1.10.3**).
move (**II-§1.10.47**).
resize (**II-§1.10.66**).

resize   §1.10.65

```
public void resize(Dimension d)
```

Resizes this component to the width and height specified by the dimension argument. Components that are in a container with a layout manager should not call this method explicitly.

PARAMETERS:

d: the new dimension for this component.

SEE ALSO:

size (**II-§1.10.72**).
reshape (**II-§1.10.64**).

resize   §1.10.66

```
public void resize(int width, int height)
```

Resizes this component to the specified width and height. Components that are in a container with a layout manager should not call this method explicitly.

PARAMETERS:

width: the new width of this component.
height: the new height of this component.

SEE ALSO:

size (**II-§1.10.72**).
reshape (**II-§1.10.64**).

setBackground   §1.10.67

```
public void setBackground(Color c)
```

Sets the background color of this component.

The setBackground method of Component calls the setBackground method (**II-§3.6.23**) of the component's peer.

PARAMETERS:

c: the color.

SEE ALSO:

getBackground (**II-§1.10.12**).

setFont §1.10.68

    public void setFont(Font f)

Sets the font of this component.

The setFont method of Component calls the setFont method (**II-§3.6.24**) of the component's peer.

PARAMETERS:

f: the font.

SEE ALSO:

getFont (**II-§1.10.14**).

setForeground §1.10.69

    public void setForeground(Color c)

Sets the foreground color of this component.

The setForeground method of Component calls the setForeground method (**II-§3.6.25**) of the component's peer.

PARAMETERS:

c: the color.

SEE ALSO:

getForeground (**II-§1.10.16**).

show §1.10.70

    public void show()

Shows this component; if this component had been made invisible by a call to the hide method (**II-§1.10.23**), makes this component visible again.

SEE ALSO:

isVisible (**II-§1.10.30**).

show §1.10.71

    public void show(boolean cond)

If the boolean argument is true, makes this component visible. If false, makes this component invisible.

PARAMETERS:

cond: if true, show this component; if false, hide this component.

SEE ALSO:

show (**II-§1.10.70**).

hide (**II-§1.10.23**).

size   §1.10.72

```
public Dimension size()
```
RETURNS:

the current size of this component.

SEE ALSO:

`resize` (**II-§1.10.65**).

toString   §1.10.73

```
public String toString()
```
RETURNS:

a string representation of this component.

OVERRIDES:

`toString` in class `Object` (**I-§1.12.9**).

update   §1.10.74

```
public void update(Graphics g)
```
Updates this component.

The AWT calls the `update` method in response to a call to `repaint` (**II-§1.10.59**). The appearance of the component on the screen has not changed since the last call to `update` or `paint`.

The `update` method of `Component`:

1. Clears this component by filling it with the background color.

2. Sets the color of the graphics context to be the foreground color of this component.
3. Calls this component's `paint` method (**II-§1.10.49**) to completely redraw this component.

The $\langle 0, 0 \rangle$ coordinate of the graphics context is the top-left corner of this component. The clipping region of the graphics context is the bounding rectangle of this component.

PARAMETERS:

`g`: the graphics context to use for updating.

validate   §1.10.75

```
public void validate()
```
Validates this component if necessary. This component and any subcomponents are laid out (**II-§1.10.33**) again, if necessary.

SEE ALSO:

`invalidate` (**II-§1.10.26**).

`LayoutManager` (**II-§1.43**).

1.11 Class Container

```
public abstract class java.awt.Container
    extends java.awt.Component (II-§1.10)
{
    // Methods
    public Component add(Component comp);                    §1.11.1
    public Component add(Component comp, int pos);          §1.11.2
    public Component add(String name, Component comp);      §1.11.3
    public void addNotify();                                §1.11.4
    public int countComponents();                           §1.11.5
    public void deliverEvent(Event evt);                    §1.11.6
    public Component getComponent(int n);                   §1.11.7
    public Component[] getComponents();                     §1.11.8
    public LayoutManager getLayout();                       §1.11.9
    public Insets insets();                                 §1.11.10
    public void layout();                                   §1.11.11
    public void list(PrintStream out, int indent);         §1.11.12
    public Component locate(int x, int y);                  §1.11.13
    public Dimension minimumSize();                         §1.11.14
    public void paintComponents(Graphics g);               §1.11.15
    protected String paramString();                         §1.11.16
    public Dimension preferredSize();                       §1.11.17
    public void printComponents(Graphics g);               §1.11.18
    public void remove(Component comp);                     §1.11.19
    public void removeAll();                                §1.11.20
    public void removeNotify();                             §1.11.21
    public void setLayout(LayoutManager mgr);              §1.11.22
    public void validate();                                 §1.11.23
}
```

Container is the abstract superclass representing all components that can hold other components.

Each container may be associated with a LayoutManager instance (**II-§1.43**) that determines the position of each of the container's subcomponents.

Methods

add   §1.11.1

```
public Component add(Component comp)
```

Adds the specified component to the end of this container.

PARAMETERS:

comp: the component to be added.

RETURNS:

the component argument.

add   §1.11.2

```
public Component add(Component comp, int pos)
```

Adds the specified component to this container at the given position.

PARAMETERS:

comp: the component to be added.
pos: the position at which to insert the component; or –1 to insert at the end.

RETURNS:

the component argument.

SEE ALSO:

remove (II-§1.11.19).

add   §1.11.3

```
public Component add(String name, Component comp)
```

Adds the specified component to the end of this container. Also adds the component to the layout manager using the name specified.

PARAMETERS:

name: a tag understood by the layout manager.
comp: the component to be added.

RETURNS:

the component argument.

SEE ALSO:

remove (II-§1.11.19).
LayoutManager (II-§1.43).

addNotify   §1.11.4

```
public void addNotify()
```

Notifies this container to create a peer.

The addNotify method of Container calls the addNotify method for each of the components in this container. It then calls its superclass's addNotify method (II-§1.10.2), to indicate that the container needs to be laid out again because its size may have changed.

Most applications do not call this method directly.

OVERRIDES:

addNotify in class Component (II-§1.10.2).

SEE ALSO:

removeNotify (II-§1.11.21).

countComponents §1.11.5

```
public int countComponents()
```

RETURNS:

the number of components in this container.

SEE ALSO:

getComponent (**II-§1.11.6**).

deliverEvent §1.11.6

```
public void deliverEvent(Event evt)
```

Delivers an event to this component or one of its subcomponents.

The `deliverEvent` method of `Container` determines whether this event properly belongs to one of its subcomponents. If so, it translates the event into the subcomponent's coordinate system and delivers the event to it by calling its `deliverEvent` method (**II-§1.10.8**).

If the event does not properly belong to one of the container's subcomponents, it calls this container's `postEvent` method (**II-§1.10.52**) on the event.

PARAMETERS:

evt: the event.

OVERRIDES:

deliverEvent in class Component (**II-§1.10.8**).

SEE ALSO:

handleEvent in class Component (**II-§1.10.22**).

getComponent §1.11.7

```
public Component getComponent(int n)
```

PARAMETERS:

n: the index of the component to get.

RETURNS:

the nth component in this container.

THROWS:

ArrayIndexOutOfBoundsException (**I-§1.25**).

If the nth value does not exist.

getComponents §1.11.8

```
public Component[] getComponents()
```

RETURNS:

an array of all the components in this container.

getLayout   §1.11.9

`public LayoutManager getLayout()`

RETURNS:

the layout manager for this container.

SEE ALSO:

`layout` (II-§1.11.11).
`setLayout` (II-§1.11.22).

insets   §1.11.10

`public Insets insets()`

Determines the insets of this container, which indicate the size of the container's border.

A `Frame`, for example, has a top inset that corresponds to the height of the frame's title bar.

The `insets` method of `Container` calls the `insets` method (II-§3.7.1) of this container's peer, if the container has a peer. Otherwise, it returns the inset `new Inset(0, 0, 0, 0)`, which indicates that the container has no border.

RETURNS:

the insets of this container.

SEE ALSO:

`LayoutManager` (II-§1.43).

layout   §1.11.11

`public void layout()`

Lays out this container.

The `layout` method of `Container` calls the `layoutContainer` method (II-§1.43.2) of the container's layout manager.

Most applications do not call this method directly. This method is called when a container calls its `validate` method (II-§1.11.23).

OVERRIDES:

`layout` in class `Component` (II-§1.10.33).

SEE ALSO:

`setLayout` (II-§1.11.22).

list §1.11.12

```
public void list(PrintStream out, int indent)
```

Prints a listing of this container to the specified output stream. The listing starts at the specified indentation.

The `list` method of `Container` prints itself by calling its superclass's `list` method (**II-§1.10.36**) and then calls `list` on each of its subcomponents with an indentation of `indent + 1`.

PARAMETERS:

out: a print stream.
indent: the number of spaces to indent.

OVERRIDES:

`list` in class Component (**II-§1.10.36**).

locate §1.11.13

```
public Component locate(int x, int y)
```

Determines the component or subcomponent of this container that contains the $\langle x, y \rangle$ coordinate. This method only looks one level deep. If the point $\langle x, y \rangle$ is inside a subcomponent that itself has subcomponents, the method does not look down the subcomponent tree.

The `locate` method of `Container` first determines if the $\langle x, y \rangle$ coordinate is `inside` (**II-§1.10.25**) its own boundaries. If not, it returns `null` immediately. If the coordinate is inside its boundaries, it calls `inside` (**II-§1.10.25**) on each of the subcomponents. If any of those calls returns `true`, that subcomponent is returned; otherwise, the container target object is returned.

PARAMETERS:

x: the x coordinate.
y: the y coordinate.

RETURNS:

this container or one of its subcomponents that contains the $\langle x, y \rangle$ coordinate; `null` if the coordinate is outside this container.

OVERRIDES:

`locate` in class Component (**II-§1.10.37**).

minimumSize §1.11.14

```
public Dimension minimumSize()
```

Determines the minimum size of this container.

The `minimumSize` method of `Container` checks to see if this container has a layout manager (**II-§1.11.9**). If so, its `minimumLayoutSize` method (**II-§1.43.3**) is called. Otherwise, its superclass's `minimumSize` method (**II-§1.10.40**) is called.

RETURNS:

the minimum size of this container.

OVERRIDES:

`minimumSize` in class `Component` (**II-§1.10.40**).

SEE ALSO:

`preferredSize` (**II-§1.11.17**).

paintComponents §1.11.15

```
public void paintComponents(Graphics g)
```

Paints each of the components in this container.

PARAMETERS:

`g`: the graphics context.

SEE ALSO:

`paint` in class `Component` (**II-§1.10.49**).
`paintAll` in class `Component` (**II-§1.10.50**).

paramString §1.11.16

```
protected String paramString()
```

Returns the parameter string representing the state of this container. This string is useful for debugging.

RETURNS:

the parameter string of this container.

OVERRIDES:

`paramString` in class `Component` (**II-§1.10.51**).

preferredSize §1.11.17

```
public Dimension preferredSize()
```

Determines the preferred size of this container.

The `preferredSize` method of `Container` checks to see if this container has a layout manager (**II-§1.11.9**). If so, its `preferredLayoutSize` method (**II-§1.43.4**) is called. Otherwise, its superclass's `preferredSize` method (**II-§1.10.53**) is called.

RETURNS:

the minimum size of this container.

OVERRIDES:

`preferredSize` in class Component (**II-§1.10.53**).

SEE ALSO:

`minimumSize` (**II-§1.11.14**).

printComponents §1.11.18

```
public void printComponents(Graphics g)
```

Prints each of the components in this container.

PARAMETERS:

`g`: the graphics context.

SEE ALSO:

`print` in class Component (**II-§1.10.56**).
`printAll` in class Component (**II-§1.10.57**).

remove §1.11.19

```
public void remove(Component comp)
```

Removes the specified component from this container. This method also causes the component to call its `removeNotify` method (**II-§1.10.58**) to remove its peer.

PARAMETERS:

`comp`: the component to be removed.

SEE ALSO:

`add` (**II-§1.11.1**).

removeAll   §1.11.20

```
public void removeAll()
```

Removes all the components from this container. This method also causes all the components in the container to call their removeNotify methods (II-§1.10.58) to remove their peers.

SEE ALSO:

add (II-§1.11.1).
remove (II-§1.11.19).

removeNotify   §1.11.21

```
public void removeNotify()
```

Notifies this container and all its subcomponents to destroy their peers.

OVERRIDES:

removeNotify in class Component (II-§1.10.58).

SEE ALSO:

addNotify (II-§1.11.4).

setLayout   §1.11.22

```
public void setLayout(LayoutManager mgr)
```

Sets the layout manager for this container.

PARAMETERS:

mgr: the new layout manager.

SEE ALSO:

layout (II-§1.11.11).
getLayout (II-§1.11.9).

validate   §1.11.23

```
public void validate()
```

Validates this container and all of its subcomponents. The AWT uses this method to cause a container to be laid out again after adding or otherwise changing the components it contains.

OVERRIDES:

validate in class Component (II-§1.10.75).

SEE ALSO:

invalidate in class Component (II-§1.10.26).

1.12 Class Dialog

```
public class java.awt.Dialog
    extends java.awt.Window (II-§1.42)
{
    // Constructors
    public Dialog(Frame parent, boolean modal);            §1.12.1
    public Dialog(Frame parent, String title,              §1.12.2
                  boolean modal);

    // Methods
    public void addNotify();                               §1.12.3
    public String getTitle();                              §1.12.4
    public boolean isModal();                              §1.12.5
    public boolean isResizable();                          §1.12.6
    protected String paramString();                        §1.12.7
    public void setResizable(boolean resizable);           §1.12.8
    public void setTitle(String title);                    §1.12.9
}
```

This class represents a dialog window, a window that takes input from the user.

Dialogs are intended to be temporary windows. They present specific, timely information to the user, or they allow the user to specify options for the current operation.

The AWT sends the dialog window all mouse, keyboard, and focus events that occur over it.

By default, the dialog window is invisible. The application must use the show method (II-§1.10.70) to cause the dialog window to appear.

The default layout for a dialog is BorderLayout.

Constructors

Dialog   §1.12.1

```
public Dialog(Frame parent, boolean modal)
```

Creates a dialog window that is initially invisible. If the `modal` flag is true, the dialog window grabs all input from the user.

The parent argument is the main application window.

PARAMETERS:

`parent`: the owner of the dialog.

`modal`: if `true`, the dialog box blocks input to other windows while it is visible.

Dialog   §1.12.2

```
public Dialog(Frame parent, String title, boolean modal)
```

Creates a titled dialog window that is initially invisible. If the `modal` flag is true, then the dialog box grabs all input from the user.

The parent argument is the main application window.

PARAMETERS:

`parent`: the owner of the dialog.

`title`: the title of the dialog.

`modal`: if `true`, dialog blocks input to other windows when shown.

Methods

addNotify   §1.12.3

```
public void addNotify()
```

This method calls the `createDialog` method (**II-§1.41.8**) of this object's toolkit (**II-§1.10.20**) in order to create a `DialogPeer` (**II-§3.8**) for this dialog window. This peer allows the application to change the look of a dialog window without changing its functionality.

Most applications do not call this method directly.

OVERRIDES:

`addNotify` in class `Window` (**II-§1.42.2**).

getTitle   §1.12.4

```
public String getTitle()
```

RETURNS:

the title of this dialog window.

SEE ALSO:

`setTitle` (**II-§1.12.9**).

isModal §1.12.5

```
public boolean isModal()
```
RETURNS:

`true` if this dialog window is modal; `false` otherwise.

isResizable §1.12.6

```
public boolean isResizable()
```
Indicates whether this dialog window is resizable. By default, a dialog window is resizable.

RETURNS:

`true` if the user can resize this dialog window; `false` otherwise.

paramString §1.12.7

```
protected String paramString()
```
Returns the parameter string representing the state of this dialog window. This string is useful for debugging.

RETURNS:

the parameter string of this dialog window.

OVERRIDES:

`paramString` in class `Container` (**II-§1.11.16**).

setResizable §1.12.8

```
public void setResizable(boolean resizable)
```
Sets the resizable flag for this dialog window.

PARAMETERS:

`resizable`: `true` if this dialog window is resizable; `false` otherwise.

setTitle §1.12.9

```
public void setTitle(String title)
```
Sets the title of this dialog window.

PARAMETERS:

`title`: the new title.

SEE ALSO:

`getTitle` (**II-§1.12.4**).

1.13 Class Dimension

```
public class java.awt.Dimension
    extends java.lang.Object (I-§1.12)
{
    // Fields
    public int height;                                          §1.13.1
    public int width;                                           §1.13.2

    // Constructors
    public Dimension();                                         §1.13.3
    public Dimension(Dimension d);                              §1.13.4
    public Dimension(int width, int height);                    §1.13.5

    // Methods
    public String toString();                                   §1.13.6
}
```

A class that encapsulates the width and height of a component in a single object.

Fields

height   §1.13.1

```
public int height
```
The height of the component.

width   §1.13.2

```
public int width
```
The width of the component.

Constructors

Dimension   §1.13.3

```
public Dimension()
```
Creates a Dimension with a width of zero and a height of zero.

Dimension §1.13.4

public Dimension(Dimension d)

Creates a Dimension whose width and height are the same as the argument.

PARAMETERS:

d: the specified dimension for the width and height values.

Dimension §1.13.5

public Dimension(int width, int height)

Creates a Dimension with the specified width and height.

PARAMETERS:

width: the width.
height: the height.

Methods

toString §1.13.6

public String toString()

RETURNS:

a string representation of this dimension.

OVERRIDES:

toString in class Object **(I-§1.12.9)**.

1.14 Class Event

```
public class java.awt.Event
    extends java.lang.Object (I-§1.12)
{
    // Fields
    public Object arg;                                      §1.14.1
    public int clickCount;                                  §1.14.2
    public Event evt;                                       §1.14.3
    public int id;                                          §1.14.4
    public int key;                                         §1.14.5
    public int modifiers;                                   §1.14.6
    public Object target;                                   §1.14.7
    public long when;                                       §1.14.8
    public int x;                                           §1.14.9
    public int y;                                           §1.14.10

    // possible values for the id field
    public final static int ACTION_EVENT;                   §1.14.11
    public final static int GOT_FOCUS;                      §1.14.12
    public final static int KEY_ACTION;                     §1.14.13
    public final static int KEY_ACTION_RELEASE;             §1.14.14
    public final static int KEY_PRESS;                      §1.14.15
    public final static int KEY_RELEASE;                    §1.14.16
    public final static int LIST_DESELECT;                  §1.14.17
    public final static int LIST_SELECT;                    §1.14.18
    public final static int LOAD_FILE;                      §1.14.19
    public final static int LOST_FOCUS;                     §1.14.20
    public final static int MOUSE_DOWN;                     §1.14.21
    public final static int MOUSE_DRAG;                     §1.14.22
    public final static int MOUSE_ENTER;                    §1.14.23
    public final static int MOUSE_EXIT;                     §1.14.24
    public final static int MOUSE_MOVE;                     §1.14.25
    public final static int MOUSE_UP;                       §1.14.26
    public final static int SAVE_FILE;                      §1.14.27
    public final static int SCROLL_ABSOLUTE;                §1.14.28
    public final static int SCROLL_LINE_DOWN;               §1.14.29
    public final static int SCROLL_LINE_UP;                 §1.14.30
    public final static int SCROLL_PAGE_DOWN;               §1.14.31
    public final static int SCROLL_PAGE_UP;                 §1.14.32
    public final static int WINDOW_DEICONIFY;               §1.14.33
    public final static int WINDOW_DESTROY;                 §1.14.34
    public final static int WINDOW_EXPOSE;                  §1.14.35
    public final static int WINDOW_ICONIFY;                 §1.14.36
    public final static int WINDOW_MOVED;                   §1.14.37

    // possible values for the key field when the
    // action is KEY_ACTION or KEY_ACTION_RELEASE
    public final static int DOWN;                           §1.14.38
```

```
public final static int END;
public final static int F1;
public final static int F2;
public final static int F3;
public final static int F4;
public final static int F5;
public final static int F6;
public final static int F7;
public final static int F8;
public final static int F9;
public final static int F10;
public final static int F11;
public final static int F12;
public final static int HOME;
public final static int LEFT;
public final static int PGDN;
public final static int PGUP;
public final static int RIGHT;
public final static int UP;

// possible masks for the modifiers field
public final static int ALT_MASK
public final static int CTRL_MASK;
public final static int SHIFT_MASK;
public final static int META_MASK;

// Constructors
public Event(Object target, int id, Object arg);
public Event(Object target, long when, int id,
             int x, int y, int key, int modifiers);
public Event(Object target, long when, int id,
             int x, int y, int key,
             int modifiers, Object arg);

// Methods
public boolean controlDown();
public boolean metaDown();
protected String paramString();
public boolean shiftDown();
public String toString();
public void translate(int dX, int dY);
}
```

END;	§1.14.39
F1;	§1.14.40
F2;	§1.14.41
F3;	§1.14.42
F4;	§1.14.43
F5;	§1.14.44
F6;	§1.14.45
F7;	§1.14.46
F8;	§1.14.47
F9;	§1.14.48
F10;	§1.14.49
F11;	§1.14.50
F12;	§1.14.51
HOME;	§1.14.52
LEFT;	§1.14.53
PGDN;	§1.14.54
PGUP;	§1.14.55
RIGHT;	§1.14.56
UP;	§1.14.57
ALT_MASK	§1.14.58
CTRL_MASK;	§1.14.59
SHIFT_MASK;	§1.14.60
META_MASK;	§1.14.61
Event(...arg);	§1.14.62
Event(...modifiers);	§1.14.63
Event(...arg);	§1.14.64
controlDown();	§1.14.65
metaDown();	§1.14.66
paramString();	§1.14.67
shiftDown();	§1.14.68
toString();	§1.14.69
translate(int dX, int dY);	§1.14.70

Event is a platform-independent class that encapsulates user events from the local Graphical User Interface (GUI) platform.

Fields

arg   §1.14.1

```
public Object arg
```

An arbitrary argument of the event. The value of this field depends on the type of event.

clickCount   §1.14.2

```
public int clickCount
```

For MOUSE_DOWN events, this field indicates the number of consecutive clicks. For other events, it is 0.

evt   §1.14.3

```
public Event evt
```

The next event. This field is set when putting events into a linked list.

id   §1.14.4

```
public int id
```

The type of the event.

key   §1.14.5

```
public int key
```

The key that was pressed in a keyboard event.

modifiers   §1.14.6

```
public int modifiers
```

The state of the modifier keys.

target   §1.14.7

```
public Object target
```

The target component. This indicates the component over which the event occurred or with which the event is associated.

when   §1.14.8

```
public long when
```

The time stamp of the event.

x   §1.14.9

```
public int x
```

The *x* coordinate of the event.

y   §1.14.10

    `public int y`

        The *y* coordinate of the event.

ACTION_EVENT   §1.14.11

    `public final static int ACTION_EVENT = 1001`

        This event indicates that the user wants some action to occur.

GOT_FOCUS   §1.14.12

    `public final static int GOT_FOCUS = 1004`

        A component gained the focus.

KEY_ACTION   §1.14.13

    `public final static int KEY_ACTION = 403`

        The user has pressed an "action" key. The key field contains one of the special values indicated in §1.14.38 to §1.14.57.

KEY_ACTION_RELEASE   §1.14.14

    `public final static int KEY_ACTION_RELEASE = 404`

        The user has released an "action" key. The key field contains one of the special values indicated in §1.14.38 to §1.14.57.

KEY_PRESS   §1.14.15

    `public final static int KEY_PRESS = 401`

        The user has pressed a normal key.

KEY_RELEASE   §1.14.16

    `public final static int KEY_RELEASE = 402`

        The user has released a normal key.

LIST_DESELECT   §1.14.17

    `public final static int LIST_DESELECT = 702`

        An item in a list has been deselected.

LIST_SELECT   §1.14.18

    `public final static int LIST_SELECT = 701`

        An item in a list has been selected.

LOAD_FILE   §1.14.19

    `public final static int LOAD_FILE = 1002`

        A file loading event.

LOST_FOCUS §1.14.20

```
public final static int LOST_FOCUS = 1005
```
A component lost the focus.

MOUSE_DOWN §1.14.21

```
public final static int MOUSE_DOWN = 501
```
The user has pressed the mouse button. The ALT_MASK flag (II-§1.14.58) indicates that the middle button has been pushed. The META_MASK flag (II-§1.14.61) indicates that the right button has been pushed.

MOUSE_DRAG §1.14.22

```
public final static int MOUSE_DRAG = 506
```
The user has moved the mouse with a button pushed. The ALT_MASK flag (II-§1.14.58) indicates that the middle button is being pushed. The META_MASK flag (II-§1.14.61) indicates that the right button is being pushed.

MOUSE_ENTER §1.14.23

```
public final static int MOUSE_ENTER = 504
```
The mouse has entered a component.

MOUSE_EXIT §1.14.24

```
public final static int MOUSE_EXIT = 505
```
The mouse has exited a component.

MOUSE_MOVE §1.14.25

```
public final static int MOUSE_MOVE = 503
```
The mouse has moved with no button pressed.

MOUSE_UP §1.14.26

```
public final static int MOUSE_UP = 502
```
The user has released the mouse button. The ALT_MASK flag (II-§1.14.58) indicates that the middle button has been pushed. The META_MASK flag (II-§1.14.61) indicates that the right button has been pushed.

SAVE_FILE §1.14.27

```
public final static int SAVE_FILE = 1003
```
A file saving event.

SCROLL_ABSOLUTE §1.14.28

```
public final static int SCROLL_ABSOLUTE = 605
```
The user has moved the bubble in a scroll bar.

SCROLL_LINE_DOWN §1.14.29

```
public final static int SCROLL_LINE_DOWN = 602
```
The user has pushed the "line down" area of a scroll bar.

SCROLL_LINE_UP §1.14.30

```
public final static int SCROLL_LINE_UP = 601
```
The user has pushed the "line up" area of a scroll bar.

SCROLL_PAGE_DOWN §1.14.31

```
public final static int SCROLL_PAGE_DOWN = 604
```
The user has pushed the "page down" area of a scroll bar.

SCROLL_PAGE_UP §1.14.32

```
public final static int SCROLL_PAGE_UP = 603
```
The user has pushed the "page up" area of a scroll bar.

WINDOW_DEICONIFY §1.14.33

```
public final static int WINDOW_DEICONIFY = 204
```
The user has asked the window manager to deiconify the window.

WINDOW_DESTROY §1.14.34

```
public final static int WINDOW_DESTROY = 201
```
The user has asked the window manager to kill the window.

WINDOW_EXPOSE §1.14.35

```
public final static int WINDOW_EXPOSE = 202
```
A window has become exposed.

WINDOW_ICONIFY §1.14.36

```
public final static int WINDOW_ICONIFY = 203
```
The user has asked the window manager to iconify the window.

WINDOW_MOVED §1.14.37

```
public final static int WINDOW_MOVED = 205
```
The window has moved.

DOWN §1.14.38

```
public final static int DOWN = 1005
```
The down key.

END §1.14.39

```
public final static int END = 1001
```
The end key.

F1   §1.14.40

    public final static int F1 = 1008
        The F1 function key.

F2   §1.14.41

    public final static int F2 = 1009
        The F2 function key.

F3   §1.14.42

    public final static int F3 = 1010
        The F3 function key.

F4   §1.14.43

    public final static int F4 = 1011
        The F4 function key.

F5   §1.14.44

    public final static int F5 = 1012
        The F5 function key.

F6   §1.14.45

    public final static int F6 = 1013
        The F6 function key.

F7   §1.14.46

    public final static int F7 = 1014
        The F7 function key.

F8   §1.14.47

    public final static int F8 = 1015
        The F8 function key.

F9   §1.14.48

    public final static int F9 = 1016
        The F9 function key.

F10   §1.14.49

    public final static int F10 = 1017
        The F10 function key.

F11   §1.14.50

    public final static int F11 = 1018
        The F11 function key.

F12 §1.14.51

```
public final static int F12 = 1019
```
The F12 function key.

HOME §1.14.52

```
public final static int HOME = 1008
```
The home key.

LEFT §1.14.53

```
public final static int LEFT = 1006
```
The left arrow key.

PGDN §1.14.54

```
public final static int PGDN = 1003
```
The page down key.

PGUP §1.14.55

```
public final static int PGUP = 1002
```
The page up key.

RIGHT §1.14.56

```
public final static int RIGHT = 1007
```
The right arrow key.

UP §1.14.57

```
public final static int UP = 1004
```
The up arrow key.

ALT_MASK §1.14.58

```
public final static int ALT_MASK = 8
```
This flag indicates that the "alt" key was down when the event occurred. For mouse events, this flag indicates that the middle button was pressed or released.

CTRL_MASK §1.14.59

```
public final static int CTRL_MASK = 2
```
This flag indicates that the control key was down when the event occurred.

SHIFT_MASK §1.14.60

```
public final static int SHIFT_MASK = 0
```
This flag indicates that the shift key was down when the event occurred.

META_MASK   §1.14.61

```
public final static int META_MASK = 4
```

This flag indicates that the meta key was down when the event occurred. For mouse events, this flag indicates that the right button was pressed or released.

Constructors

Event   §1.14.62

```
public Event(Object target, int id, Object arg)
```

Creates an Event with the specified target component, event type, and argument.

PARAMETERS:

target: the target component.
id: the event type.
arg: the specified argument.

Event   §1.14.63

```
public Event(Object target, long when, int id,
            int x, int y, int key, int modifiers)
```

Creates an Event with the specified target component, time stamp, event type, x and y coordinates, keyboard key, state of the modifier keys, and an argument set to null.

PARAMETERS:

target: the target component.
when: the time stamp.
id: the event type.
x: the x coordinate.
y: the y coordinate.
key: the key pressed in a keyboard event.
modifiers: the state of the modifier keys.

Event §1.14.64

```
public Event(Object target, long when, int id, int x,
            int y, int key, int modifiers, Object arg)
```

Creates an Event with the specified target component, time stamp, event type, *x* and *y* coordinates, keyboard key, state of the modifier keys, and argument.

PARAMETERS:

target: the target component.
when: the time stamp.
id: the event type.
x: the *x* coordinate.
y: the *y* coordinate.
key: the key pressed in a keyboard event.
modifiers: the state of the modifier keys.
arg: the specified argument.

Methods

controlDown §1.14.65

```
public boolean controlDown()
```

RETURNS:

true if this event indicates that the control key was down; false otherwise.

SEE ALSO:

modifiers (II-§1.14.6).
shiftDown (II-§1.14.68).
metaDown (II-§1.14.66).

metaDown §1.14.66

```
public boolean metaDown()
```

RETURNS:

true if this event indicates that the meta key was down; false otherwise.

SEE ALSO:

modifiers (II-§1.14.6).
shiftDown (II-§1.14.68).
controlDown (II-§1.14.65).

paramString   §1.14.67

```
protected String paramString()
```

Returns the parameter string representing this event. This string is useful for debugging.

RETURNS:

the parameter string of this event.

shiftDown   §1.14.68

```
public boolean shiftDown()
```

RETURNS:

true if this event indicates that the shift key was down; false otherwise.

SEE ALSO:

modifiers **(II-§1.14.6)**.
controlDown **(II-§1.14.65)**.
metaDown **(II-§1.14.66)**.

toString   §1.14.69

```
public String toString()
```

RETURNS:

a string representation of this event.

OVERRIDES:

toString in class Object **(I-§1.12.9)**.

translate   §1.14.70

```
public void translate(int dx, int dy)
```

Translates this event so that its x and y coordinates are increased by dx and dy, respectively.

PARAMETERS:

dx: the amount to translate the x coordinate.
dy: the amount to translate the y coordinate.

1.15 Class FileDialog

```
public class java.awt.FileDialog
    extends java.awt.Dialog (II-§1.12)
{
    // Fields
    public final static int LOAD;                        §1.15.1
    public final static int SAVE;                        §1.15.2

    // Constructors
    public FileDialog(Frame parent, String title);       §1.15.3
    public FileDialog(Frame parent, String title,        §1.15.4
                       int mode);
    // Methods
    public void addNotify();                             §1.15.5
    public String getDirectory();                        §1.15.6
    public String getFile();                             §1.15.7
    public FilenameFilter getFilenameFilter();           §1.15.8
    public int getMode();                                §1.15.9
    protected String paramString();                      §1.15.10
    public void setDirectory(String dir);                §1.15.11
    public void setFile(String file);                    §1.15.12
    public void setFilenameFilter(FilenameFilter filter); §1.15.13
}
```

The class FileDialog displays a dialog window from which the user can select a file.

Since it is a modal dialog, when its show method (II-§1.42.7) is called, it blocks the rest of the application until the user has chosen a file.

The AWT sends the file dialog window all mouse, keyboard, and focus events that occur over it.

Fields

LOAD §1.15.1

```
public final static int LOAD = 0
```

This constant value indicates that the file dialog window is intended to determine a file from which to read.

SAVE §1.15.2

```
public final static int SAVE = 1
```

This constant value indicates that the file dialog window is intended to determine a file to which to write.

Constructors

FileDialog   §1.15.3

  `public FileDialog(Frame parent, String title)`

  Creates a file dialog window with the specified title for loading a file. The files shown are those in the current directory.

  PARAMETERS:

  `parent`: the owner of the dialog.
  `title`: the title of the dialog.

FileDialog   §1.15.4

  `public FileDialog(Frame parent, String title, int mode)`

  Creates a file dialog window with the specified title for loading or saving a file.

  The `mode` argument must have the value `LOAD` **(II-§1.15.1)** or `SAVE` **(II-§1.15.2)**. The value `LOAD` indicates that the file dialog is finding a file to read. The value `SAVE` indicates that the file dialog is finding a place to write a file.

  PARAMETERS:

  `parent`: the owner of the dialog.
  `title`: the title of the dialog.
  `mode`: the mode of the dialog.

Methods

addNotify   §1.15.5

  `public void addNotify()`

  This method calls the `createFileDialog` method **(II-§1.41.9)** of this object's toolkit **(II-§1.10.20)** in order to create a `FileDialogPeer` **(II-§3.9)** for this file dialog window. The peer allows the application to change the look of a file dialog window without changing its functionality.

  Most applications do not call this method directly.

  OVERRIDES:

  `addNotify` in class `Dialog` **(II-§1.12.3)**.

getDirectory   §1.15.6

  `public String getDirectory()`

  RETURNS:

  the directory of this dialog.

getFile §1.15.7

    `public String getFile()`

    RETURNS:

    the currently selected file of this file dialog window, or `null` if none is selected.

getFilenameFilter §1.15.8

    `public FilenameFilter getFilenameFilter()`

    Determines this file dialog's filename filter. A filename filter **(I-§2.26)** allows the user to specify which files appear in the file dialog window.

    RETURNS:

    this file dialog's filename filter

getMode §1.15.9

    `public int getMode()`

    Indicates whether this file dialog box is for loading from a file or for saving to a file.

    RETURNS:

    the mode of this file dialog window; the value is either LOAD **(II-§1.15.1)** or SAVE **(II-§1.15.2)** .

paramString §1.15.10

    `protected String paramString()`

    Returns the parameter string representing the state of this file dialog window. This string is useful for debugging.

    RETURNS:

    the parameter string of this file dialog window.

    OVERRIDES:

    paramString in class `Dialog` **(II-§1.12.7)**.

setDirectory §1.15.11

    `public void setDirectory(String dir)`

    Sets the directory of this file dialog window to be the specified directory.

    PARAMETERS:

    `dir`: the specific directory.

setFile   §1.15.12

    `public void setFile(String file)`

    Sets the selected file for this file dialog window to be the specified file. This file becomes the default file if it is set before the file dialog window is first shown.

PARAMETERS:

`file`: the file being set.

setFilenameFilter   §1.15.13

    `public void setFilenameFilter(FilenameFilter filter)`

    Sets the filename filter **(I-§2.26)** for this file dialog window to the specified filter.

PARAMETERS:

`filter`: the specified filter.

1.16 Class FlowLayout

```
public class java.awt.FlowLayout
    extends java.lang.Object (I-§1.12)
    implements java.awt.LayoutManager (II-§1.43)
{
    // Fields
    public final static int CENTER;                         §1.16.1
    public final static int LEFT;                           §1.16.2
    public final static int RIGHT;                          §1.16.3

    // Constructors
    public FlowLayout();                                    §1.16.4
    public FlowLayout(int align);                           §1.16.5
    public FlowLayout(int align, int hgap, int vgap);       §1.16.6

    // Methods
    public void addLayoutComponent(String name,             §1.16.7
                              Component comp);
    public void layoutContainer(Container target);          §1.16.8
    public Dimension minimumLayoutSize(Container target);   §1.16.9
    public Dimension preferredLayoutSize(Container target); §1.16.10
    public void removeLayoutComponent(Component comp);      §1.16.11
    public String toString();                               §1.16.12
}
```

    A flow layout arranges components in a left-to-right flow, much like lines of text in a paragraph. Flow layouts are typically used to arrange buttons in a panel.

For example, the following picture shows an applet using the flow layout manager (its default layout manager) to position three buttons:

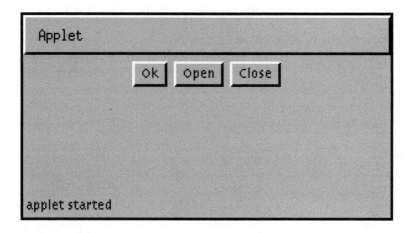

Here is the applet code:

```
import java.awt.*;
import java.applet.Applet;

public class myButtons extends Applet {
Button button1, button2, button3;
public void init() {
    button1 = new Button("Ok");
    button2 = new Button("Open");
    button3 = new Button("Close");
    add(button1);
    add(button2);
    add(button3);
    }
}
```

A flow layout lets each component take its natural (preferred) size.

Fields

CENTER   §1.16.1

```
public final static int CENTER = 1
```
This value indicates that each row of components should be centered.

LEFT   §1.16.2

```
public final static int LEFT = 0
```

This value indicates that each row of components should be left-justified.

RIGHT   §1.16.3

```
public final static int RIGHT = 2
```

This value indicates that each row of components should be right-justified.

Constructors

FlowLayout   §1.16.4

```
public FlowLayout()
```

Creates a new flow layout manager with a centered alignment and a default 5-pixel horizontal and vertical gap.

FlowLayout   §1.16.5

```
public FlowLayout(int align)
```

Creates a new flow layout manager with the indicated alignment and a default 5-pixel horizontal and vertical gap.

The alignment argument must be one of LEFT, RIGHT, or CENTER.

PARAMETERS:

align: the alignment value.

FlowLayout   §1.16.6

```
public FlowLayout(int align, int hgap, int vgap)
```

Creates a new flow layout manager with the indicated alignment and the indicated horizontal and vertical gaps.

The alignment argument must be one of LEFT, RIGHT, or CENTER.

PARAMETERS:

align: the alignment value.
hgap: the horizontal gap between components.
vgap: the vertical gap between components.

Methods

addLayoutComponent §1.16.7

```
public void addLayoutComponent(String name, Component comp)
```

This method is not used by the flow layout manager.

PARAMETERS:

name: a tag.
comp: the component to be added.

layoutContainer §1.16.8

```
public void layoutContainer(Container target)
```

Lays out the container argument using this layout.

This method lets each component take its preferred size.

Most applications do not call this method directly. This method is called when a container calls its layout method (**II-§1.11.11**).

PARAMETERS:

target: the container in which to do the layout.

SEE ALSO:

Container (**II-§1.11**).

minimumLayoutSize §1.16.9

```
public Dimension minimumLayoutSize(Container target)
```

Determines the minimum size of the target container using this flow layout.

The minimum width needed to lay out the container's components is the total minimum width of each of the components, plus (ncomponents + 1) times the horizontal gap, plus the left and right inset, where ncomponents is the number of components in the container.

The minimum height needed to lay out the container's components is the greatest minimum height of the components, plus twice the vertical gap, plus the top and bottom insets.

Most applications do not call this method directly. This method is called when a container calls its layout method (**II-§1.11.11**).

PARAMETERS:

target: the container in which to do the layout.

RETURNS:

the minimum dimensions needed to lay out the subcomponents of the specified container.

SEE ALSO:

preferredLayoutSize (**II-§1.16.10**).

preferredLayoutSize   **§1.16.10**

    public Dimension preferredLayoutSize(Container target)

Determines the preferred size of the `target` container using this flow layout.

The preferred width to lay out the container's components is the total preferred width of each of the components, plus (`ncomponents` + 1) times the horizontal gap, plus the left and right inset, where `ncomponents` is the number of components in the container.

The preferred height to lay out the container's components is the greatest preferred height of the components, plus twice the vertical gap, plus the top and bottom insets.

Most applications do not call this method directly. This method is called when a container calls its `preferredSize` method (**II-§1.11.17**).

PARAMETERS:

parent: the container in which to do the layout.

RETURNS:

the preferred dimensions to lay out the subcomponents of the specified container.

SEE ALSO:

Container (**II-§1.11**).
minimumLayoutSize (**II-§1.16.9**).

removeLayoutComponent   **§1.16.11**

    public void removeLayoutComponent(Component comp)

Removes the specified component from this layout.

Most applications do not call this method directly. This method is called when a container calls its `remove` (**II-§1.11.19**) or `removeAll` (**II-§1.11.20**) methods.

PARAMETERS:

comp: the component to be removed.

toString   **§1.16.12**

    public String toString()

RETURNS:

a string representation of this layout.

OVERRIDES:

toString in class Object (**I-§1.12.9**).

1.17 Class Font

```
public class java.awt.Font
    extends java.lang.Object (I-§1.12)
{
    // Fields
    protected String name;                                        §1.17.1
    protected int size;                                           §1.17.2
    protected int style;                                          §1.17.3

    // style has the following bit masks
    public final static int BOLD;                                 §1.17.4
    public final static int ITALIC;                               §1.17.5
    public final static int PLAIN;                                §1.17.6

    // Constructors
    public Font(String name, int style, int size);               §1.17.7

    // Methods
    public boolean equals(Object obj);                            §1.17.8
    public String getFamily();                                    §1.17.9
    public static Font getFont(String nm);                        §1.17.10
    public static Font getFont(String nm, Font font);             §1.17.11
    public String getName();                                      §1.17.12
    public int getSize();                                         §1.17.13
    public int getStyle();                                        §1.17.14
    public int hashCode();                                        §1.17.15
    public boolean isBold();                                      §1.17.16
    public boolean isItalic();                                    §1.17.17
    public boolean isPlain();                                     §1.17.18
    public String toString();                                     §1.17.19
}
```

This class represents a font.

Fields

name   §1.17.1

    protected String name

      The logical name of this font.

size   §1.17.2

    protected int size

      The point size of this font.

style   §1.17.3

    protected int style

The style of the font. This is the sum of the constants PLAIN, BOLD, or
ITALIC.

BOLD   §1.17.4

    public final static int BOLD = 1

The bold style constant. This can be combined with the other style constants for mixed styles.

ITALIC   §1.17.5

    public final static int ITALIC = 2

The italicized style constant. This can be combined with the other style
constants for mixed styles.

PLAIN   §1.17.6

    public final static int PLAIN = 0

The plain style constant.

Constructors

Font   §1.17.7

    public Font(String name, int style, int size)

Creates a new font with the specified name, style, and point size.

PARAMETERS:
name: the font name.
style: the constant style used.
size: the point size of the font.

SEE ALSO:
getFontList in class Toolkit (II-§1.41.24).

Methods

equals §1.17.8

```
public boolean equals(Object obj)
```

The result is `true` if and only if the argument is not `null` and is a `Font` object with the same name, same style, and same point size as this `Font`.

PARAMETERS:

`obj`: the object to compare with.

RETURNS:

`true` if the objects are the same; `false` otherwise.

OVERRIDES:

`equals` in class `Object` (**I-§1.12.3**).

getFamily §1.17.9

```
public String getFamily()
```

RETURNS:

the platform-specific family name of this font.

SEE ALSO:

getName (**II-§1.17.12**).

getFont §1.17.10

```
public static Font getFont(String nm)
```

The first argument is treated as the name of a system property to be obtained as if by the method `System.getProperty` (**I-§1.18.10**). The string value of this property is then interpreted as a font, as described in the `get-Font` method of two arguments (**II-§1.17.11**).

If the specified property is not found, `null` is returned.

PARAMETERS:

`nm`: the property name.

RETURNS:

the Font value of the property.

getFont §1.17.11

```
public static Font getFont(String nm, Font font)
```

The first argument is treated as the name of a system property to be obtained as if by the method `System.getProperty` (**I-§1.18.10**). The string value of this property is then interpreted as a font.

The property value should be one of the following forms:

fontname–style–pointsize

fontname–pointsize

fontname–style

fontname

where *style* is one of the three strings "bold", "bolditalic", or "italic" and point size is a decimal representation of the point size.

The default style is PLAIN. The default point size is 12.

If the specified property is not found, the font argument is returned instead.

PARAMETERS:

nm: the property name.
font: a default font to return if property nm is not defined.

RETURNS:

the Font value of the property.

getName   §1.17.12

    public String getName()

RETURNS:

the logical name of this font.

SEE ALSO:

getFamily (II-§1.17.9).

getSize   §1.17.13

    public int getSize()

RETURNS:

the point size of this font.

getStyle   §1.17.14

    public int getStyle()

RETURNS:

the style of this font.

SEE ALSO:

isPlain (II-§1.17.18).
isBold (II-§1.17.16).
isItalic (II-§1.17.17).

hashCode §1.17.15

    `public int hashCode()`

    RETURNS:

    a hash code value for this font.

    OVERRIDES:

    hashCode in class `Object` (**I-§1.12.6**).

isBold §1.17.16

    `public boolean isBold()`

    RETURNS:

    `true` if this font is bold; `false` otherwise.

    SEE ALSO:

    getStyle (**II-§1.17.16**).

isItalic §1.17.17

    `public boolean isItalic()`

    RETURNS:

    `true` if this font is italic; `false` otherwise.

    SEE ALSO:

    getStyle (**II-§1.17.14**).

isPlain §1.17.18

    `public boolean isPlain()`

    RETURNS:

    `true` if this font is neither bold nor italic; `false` otherwise.

    SEE ALSO:

    getStyle (**II-§1.17.14**).

toString §1.17.19

    `public String toString()`

    RETURNS:

    a string representation of this font.

    OVERRIDES:

    toString in class `Object` (**I-§1.12.9**).

1.18 Class FontMetrics

```
public abstract class java.awt.FontMetrics
    extends java.lang.Object (I-§1.12)
{
    // Fields
    protected Font font;                                    §1.18.1

    // Constructors
    protected FontMetrics(Font font);                       §1.18.2

    // Methods
    public int bytesWidth(byte data[], int off, int len);   §1.18.3
    public int charsWidth(char data[], int off, int len);   §1.18.4
    public int charWidth(char ch);                          §1.18.5
    public int charWidth(int ch);                           §1.18.6
    public int getAscent();                                 §1.18.7
    public int getDescent();                                §1.18.8
    public Font getFont();                                  §1.18.9
    public int getHeight();                                 §1.18.10
    public int getLeading();                                §1.18.11
    public int getMaxAdvance();                             §1.18.12
    public int getMaxAscent();                              §1.18.13
    public int getMaxDescent();                             §1.18.14
    public int[] getWidths();                               §1.18.15
    public int stringWidth(String str);                     §1.18.16
    public String toString();                               §1.18.17
}
```

This class represents a font metrics object, which gives information about the rendering of a particular font on a particular screen.

When an application asks the AWT to place a character at the position $\langle x, y \rangle$, the character is placed so that its reference point (shown as the dot in the picture on the right) is put at that position. The reference point specifies a horizontal line called the *baseline* of the character. In normal printing, the baselines of the characters should align. In addition, every character in a font has an *ascent*, a *descent*, and an *advance width*. The ascent is the amount by which the character ascends above the baseline. The descent is the amount by which the character descends below the baseline.

The advance width indicates the position at which AWT should place the next character. If the current character is placed with its reference point at the position $\langle x, y \rangle$, and the character's advance width is w, then the following character is placed with its reference point at the position $\langle x + w, y \rangle$. The advance width is often the same as the width of character's bounding box, but need not be so. In particular, slanted and italic fonts often have characters whose top right corner extends slightly beyond the advance width.

An array of characters or a string can also have an ascent, a descent, and an advance width. The ascent of the array is the maximum ascent of any character in the array. The descent is the maximum descent of any character in the array. The advance width is the sum of the advance widths of each of the characters in the array.

The default implementations of these methods are inefficient; they are usually overridden by more efficient toolkit-specific implementations.

Fields

font §1.18.1

    `protected Font font`

      The actual font.

    SEE ALSO:

    `getFont` **(II-§1.18.9)**.

Constructors

FontMetrics §1.18.2

    `protected FontMetrics(Font font)`

      Creates a new `FontMetrics` object for finding out height and width information about the specified font and specific character glyphs in that font.

    PARAMETERS:

    `font`: the font.

    SEE ALSO:

    `Font` **(II-§1.17)**.

Methods

bytesWidth §1.18.3

```
public int bytesWidth(byte data[], int off, int len)
```

PARAMETERS:

data: an array of characters.
off: the start offset of the data.
len: the number of bytes to be measured.

RETURNS:

the advance width of the subarray of the specified byte array in the font
described by this font metric.

SEE ALSO:

stringWidth (II-§1.18.16).
charsWidth (II-§1.18.4).

charsWidth §1.18.4

```
public int charsWidth(char data[], int off, int len)
```

PARAMETERS:

data: an array of characters.
off: the start offset of the data.
len: the number of bytes measured.

RETURNS:

the advance width of the subarray of the specified char array in the font
described by this font metric.

SEE ALSO:

stringWidth (II-§1.18.16).
bytesWidth (II-§1.18.3).

charWidth §1.18.5

```
public int charWidth(char ch)
```

PARAMETERS:

ch: a char.

RETURNS:

the advance width of the specified char in the font described by this font
metric.

SEE ALSO:

stringWidth (II-§1.18.16).

charWidth   §1.18.6

```
public int charWidth(int ch)
```
PARAMETERS:

ch: a char.

RETURNS:

the advance width of the specified character in the font described by this font
   metric.

SEE ALSO:

stringWidth **(II-§1.18.16)**.

getAscent   §1.18.7

```
public int getAscent()
```

Determines the *font ascent* of the font described by this font metric. The
font ascent is the distance from the baseline to the top of most alphanumeric
characters. Some characters in the font may extend above this distance.

RETURNS:

the font ascent of the font.

SEE ALSO:

getMaxAscent **(II-§1.18.13)**.

getDescent   §1.18.8

```
public int getDescent()
```

Determines the *font descent* of the font described by this font metric. The
font descent is the distance from the baseline to the bottom of most alphanumeric characters. Some characters in the font may extend below this distance.

RETURNS:

the font descent of the font.

SEE ALSO:

getMaxDescent **(II-§1.18.14)**.

getFont   §1.18.9

```
public Font getFont()
```
RETURNS:

the font described by this font metric.

getHeight   §1.18.10

```
public int getHeight()
```

Determines the *standard height* of a line of text in the font described by this font metric. This standard height is the distance between the baselines of adjacent lines of text. It is computed as the sum

```
getLeading() + getAscent() + getDescent()
```

There is no guarantee that lines of text spaced at this distance must be disjoint; such lines may overlap if some characters overshoot either the standard ascent or the standard descent.

RETURNS:

the standard height of the font.

getLeading   §1.18.11

```
public int getLeading()
```

Determines the *standard leading* of the font described by this font metric. The standard leading (interline spacing) is the logical amount of space to be reserved between the descent of one line of text and the ascent of the next line. The height metric is calculated to include this extra space.

RETURNS:

the standard leading of the font.

getMaxAdvance   §1.18.12

```
public int getMaxAdvance()
```

RETURNS:

the maximum advance width of any character in the font, or –1 if the maximum advance is not known.

getMaxAscent   §1.18.13

```
public int getMaxAscent()
```

Determines the maximum ascent of the font described by this font metric. No character extends further above the baseline than this height.

RETURNS:

the maximum ascent of any character in the font.

SEE ALSO:

getAscent (II-§1.18.7).

getMaxDescent §1.18.14

```
public int getMaxDescent()
```

Determines the maximum descent of the font described by this font metric. No character extends further below the baseline than this height.

RETURNS:

the maximum descent of any character in the font.

SEE ALSO:

getDescent (II-§1.18.8).

getWidths §1.18.15

```
public int[] getWidths()
```

RETURNS:

any array giving the advance widths of the first 256 characters in the font described by this font metric.

stringWidth §1.18.16

```
public int stringWidth(String str)
```

PARAMETERS:

str: a string.

RETURNS:

the advance width of the specified string in the font described by this font metric.

SEE ALSO:

charsWidth (II-§1.18.4).
bytesWidth (II-§1.18.3).

toString §1.18.17

```
public String toString()
```

RETURNS:

a string representation of this font metric.

OVERRIDES:

toString in class Object (I-§1.12.9).

1.19 Class Frame

```
public class java.awt.Frame
    extends java.awt.Window (II-§1.42)
    implements java.awt.MenuContainer (II-§1.44)
{
    // possible cursor types for the setCursor method
    public final static int CROSSHAIR_CURSOR;          §1.19.1
    public final static int DEFAULT_CURSOR;            §1.19.2
    public final static int E_RESIZE_CURSOR;           §1.19.3
    public final static int HAND_CURSOR;               §1.19.4
    public final static int MOVE_CURSOR;               §1.19.5
    public final static int N_RESIZE_CURSOR;           §1.19.6
    public final static int NE_RESIZE_CURSOR;          §1.19.7
    public final static int NW_RESIZE_CURSOR;          §1.19.8
    public final static int S_RESIZE_CURSOR;           §1.19.9
    public final static int SE_RESIZE_CURSOR;          §1.19.10
    public final static int SW_RESIZE_CURSOR;          §1.19.11
    public final static int TEXT_CURSOR;               §1.19.12
    public final static int W_RESIZE_CURSOR;           §1.19.13
    public final static int WAIT_CURSOR;               §1.19.14

    // Constructors
    public Frame();                                    §1.19.15
    public Frame(String title);                        §1.19.16

    // Methods
    public void addNotify();                           §1.19.17
    public void dispose();                             §1.19.18
    public int getCursorType();                        §1.19.19
    public Image getIconImage();                       §1.19.20
    public MenuBar getMenuBar();                       §1.19.21
    public String getTitle();                          §1.19.22
    public boolean isResizable();                      §1.19.23
    protected String paramString();                    §1.19.24
    public void remove(MenuComponent m);               §1.19.25
    public void setCursor(int cursorType);             §1.19.26
    public void setIconImage(Image image);             §1.19.27
    public void setMenuBar(MenuBar mb);                §1.19.28
    public void setResizable(boolean resizable);       §1.19.29
    public void setTitle(String title);                §1.19.30
}
```

A frame is a top-level window with a title and a border. A frame can also have a menu bar. The AWT sends the frame all mouse, keyboard, and focus events that occur over it.

Fields

CROSSHAIR_CURSOR §1.19.1

    `public final static int CROSSHAIR_CURSOR = 1`

       A cross-hair shaped cursor.

DEFAULT_CURSOR §1.19.2

    `public final static int DEFAULT_CURSOR = 0`

       The default cursor.

E_RESIZE_CURSOR §1.19.3

    `public final static int E_RESIZE_CURSOR = 11`

       A cursor indicating that the right-hand border is being resized.

HAND_CURSOR §1.19.4

    `public final static int HAND_CURSOR = 12`

       A hand-shaped cursor.

MOVE_CURSOR §1.19.5

    `public final static int MOVE_CURSOR = 13`

       A cursor indicating that an object is being moved.

N_RESIZE_CURSOR §1.19.6

    `public final static int N_RESIZE_CURSOR = 8`

       A cursor indicating that the top border is being resized.

NE_RESIZE_CURSOR §1.19.7

    `public final static int NE_RESIZE_CURSOR = 7`

       A cursor indicating that the top right corner is being resized.

NW_RESIZE_CURSOR §1.19.8

    `public final static int NW_RESIZE_CURSOR = 6`

       A cursor indicating that the top left corner is being resized.

S_RESIZE_CURSOR §1.19.9

    `public final static int S_RESIZE_CURSOR = 9`

       A cursor indicating that the bottom edge is being resized.

SE_RESIZE_CURSOR §1.19.10

    `public final static int SE_RESIZE_CURSOR = 5`

       A cursor indicating that the bottom right edge is being resized.

SW_RESIZE_CURSOR   §1.19.11

  `public final static int SW_RESIZE_CURSOR = 4`

   A cursor indicating that the bottom left edge is being resized.

TEXT_CURSOR   §1.19.12

  `public final static int TEXT_CURSOR = 2`

   A cursor for text insertion.

W_RESIZE_CURSOR   §1.19.13

  `public final static int W_RESIZE_CURSOR = 10`

   A cursor indicating that the left edge is being resized.

WAIT_CURSOR   §1.19.14

  `public final static int WAIT_CURSOR = 3`

   A cursor indicating that a long-running operation is taking place.

Constructors

Frame   §1.19.15

  `public Frame()`

   Constructs a new frame; it is initially invisible and has no title.

Frame   §1.19.16

  `public Frame(String title)`

   Constructs a new frame; it is initially invisible and has the specified title.

  PARAMETERS:

  `title`: the title.

Methods

addNotify   §1.19.17

  `public void addNotify()`

   This method calls the `createFrame` method (**II-§1.41.10**) of this object's toolkit (**II-§1.10.20**) in order to create a `FramePeer` (**II-§3.10**) for this frame. This peer allows the application to change the look of a frame without changing its functionality.

   Most applications do not call this method directly.

  OVERRIDES:

  `addNotify` in class `Window` (**II-§1.42.2**).

dispose   §1.19.18

> `public void dispose()`
>
> Disposes of this frame, its menu bar, and any system resources used by this frame.
>
> **OVERRIDES:**
>
> `dispose` in class `Window` (**II-§1.42.3**).

getCursorType   §1.19.19

> `public int getCursorType()`
>
> **RETURNS:**
>
> the cursor type of this frame.

getIconImage   §1.19.20

> `public Image getIconImage()`
>
> **RETURNS:**
>
> the icon image for this frame, or `null` if this frame doesn't have an icon image.

getMenuBar   §1.19.21

> `public MenuBar getMenuBar()`
>
> **RETURNS:**
>
> the menu bar for this frame, or `null` if this frame doesn't have a menu bar.

getTitle   §1.19.22

> `public String getTitle()`
>
> **RETURNS:**
>
> the title of this frame, or `null` if this frame doesn't have a title.
>
> **SEE ALSO:**
>
> `setTitle` (**II-§1.19.30**).

isResizable   §1.19.23

> `public boolean isResizable()`
>
> Indicates whether this frame is resizable. By default, all frames are resizable.
>
> **RETURNS:**
>
> `true` if the user can resize this frame; `false` otherwise.

paramString   §1.19.24

```
protected String paramString()
```

Returns the parameter string representing the state of this frame. This string is useful for debugging.

RETURNS:

the parameter string of this frame.

OVERRIDES:

paramString in class Container (**II-§1.11.16**).

remove   §1.19.25

```
public void remove(MenuComponent m)
```

Removes the specified menu bar from this frame.

PARAMETERS:

m: the menu component to remove.

setCursor   §1.19.26

```
public void setCursor(int cursorType)
```

Sets the cursor image for this frame to be one of the predefined cursors.

PARAMETERS:

cursorType: one of the predefined cursor constants defined above
(**II-§1.19.1–§1.19.14**).

setIconImage   §1.19.27

```
public void setIconImage(Image image)
```

Sets the image to display when this frame is iconized. The default icon is platform-specific. Not all platforms support the concept of iconizing a window.

PARAMETERS:

image: the icon image to be displayed.

setMenuBar   §1.19.28

```
public void setMenuBar(MenuBar mb)
```

Sets the menu bar of this frame to the specified menu bar.

PARAMETERS:

mb: the new menu bar.

setResizable §1.19.29

```
public void setResizable(boolean resizable)
```

Determines whether this frame should be resizable. By default, a frame is resizable.

PARAMETERS:

resizable: true if this frame should be resizable; false otherwise.

setTitle §1.19.30

```
public void setTitle(String title)
```

Sets the title of this frame to the specified title.

PARAMETERS:

title: the new title of this frame, or null to remove the title.

SEE ALSO:

getTitle (II-§1.19.22).

1.20 Class Graphics

```
public abstract class java.awt.Graphics
    extends java.lang.Object (I-§1.12)
{
    // Constructors
    protected Graphics();                                          §1.20.1

    // Methods
    public abstract void clearRect(int x, int y,                  §1.20.2
                                int width, int height);
    public abstract void clipRect(int x, int y,                   §1.20.3
                                int width, int height);
    public abstract void                                          §1.20.4
        copyArea(int x, int y, int width,
                int height, int dx, int dy);
    public abstract Graphics create();                            §1.20.5
    public Graphics create(int x, int y,                          §1.20.6
                            int width, int height);
    public abstract void dispose();                               §1.20.7
    public void draw3DRect(int x, int y, int width,               §1.20.8
                            int height, boolean raised);
    public abstract voiddrawArc(int x, int y, int width,          §1.20.9
                            int height, int startAngle,
                            int arcAngle);
    public void drawBytes(byte data[], int offset,                §1.20.10
                            int length, int x, int y);
    public void drawChars(char data[], int offset,                §1.20.11
                            int length, int x, int y);
    public abstract boolean                                       §1.20.12
        drawImage(Image img, int x, int y, Color bgcolor,
                ImageObserver observer);
    public abstract boolean                                       §1.20.13
        drawImage(Image img, int x, int y,
                ImageObserver observer);
    public abstract boolean                                       §1.20.14
        drawImage(Image img, int x, int y,
                int width, int height, Color bgcolor,
                ImageObserver observer);
    public abstract boolean                                       §1.20.15
        drawImage(Image img, int x, int y,
                int width, int height,
                ImageObserver observer);
    public abstract void drawLine(int x1, int y1,                 §1.20.16
                            int x2, int y2);
    public abstract void drawOval(int x, int y,                   §1.20.17
                                int width, int height);
```

```
public abstract void                                    §1.20.18
    drawPolygon(int xPoints[], int yPoints[],
                int nPoints);
public void drawPolygon(Polygon p);                     §1.20.19
public void drawRect(int x, int y,                      §1.20.20
                    int width, int height);
public abstract void                                    §1.20.21
    drawRoundRect(int x, int y, int width,
                  int height, int arcWidth,
                  int arcHeight);
public abstract void                                    §1.20.22
    drawString(String str, int x, int y);
public void                                             §1.20.23
    fill3DRect(int x, int y, int width,
                int height, boolean raised);
public abstract void                                    §1.20.24
    fillArc(int x, int y, int width,
            int height, int startAngle,
            int arcAngle);
public abstract void                                    §1.20.25
    fillOval(int x, int y, int width, int height);
public abstract void                                    §1.20.26
    fillPolygon(int xPoints[], int yPoints[],
                int nPoints);
public void fillPolygon(Polygon p);                     §1.20.27
public abstract void                                    §1.20.28
    fillRect(int x, int y, int width, int height);
public abstract void                                    §1.20.29
    fillRoundRect(int x, int y, int width, int height,
                  int arcWidth, int arcHeight);
public void finalize();                                 §1.20.30
public abstract Rectangle getClipRect();                §1.20.31
public abstract Color getColor();                       §1.20.32
public abstract Font getFont();                         §1.20.33
public FontMetrics getFontMetrics();                    §1.20.34
public abstract FontMetrics getFontMetrics(Font f);     §1.20.35
public abstract void setColor(Color c);                 §1.20.36
public abstract void setFont(Font font);                §1.20.37
public abstract void setPaintMode();                    §1.20.38
public abstract void setXORMode(Color c1);              §1.20.39
public String toString();                               §1.20.40
public abstract void  translate(int x, int y);          §1.20.41
}
```

The Graphics class is the abstract base class for all graphics contexts which allow an application to draw onto components or onto off-screen images.

Unless otherwise stated, all graphics operations performed with a graphics context object only modify bits within the graphic context's clipping region (**II-§1.20.3**). All drawing or writing is done in the current color (**II-§1.20.36**), using the current paint mode (**II-§1.20.38, §1.20.39**), and in the current font (**II-§1.20.37**).

Constructors

Graphics   §1.20.1

```
protected Graphics()
```

This constructor is the default contructor for a graphics context.

Since `Graphics` is an abstract class, applications cannot call this constructor directly. Graphics contexts are obtained from other graphics contexts (**II-§1.20.5**) or are created by a component (**II-§1.10.17**).

Methods

clearRect   §1.20.2

```
public abstract void
clearRect(int x, int y, int width, int height)
```

Clears the specified rectangle by filling it with the background color of the screen.[5] This operation does not use the current paint mode (**II-§1.20.38, §1.20.39**).

PARAMETERS:

`x`: the *x* coordinate.
`y`: the *y* coordinate.
`width`: the width of the rectangle.
`height`: the height of the rectangle.

SEE ALSO:

`fillRect` (**II-§1.20.28**).
`drawRect` (**II-§1.20.20**).

---

[5]. In Java 1.0, the background color of offscreen images is white. In Java 1.1, the background color of offscreen images may be system dependent. Applications should use `setColor` (**II-§1.20.36**) followed by `fillRect` (**II-§1.20.28**) to ensure that an offscreen image is cleared to a specific color.

clipRect §1.20.3

```
public abstract void
clipRect(int x, int y, int width, int height)
```

Sets a clipping rectangle for this graphics context. The resulting clipping area is the intersection of the current clipping area and the specified rectangle.

Graphics operations performed with this graphics context have no effect outside the clipping area.

PARAMETERS:

x: the x coordinate.
y: the y coordinate.
width: the width of the rectangle.
height: the height of the rectangle.

SEE ALSO:

getClipRect (II-§1.20.31).

copyArea §1.20.4

```
public abstract void
copyArea(int x, int y, int width, int height,
         int dx, int dy)
```

Copies an area. The source is the rectangle with origin $\langle x, y \rangle$, and size specified by the width and height arguments. The destination is the rectangle with origin $\langle x + dx, y + dy \rangle$ and the same width and height.

The clipping rectangle of this graphics context affects only the destination, not the source.

PARAMETERS:

x: the x coordinate of the source.
y: the y coordinate of the source.
width: the width.
height: the height.
dx: the horizontal distance.
dy: the vertical distance.

create §1.20.5

```
public abstract Graphics create()
```

RETURNS:

a new graphics context that is a copy of this graphics context.

create   **§1.20.6**

```
public Graphics
create(int x, int y, int width, int height)
```

Creates a new graphics context. The new graphics context is identical to this graphics context, except in two respects:

♦ The new context is translated by $\langle x, y \rangle$. That is to say, the point $\langle 0, 0 \rangle$ in the new graphics context is the same as $\langle x, y \rangle$ in this graphics context.

♦ The graphics context has an additional clipping rectangle with origin $\langle 0, 0 \rangle$, and size specified by the width and height arguments, in addition to whatever (translated) clipping rectangle it inherited from this graphics context.

PARAMETERS:

x: the *x* coordinate.
y: the *y* coordinate.
width: the width of the clipping rectangle.
height: the height of the clipping rectangle.

RETURNS:

a new graphics context.

SEE ALSO:

translate (II-§1.20.41).

dispose   **§1.20.7**

```
public abstract void dispose()
```

Disposes of this graphics context.
The graphics context cannot be used after it has been disposed.

SEE ALSO:

finalize (II-§1.20.30).

draw3DRect   **§1.20.8**

```
public void draw3DRect(int x, int y, int width,
                       int height, boolean raised)
```

Draws a highlighted 3-D rectangle.

PARAMETERS:

x: the *x* coordinate.
y: the *y* coordinate.
width: the width of the rectangle.
height: the height of the rectangle.
raised: if true, the rectangle appears raised; if false, it appears lowered.

drawArc §1.20.9

```
public abstract void
drawArc(int x, int y, int width, int height,
        int startAngle, int arcAngle)
```

Draws a single circular or elliptical arc.

The center of the arc is the center of the rectangle whose origin is ⟨x, y⟩ and whose size is specified by the `width` and `height` arguments.

The two axes of the arc are given by the `width` and `height` arguments.

The arc is drawn from `startAngle` to `startAngle + arcAngle`. The start angle and arc angle are in degrees, not radians.

A start angle of 0 indicates the 3-o'clock position. A positive arc angle indicates a counterclockwise rotation; a negative arc angle indicates a clockwise rotation.

PARAMETERS:

`x`: the *x* coordinate.
`y`: the *y* coordinate.
`width`: the width of the rectangle.
`height`: the height of the rectangle.
`startAngle`: the beginning angle.
`arcAngle`: the angle of the arc (relative to `startAngle`).

SEE ALSO:

`fillArc` **(II-§1.20.24)**.

drawBytes §1.20.10

```
public void drawBytes(byte data[], int offset,
                      int length, int x, int y)
```

Draws the text given by the specified byte array using this graphics context's current font and color. The baseline of the first character is at position ⟨x, y⟩ in this graphics context's coordinate system.

PARAMETERS:

`data`: the data to be drawn.
`offset`: the start offset in the data.
`length`: the number of bytes that are drawn.
`x`: the *x* coordinate.
`y`: the *y* coordinate.

SEE ALSO:

`drawString` **(II-§1.20.22)**.
`drawChars` **(II-§1.20.11)**.

drawChars   §1.20.11

```
public void drawChars(char data[], int offset,
                      int length, int x, int y)
```

Draws the text given by the specified character array using this graphics context's current font and color. The baseline of the first character is at position $\langle x, y \rangle$ in the graphics context's coordinate system.

PARAMETERS:

data: the array of characters to be drawn.
offset: the start offset in the data.
length: the number of characters to be drawn.
x: the *x* coordinate.
y: the *y* coordinate.

SEE ALSO:

drawString (II-§1.20.22).
drawBytes (II-§1.20.10).

drawImage   §1.20.12

```
public abstract boolean
drawImage(Image img, int x, int y, Color bgcolor,
          ImageObserver observer)
```

Draws the specified image with its top left corner at $\langle x, y \rangle$ in this graphics context's coordinate space. Transparent pixels in the image are drawn in the specified background color.

If the image has not yet been completely loaded, the image observer's imageUpdate (II-§2.11.9) method is notified as more of the image becomes available.

PARAMETERS:

img: the specified image to be drawn.
x: the *x* coordinate.
y: the *y* coordinate.
bgcolor: the background color.
observer: object to notify when the image is loaded.

RETURNS:

true if all bits of the image are available; false otherwise.

SEE ALSO:

Image (II-§1.24).
ImageObserver (II-§2.11).

drawImage §1.20.13

```
public abstract boolean
drawImage(Image img, int x, int y, ImageObserver observer)
```

Draws the specified image with its top left corner at $\langle x, y \rangle$ in this graphics context's coordinate space. Transparent pixels in the image do not affect whatever pixels are already there.

If the image has not yet been completely loaded, the image observer's imageUpdate (**II-§2.11.9**) method is notified as more of the image becomes available.

PARAMETERS:

img: the specified image to be drawn.
x: the x coordinate.
y: the y coordinate.
observer: object to notify when the image is loaded.

RETURNS:

true if all bits of the image are available; false otherwise.

SEE ALSO:

Image (**II-§1.24**).
ImageObserver (**II-§2.11**).

drawImage   §1.20.14

```
public abstract boolean
drawImage(Image img, int x, int y, int width,
          int height, Color bgcolor, ImageObserver observer)
```

Draws the specified image inside the specified rectangle of this graphics context's coordinate space. The image is scaled if necessary. Transparent pixels in the image are drawn in the specified background color.

If the image has not yet been completely loaded, the image observer's imageUpdate (**II-§2.11.9**) method is notified as more of the image becomes available.

PARAMETERS:

img: the specified image to be drawn.
x: the *x* coordinate.
y: the *y* coordinate.
width: the width of the rectangle.
height: the height of the rectangle.
bgcolor: background color for the image.
observer: object to notify when the image is loaded.

RETURNS:

true if all bits of the image are available; false otherwise.

SEE ALSO:

Image (**II-§1.24**).
ImageObserver (**II-§2.11**).

drawImage §1.20.15

```
public abstract boolean
drawImage(Image img, int x, int y, int width,
        int height, ImageObserver observer)
```

Draws the specified image inside the specified rectangle of this graphics context's coordinate space. The image is scaled if necessary. Transparent pixels in the image do not affect whatever pixels are already there.

If the image has not yet been completely loaded, the image observer's imageUpdate **(II-§2.11.9)** method is notified as more of the image becomes available.

PARAMETERS:

img: the specified image to be drawn.
x: the x coordinate.
y: the y coordinate.
width: the width of the rectangle.
bgcolor: background color for the image.
observer: object to notify when the image is loaded.

RETURNS:

true if all bits of the image are available; false otherwise.

SEE ALSO:

Image **(II-§1.24)**.
ImageObserver **(II-§2.11)**.

drawLine §1.20.16

```
public abstract void
drawLine(int x1, int y1, int x2, int y2)
```

Draws a line from $\langle x1, y1 \rangle$ to $\langle x2, y2 \rangle$ in this graphics context's coordinate system.

The line is drawn below and to the right of the logical coordinates.

PARAMETERS:

x1: the first point's x coordinate.
y1: the first point's y coordinate.
x2: the second point's x coordinate.
y2: the second point's y coordinate.

drawOval §1.20.17

```
public abstract void
drawOval(int x, int y, int width, int height)
```

Draws a circle or an ellipse such that it fits within the rectangle specified by the x, y, width, and height arguments.

The center of the oval is the center of the rectangle whose origin is ⟨x, y⟩ in this graphics context's coordinate system and whose size is specified by the width and height arguments.

PARAMETERS:

x: the *x* coordinate.
y: the *y* coordinate.
width: the width of the rectangle.
height: the height of the rectangle.

SEE ALSO:

fillOval (II-§1.20.25).

drawPolygon §1.20.18

```
public abstract void
drawPolygon(int xPoints[], int yPoints[], int nPoints)
```

Draws a closed polygon defined by an array of x coordinates and y coordinates.

This method draws the polygon defined by npoint line segments, where the first npoint−1 line segments are line segments from ⟨xpoints[$i-1$], ypoints[$i-1$]⟩ to ⟨xpoints[i], ypoints[i]⟩, for $1 \le i <$ npoints. The last line segment starts at the final point and ends at the first point.

PARAMETERS:

xPoints: an array of x coordinates.
yPoints: an array of y coordinates.
nPoints: the total number of points.

SEE ALSO:

fillPolygon (II-§1.20.26).

drawPolygon §1.20.19

```
public void drawPolygon(Polygon p)
```

Draws a polygon defined by the specified polygon argument.

PARAMETERS:

p: a polygon.

SEE ALSO:

fillPolygon (II-§1.20.26).

drawRect §1.20.20

```
public void drawRect(int x, int y, int width, int height)
```

Draws the outline of the specified rectangle using the current color. The left and right edges of the rectangle are at x and x + width, respectively. The top and bottom edges of the rectangle are at y and y + height respectively.

PARAMETERS:

x: the *x* coordinate.
y: the *y* coordinate.
width: the width of the rectangle.
height: the height of the rectangle.

SEE ALSO:

fillRect (**II-§1.20.28**).
clearRect (**II-§1.20.2**).

drawRoundRect §1.20.21

```
public abstract void
drawRoundRect(int x, int y, int width, int height,
            int arcWidth, int arcHeight)
```

Draws an outlined round-cornered rectangle using this graphics context's current color. The left and right edges of the rectangle are at x and x + width, respectively. The top and bottom edges of the rectangle are at y and y + height .

PARAMETERS:

x: the *x* coordinate.
y: the *y* coordinate.
width: the width of the rectangle.
height: the height of the rectangle.
arcWidth: the horizontal diameter of the arc at the four corners.
arcHeight: the vertical diameter of the arc at the four corners.

SEE ALSO:

fillRoundRect (**II-§1.20.29**).

drawString   §1.20.22

```
public abstract void drawString(String str, int x, int y)
```

Draws the string using this graphics context's current font and color. The baseline of the first character is at position $\langle x, y \rangle$ in the graphics context's coordinate system.

PARAMETERS:

str: the string to be drawn.
x: the *x* coordinate.
y: the *y* coordinate.

SEE ALSO:

drawChars (**II-§1.20.11**).
drawBytes (**II-§1.20.10**).

fill3DRect   §1.20.23

```
public void fill3DRect(int x, int y, int width,
                         int height, boolean raised)
```

Draws a highlighted 3-D rectangle that is filled with this graphics context's current color.

PARAMETERS:

x: the *x* coordinate.
y: the *y* coordinate.
width: the width of the rectangle.
height: the height of the rectangle.
raised: if true, the rectangle is raised; if false, it is lowered.

fillArc §1.20.24

```
public abstract void
fillArc(int x, int y, int width, int height,
        int startAngle, int arcAngle)
```

Draws a single circular or elliptical arc that is filled with this graphics context's current color. The result is a pie shape.

The center of the arc is the center of the rectangle whose origin is ⟨x, y⟩ and whose size is specified by the width and height arguments.

The two axes of the arc are given by the width and height arguments.

The arc is drawn from startAngle to startAngle + arcAngle. The start angle and arc angle are in degrees, not radians.

A start angle of 0 indicates the 3-o'clock position. A positive arc angle indicates a counterclockwise rotation; a negative arc angle indicates a clockwise rotation.

PARAMETERS:

x: the *x* coordinate.
y: the *y* coordinate.
width: the width of the rectangle.
height: the height of the rectangle.
startAngle: the beginning angle.
arcAngle: the angle of the arc (relative to startAngle).

SEE ALSO:

drawArc (**II-§1.20.9**).

fillOval §1.20.25

```
public abstract void
fillOval(int x, int y, int width, int height)
```

Draws a filled circle or a filled ellipse using this graphics context's current color.

The center of the oval is the center of the rectangle whose origin is ⟨x, y⟩ in the graphics context's coordinate system and whose size is specified by the width and height arguments.

PARAMETERS:

x: the *x* coordinate.
y: the *y* coordinate.
width: the width of the rectangle.
height: the height of the rectangle.

SEE ALSO:

drawOval (**II-§1.20.17**).

fillPolygon   §1.20.26

```
public abstract void
fillPolygon(int xPoints[], int yPoints[], int nPoints)
```

Fills a polygon defined by an array of x coordinates and y coordinates with this graphics context's current color.

This method fills the polygon defined by npoint line segments, where the first npoint-1 line segments are line segments from $\langle \text{xpoints}[i-1], \text{ypoints}[i-1]\rangle$ to $\langle \text{xpoints}[i], \text{ypoints}[i]\rangle$, for $1 \leq i < \text{npoints}$. The last line segment starts at the final point and ends at the first point.

The area inside the polygon is defined using an "even$-$odd" fill rule, also known as the "alternating rule."

PARAMETERS:

xPoints: an array of x coordinates.
yPoints: an array of y coordinates.
nPoints: the total number of points.

SEE ALSO:

drawPolygon (**II-§1.20.18**).

fillPolygon   §1.20.27

```
public void fillPolygon(Polygon p)
```

Fills a polygon defined by the specified polygon argument with this graphics context's current color.

The area inside the polygon is defined using an "even-odd" fill rule, also known as the "alternating rule."

PARAMETERS:

p: the polygon.

SEE ALSO:

drawPolygon (**II-§1.20.19**).

fillRect §1.20.28

```
public abstract void
fillRect(int x, int y, int width, int height)
```

Fills the specified rectangle with this graphics context's current color. The left and right edges are at x and x + width − 1, respectively. The top and bottom edges are at y and y + height − 1, respectively.

PARAMETERS:

x: the *x* coordinate.
y: the *y* coordinate.
width: the width of the rectangle.
height: the height of the rectangle.

SEE ALSO:

drawRect (**II-§1.20.20**).
clearRect (**II-§1.20.2**).

fillRoundRect §1.20.29

```
public abstract void
fillRoundRect(int x, int y, int width, int height,
              int arcWidth, int arcHeight)
```

Fills an outlined rounded corner rectangle with this graphics context's current color. The left and right edges are at x and x + width − 1, respectively. The top and bottom edges are at y and y + height − 1, respectively.

PARAMETERS:

x: the *x* coordinate.
y: the *y* coordinate.
width: the width of the rectangle.
height: the height of the rectangle.
arcWidth: the horizontal diameter of the arc at the four corners.
arcHeight: the vertical diameter of the arc at the four corners.

SEE ALSO:

drawRoundRect (**II-§1.20.21**).

finalize §1.20.30

```
public void finalize()
```

The finalize method ensures that this graphics context's dispose method (**II-§1.20.7**) is called when this graphics context is no longer referenced.

OVERRIDES:

finalize in class Object (**I-§1.12.4**).

getClipRect   §1.20.31
> `public abstract Rectangle getClipRect()`
>
> **RETURNS:**
>
> the bounding rectangle of this graphics context's clipping area.
>
> **SEE ALSO:**
>
> `clipRect` **(II-§1.20.3)**.

getColor   §1.20.32
> `public abstract Color getColor()`
>
> **RETURNS:**
>
> this graphics context's current color.
>
> **SEE ALSO:**
>
> `setColor` **(II-§1.20.36)**.

getFont   §1.20.33
> `public abstract Font getFont()`
>
> **RETURNS:**
>
> this graphics context's current font.
>
> **SEE ALSO:**
>
> `setFont` **(II-§1.20.37)**.

getFontMetrics   §1.20.34
> `public FontMetrics getFontMetrics()`
>
> **RETURNS:**
>
> the font metrics of this graphics context's current font.
>
> **SEE ALSO:**
>
> `getFont` **(II-§1.20.33)**.

getFontMetrics   §1.20.35
> `public abstract FontMetrics getFontMetrics(Font f)`
>
> **PARAMETERS:**
>
> `f`: the specified font.
>
> **RETURNS:**
>
> the font metrics for the specified font.
>
> **SEE ALSO:**
>
> `getFont` **(II-§1.20.33)**.

setColor §1.20.36

```
public abstract void setColor(Color c)
```

Sets this graphics context's current color to the specified color. All subsequent graphics operations using this graphics context use this specified color.

PARAMETERS:

c: the color.

SEE ALSO:

Color (II-§1.9).

getColor (II-§1.20.32).

setFont §1.20.37

```
public abstract void setFont(Font font)
```

Sets this graphics context's font to the specified font.

All subsequent text operations [such as drawString (II-§1.20.22), drawBytes (II-§1.20.10), and drawChars (II-§1.20.11)] using this graphics context use this font.

PARAMETERS:

font: the font.

setPaintMode §1.20.38

```
public abstract void setPaintMode()
```

Sets the paint mode of this graphics context to overwrite the destination with this graphics context's current color.

setXORMode §1.20.39

```
public abstract void setXORMode(Color c1)
```

Sets the paint mode of this graphics context to alternate between this graphics context's current color and the new specified color.

When drawing operations are performed, pixels which are the current color are changed to the specified color, and vice versa.

Pixels that are of colors other than those two colors are changed in an unpredictable but reversible manner; if the same figure is drawn twice, then all pixels are restored to their original values.

PARAMETERS:

c1: the second color.

toString   §1.20.40

```
public String toString()
```
RETURNS:

a string representation of this graphics context.

OVERRIDES:

toString in class Object (**I-§1.12.9**).

translate   §1.20.41

```
public abstract void translate(int x, int y)
```

   Modifies this graphics context so that its new origin corresponds to the point $\langle x, y \rangle$ in this graphics context's original coordinate system.

PARAMETERS:

x: the *x* coordinate.
y: the *y* coordinate.

1.21 Class GridBagConstraints

```
public class java.awt.GridBagConstraints
     extends java.lang.Object (I-§1.12)
     implements java.lang.Cloneable (I-§1.22)
{
     // Fields
     public int anchor;                              §1.21.1
     public int fill;                                §1.21.2
     public int gridheight;                          §1.21.3
     public int gridwidth;                           §1.21.4
     public int gridx;                               §1.21.5
     public int gridy;                               §1.21.6
     public Insets insets;                           §1.21.7
     public int ipadx;                               §1.21.8
     public int ipady;                               §1.21.9
     public double weightx;                          §1.21.10
     public double weighty;                          §1.21.11

     // the anchor field has one of the following values
     public final static int CENTER;                 §1.21.12
     public final static int EAST;                   §1.21.13
     public final static int NORTH;                  §1.21.14
     public final static int NORTHEAST;              §1.21.15
     public final static int NORTHWEST;              §1.21.16
     public final static int SOUTH;                  §1.21.17
     public final static int SOUTHEAST;              §1.21.18
     public final static int SOUTHWEST;              §1.21.19
     public final static int WEST;                   §1.21.20

     // the fill field has one of the following values
     public final static int BOTH;                   §1.21.21
     public final static int HORIZONTAL;             §1.21.22
     public final static int NONE;                   §1.21.23
     public final static int VERTICAL;               §1.21.24

     // default value for gridheight, gridwidth
     public final static int REMAINDER;              §1.21.25

     // default value for gridx, gridy
     public final static int RELATIVE;               §1.21.26

     // Constructors
     public GridBagConstraints();                    §1.21.27

     // Methods
     public Object clone();                          §1.21.28
}
```

The `GridBagConstraints` class specifies constraints for components that are laid out using the `GridBagLayout` class (**II-§1.22**).

Fields

anchor §1.21.1

```
public int anchor
```

This field is used when the component is smaller than its display area. It determines where, within the area, to place the component. Valid values are the following:

```
CENTER
NORTH
NORTHEAST
EAST
SOUTHEAST
SOUTH
SOUTHWEST
WEST
NORTHWEST
```

The default value is `CENTER`.

fill §1.21.2

```
public int fill
```

This field is used when the component's display area is larger than the component's requested size. It determines whether to resize the component, and if so, how.

Valid values are the following:

- ◆ `NONE`: Do not resize the component.

- ◆ `HORIZONTAL`: Make the component wide enough to fill its display area horizontally, but do not change its height.

- ◆ `VERTICAL`: Make the component tall enough to fill its display area vertically, but do not change its width.

- ◆ `BOTH`: Make the component fill its display area entirely.

The default value is `NONE`.

gridheight §1.21.3

```
public int gridheight
```

Specifies the number of cells in a column for the component's display area.

Use REMAINDER to specify that the component be the last one in its column. Use RELATIVE to specify that the component be the next-to-last one in its column.

The default value is 1.

gridwidth §1.21.4

```
public int gridwidth
```

Specifies the number of cells in a row for the component's display area.

Use REMAINDER to specify that the component be the last one in its row. Use RELATIVE to specify that the component be the next-to-last one in its row.

The default value is 1.

gridx §1.21.5

```
public int gridx
```

Specifies the cell at the left of the component's display area, where the leftmost cell has gridx = 0. The value RELATIVE specifies that the component be placed just to the right of the component that was added to the container just before this component was added.

The default value is Relative.

gridy §1.21.6

```
public int gridy
```

Specifies the cell at the top of the component's display area, where the topmost cell has gridy = 0. The value RELATIVE specifies that the component be placed just below the component that was added to the container just before this component was added.

The default value is Relative.

insets §1.21.7

```
public Insets insets
```

This field specifies the external padding of the component, the minimum amount of space between the component and the edges of its display area.

The default value is new Insets(0, 0, 0, 0).

ipadx   §1.21.8

```
public int ipadx
```

This field specifies the internal padding, that is, how much space to add to the minimum width of the component. The width of the component is at least its minimum width plus ipadx*2 pixels.

The default value is 0.

ipady   §1.21.9

```
public int ipady
```

This field specifies the internal padding, how much to add to the minimum height of the component. The height of the component is at least its minimum height plus ipady*2 pixels.

The default value is 0.

weightx   §1.21.10

```
public double weightx
```

This field specifies how to distribute extra vertical space.

The grid bag layout manager calculates the weight of a row to be the maximum weightx of all the components in a row. If the resulting layout is smaller vertically than the area it needs to fill, the extra space is distributed to each row in proportion to its weight. A row that has weight 0 receives no extra space.

If all the weights are zero, all the extra space appears between the grids of the cell and the top and bottom edges.

The default value of this field is 0.

weighty   §1.21.11

```
public double weighty
```

This field specifies how to distribute extra horizontal space.

The grid bag layout manager calculates the weight of a column to be the maximum weighty of all the components in a row. If the resulting layout is smaller horizontally than the area it needs to fill, the extra space is distributed to each column in proportion to its weight. A column that has weight 0 receives no extra space.

If all the weights are zero, all the extra space appears between the grids of the cell and the right and left edges.

The default value of this field is 0.

CENTER   §1.21.12

```
public final static int CENTER = 10
```

Put the component in the center of its display area.

EAST   §1.21.13

```
public final static int EAST = 13
```
Put the component on the right side of its display area, centered vertically.

NORTH   §1.21.14

```
public final static int NORTH = 11
```
Put the component at the top of its display area, centered horizontally.

NORTHEAST   §1.21.15

```
public final static int NORTHEAST = 12
```
Put the component in the top right corner of its display area.

NORTHWEST   §1.21.16

```
public final static int NORTHWEST = 18
```
Put the component in the top left corner of its display area.

SOUTH   §1.21.17

```
public final static int SOUTH = 15
```
Put the component at the bottom of its display area, centered horizontally.

SOUTHEAST   §1.21.18

```
public final static int SOUTHEAST = 14
```
Put the component in the bottom right corner of its display area.

SOUTHWEST   §1.21.19

```
public final static int SOUTHWEST = 16
```
Put the component in the bottom left corner of its display area.

WEST   §1.21.20

```
public final static int WEST = 17
```
Put the component on the left side of its display area, centered vertically.

BOTH   §1.21.21

```
public final static int BOTH = 1
```
Resize the component both horizontally and vertically.

HORIZONTAL   §1.21.22

```
public final static int HORIZONTAL = 2
```
Resize the component horizontally but not vertically.

NONE   §1.21.23

> `public final static int NONE = 0`
>> Do not resize the component.

VERTICAL   §1.21.24

> `public final static int VERTICAL = 3`
>> Resize the component vertically but not horizontally.

REMAINDER   §1.21.25

> `public final static int REMAINDER = 0`
>> Specify that the component is the last component in its column or row.

RELATIVE   §1.21.26

> `public final static int RELATIVE = -1`
>> Specify that this component is the next-to-last component in its column or row (`gridwidth`, `gridheight`), or that this component be placed next to the previously added component (`gridx`, `gridy`).

Constructors

GridBagConstraints   §1.21.27

> `public GridBagConstraints()`
>> Creates a grid bag constraint object with all the fields set to their default value.

Methods

clone   §1.21.28

> `public Object clone()`
> **RETURNS:**
> a copy of this grid bag constraint.
> **OVERRIDES:**
> clone in class Object (**I-§1.12.2**).

1.22 Class GridBagLayout

```
public class java.awt.GridBagLayout
    extends java.lang.Object (I-§1.12)
    implements java.awt.LayoutManager (II-§1.43)
{
    // Fields
    protected final static int MAXGRIDSIZE;            §1.22.1
    protected final static int MINSIZE;                §1.22.2

    // Constructors
    public GridBagLayout();                            §1.22.3

    // Methods
    public void addLayoutComponent(String name,        §1.22.4
                             Component comp);
    public GridBagConstraints                          §1.22.5
        getConstraints(Component comp);
    public void layoutContainer(Container target);     §1.22.6
    protected GridBagConstraints                       §1.22.7
        lookupConstraints(Component comp);
    public Dimension minimumLayoutSize(Container target);   §1.22.8
    public Dimension preferredLayoutSize(Container target); §1.22.9
    public void removeLayoutComponent(Component comp);      §1.22.10
    public void                                        §1.22.11
        setConstraints(Component comp,
                    GridBagConstraints constraints);
    public String toString();                          §1.22.12
}
```

The grid bag layout manager is a flexible layout manager that aligns components horizontally and vertically, without requiring that the components be the same size.

Each grid bag layout manager uses a rectangular grid of cells, with each component occupying one or more cells (called its *display area*). Each component in a grid bag layout is associated with a set of constraints contained within a GridBagConstraints instance that specifies how the component is to be laid out within its display area.

The manner in which the grid bag layout manager places a set of components depends on each component's constraints and its minimum size, as well as the preferred size of the components' container.

To use a grid bag layout effectively, one or more components must have a customized GridBagConstraints object created for them.

The fields of the GridBagConstraints object are described more fully in **II-§1.21**.

The following figure shows 10 components (all buttons) managed by a grid bag layout manager:

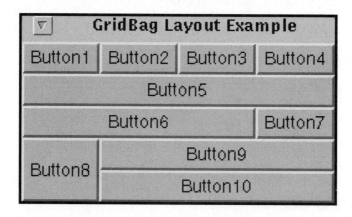

Each of the 10 components has the `fill` field of its constraint set to Grid-BagConstraints.BOTH. In addition, the buttons have the following nondefault constraints:

♦ Button1, Button2, Button3: `weightx` = 1.0

♦ Button4: `weightx` = 1.0, `gridwidth` = GridBagConstraints.REMAINDER

♦ Button5: `gridwidth` = GridBagConstraints.REMAINDER

♦ Button6: `gridwidth` = GridBagConstraints.RELATIVE

♦ Button7: `gridwidth` = GridBagConstraints.REMAINDER

♦ Button8: `gridheight` = 2, `weighty` = 1.0

♦ Button9, Button10: `gridwidth` = GridBagConstraints.REMAINDER

Here is the code that implements the example shown above:

```
import java.awt.*;
import java.util.*;
import java.applet.Applet;
public class GridBagEx1 extends Applet {
    protected void makebutton(String name,
                              GridBagLayout gridbag,
                              GridBagConstraints c) {
        Button button = new Button(name);
        gridbag.setConstraints(button, c);
        add(button);
    }
```

```java
    public void init() {
        GridBagLayout gridbag = new GridBagLayout();
        GridBagConstraints c = new GridBagConstraints();
        setFont(new Font("Helvetica", Font.PLAIN, 14));
        setLayout(gridbag);
        c.fill = GridBagConstraints.BOTH;
        c.weightx = 1.0;
        makebutton("Button1", gridbag, c);
        makebutton("Button2", gridbag, c);
        makebutton("Button3", gridbag, c);

        // end row
        c.gridwidth = GridBagConstraints.REMAINDER;
        makebutton("Button4", gridbag, c);
        c.weightx = 0.0;    //reset to the default
        makebutton("Button5", gridbag, c); //another row

        // next-to last in row
        c.gridwidth = GridBagConstraints.RELATIVE;
        makebutton("Button6", gridbag, c);
        c.gridwidth = GridBagConstraints.REMAINDER; //end row
        makebutton("Button7", gridbag, c);
        c.gridwidth = 1;         // reset to the default
        c.gridheight = 2;
        c.weighty = 1.0;
        makebutton("Button8", gridbag, c);
        c.weighty = 0.0;    //reset to the default

        // end row
        c.gridwidth = GridBagConstraints.REMAINDER;
        c.gridheight = 1;    // reset to the default
        makebutton("Button9", gridbag, c);
        makebutton("Button10", gridbag, c);
        resize(300, 100);
    }

    public static void main(String args[]) {
        Frame f = new Frame("GridBag Layout Example");
        GridBagEx1 ex1 = new GridBagEx1();
        ex1.init();
        f.add("Center", ex1);
        f.pack();
    f.show();
    }
}
```

Fields

MAXGRIDSIZE   §1.22.1

    `protected final static int MAXGRIDSIZE = 128`

        The maximum number of grid positions (both horizontally and vertically) that can be laid out by the grid bag layout.

MINSIZE   §1.22.2

    `protected final static int MINSIZE = 1`

        The smallest grid that can be laid out by the grid bag layout.

Constructors

GridBagLayout   §1.22.3

    `public GridBagLayout()`

        Creates a grid bag layout manager.

Methods

---

addLayoutComponent   §1.22.4

    `public void addLayoutComponent(String name, Component comp)`

        This method is not used by the grid bag layout manager.

PARAMETERS:

name: a tag understood by the layout manager.
comp: the component to be added.

getConstraints   §1.22.5

    `public GridBagConstraints getConstraints(Component comp)`

PARAMETERS:

comp: the component to be queried.

RETURNS:

the constraint for the specified component in this grid bag layout; a copy of the constraint object is returned.

layoutContainer   **§1.22.6**

> `public void layoutContainer(Container target)`

Lays out the container argument using this grid bag layout.

This method reshapes the components in the specified container in order to satisfy the constraints of this `GridBagLayout` object.

Most applications do not call this method directly. This method is called when a container calls its `layout` method (**II-§1.11.11**).

PARAMETERS:

`target`: the container in which to do the layout.

SEE ALSO:

`Container` (**II-§1.11**).

lookupConstraints   **§1.22.7**

> `protected GridBagConstraints`
> `lookupConstraints(Component comp)`

Retrieves the constraints for the specified component in this grid bag layout. The return value is not a copy, but is the actual `GridBagConstraints` object used by the layout mechanism.

PARAMETERS:

`comp`: the component to be queried.

RETURNS:

the contraints for the specified component.

minimumLayoutSize   **§1.22.8**

> `public Dimension minimumLayoutSize(Container target)`

Determines the minimum size of the `target` container using this grid bag layout.

This method is called when a container calls its `layout` method (**II-§1.11.11**). Most applications do not call this method directly.

PARAMETERS:

`target`: the container in which to do the layout.

RETURNS:

the minimum dimensions needed to lay out the subcomponents of the specified container.

SEE ALSO:

`preferredLayoutSize` (**II-§1.22.9**).

preferredLayoutSize   **§1.22.9**

```
public Dimension preferredLayoutSize(Container target)
```

Determines the preferred size of the `target` container using this grid bag layout.

Most applications do not call this method directly. This method is called when a container calls its `preferredSize` method **(II-§1.11.17)**.

PARAMETERS:

`target`: the container in which to do the layout.

RETURNS:

the preferred dimensions to lay out the subcomponents of the specified container.

SEE ALSO:

`minimumLayoutSize` **(II-§1.22.8)**.

removeLayoutComponent   **§1.22.10**

```
public void removeLayoutComponent(Component comp)
```

Removes the specified component from this layout.

Most applications do not call this method directly. This method is called when a container calls its `remove` **(II-§1.11.19)** or `removeAll` **(II-§1.11.20)** methods.

PARAMETERS:

`comp`: the component to be removed.

setConstraints   **§1.22.11**

```
public void setConstraints(Component comp,
                           GridBagConstraints constraints)
```

Sets the constraints for the specified component in this layout.

PARAMETERS:

`comp`: the component to be modified.
`constraints`: the constraints to be applied.

toString   **§1.22.12**

```
public String toString()
```

RETURNS:

a string representation of this grid bag layout.

OVERRIDES:

`toString` in class `Object` **(I-§1.12.9)**.

1.23 Class GridLayout

```
public class java.awt.GridLayout
    extends java.lang.Object (I-§1.12)
    implements java.awt.LayoutManager (II-§1.43)
{
    // Constructors
    public GridLayout(int rows, int cols);                        §1.23.1
    public GridLayout(int rows, int cols,                         §1.23.2
                      int hgap, int vgap);
    // Methods
    public void addLayoutComponent(String name,                   §1.23.3
                                   Component comp);
    public void layoutContainer(Container target);                §1.23.4
    public Dimension minimumLayoutSize(Container target);         §1.23.5
    public Dimension preferredLayoutSize(Container target);       §1.23.6
    public void removeLayoutComponent(Component comp);            §1.23.7
    public String toString();                                     §1.23.8
}
```

This grid layout manager causes the container's components to be laid out in a rectangular grid. The container is split into equal-sized rectangles: one component is placed into each rectangle.

For example, the following code says to lay out the six buttons into three rows and two columns:

```
import java.awt.*;
import java.applet.Applet;
public class buttonGrid extends Applet {
  public void init() {
    setLayout(new GridLayout(3,2));
    add(new Button("1"));
    add(new Button("2"));
    add(new Button("3"));
    add(new Button("4"));
    add(new Button("5"));
    add(new Button("6"));
  }
}
```

It produces the following output:

Constructors

GridLayout   §1.23.1

    public GridLayout(int rows, int cols)

Creates a grid layout with the specified number of rows and columns. All components in the layout are given equal size.

One, but not both, of `rows` and `columns` can be zero, which means that any number of objects can be placed in a row or in a column.

PARAMETERS:

`rows`: the rows; zero means "any number."
`cols`: the columns; zero means "any number."

GridLayout   §1.23.2

    public GridLayout(int rows, int cols, int hgap, int vgap)

Creates a grid layout with the specified number of rows and columns. All components in the layout are given equal size.

In addition, the horizontal and vertical gaps are set to the specified values. The horizontal gaps are placed at the left and right edges and between each of the columns. The vertical gaps are placed at the top and bottom edges and between each of the rows.

One, but not both, of `rows` and `columns` can be zero, which means that any number of objects can be placed in a row or in a column.

PARAMETERS:

`rows`: the rows; zero means "any number. "
`cols`: the columns; zero means "any number."
`hgap`: the horizontal gap.
`vgap`: the vertical gap.

Methods

addLayoutComponent §1.23.3

```
public void addLayoutComponent(String name, Component comp)
```

This method is not used by the grid layout manager.

PARAMETERS:

name: a tag.
comp: the component to be added.

layoutContainer §1.23.4

```
public void layoutContainer(Container target)
```

Lays out the container argument using this layout.

This method reshapes the components in the specified target container in order to satisfy the constraints of the GridLayout object.

The grid layout manager determines the size of individual components by dividing the free space in the container into equal-sized portions according to the number of rows and columns in the layout. The container's free space equals the container's size minus any insets and any specified horizontal or vertical gap. All components in a grid layout are given the same size.

Most applications do not call this method directly. This method is called when a container calls its layout method (**II-§1.11.11**).

PARAMETERS:

target: the container in which to do the layout.

SEE ALSO:

Container (**II-§1.11**).

minimumLayoutSize   §1.23.5

```
public Dimension minimumLayoutSize(Container target)
```

Determines the minimum size of the container argument using this grid layout.

The minimum width of a grid layout is the largest minimum width of any of the widths in the container times the number of columns, plus the horizontal padding times the number of columns plus 1, plus the left and right insets of the target container.

The minimum height of a grid layout is the largest minimum height of any of the widths in the container times the number of rows, plus the vertical padding times the number of rows plus 1, plus the top and left insets of the target container.

Most applications do not call this method directly. This method is called when a container calls its `layout` method (**II-§1.11.11**).

PARAMETERS:

`target`: the container in which to do the layout.

RETURNS:

the minimum dimensions needed to lay out the subcomponents of the specified container.

SEE ALSO:

`preferredLayoutSize` (**II-§1.23.6**).

preferredLayoutSize §1.23.6

```
public Dimension preferredLayoutSize(Container target)
```

Determines the preferred size of the container argument using this grid layout.

The preferred width of a grid layout is the largest preferred width of any of the widths in the container times the number of columns, plus the horizontal padding times the number of columns plus 1, plus the left and right insets of the target container.

The preferred height of a grid layout is the largest preferred height of any of the widths in the container times the number of rows, plus the vertical padding times the number of rows plus 1, plus the top and left insets of the target container.

Most applications do not call this method directly. This method is called when a container calls its `preferredSize` method (**II-§1.11.17**).

PARAMETERS:

`target`: the container in which to do the layout.

RETURNS:

the preferred dimensions to lay out the subcomponents of the specified container.

SEE ALSO:

`minimumLayoutSize` (**II-§1.23.5**).

removeLayoutComponent §1.23.7

```
public void removeLayoutComponent(Component comp)
```

This method is not used by the grid layout manager.

PARAMETERS:

`comp`: the component to be removed.

toString §1.23.8

```
public String toString()
```

RETURNS:

a string representation of this grid layout.

OVERRIDES:

`toString` in class `Object` (**I-§1.12.9**).

1.24 Class Image

```
public abstract class java.awt.Image
    extends java.lang.Object (I-§1.12)
{
    // Fields
    public final static Object UndefinedProperty;          §1.24.1

    // Constructors
    public Image();                                        §1.24.2

    // Methods
    public abstract void flush();                          §1.24.3
    public abstract Graphics getGraphics();                §1.24.4
    public abstract int getHeight(ImageObserver observer); §1.24.5
    public abstract Object                                 §1.24.6
        getProperty(String name, ImageObserver observer);
    public abstract ImageProducer getSource();             §1.24.7
    public abstract int getWidth(ImageObserver observer);  §1.24.8
}
```

The abstract class Image is the superclass of all classes that represent graphical images.

Fields

UndefinedProperty   §1.24.1

```
    public final static Object UndefinedProperty
        = new Object()
```

The UndefinedProperty object should be returned whenever a property which was not defined for a particular image is fetched.

Constructors

Image   §1.24.2

```
    public Image()
```

The default constructor for an image.

Methods

flush §1.24.3

`public abstract void flush()`

Flushes all resources being used by this `Image` object.

These resources include any pixel data that are being cached for rendering to the screen, as well as any system resources that are being used to store data or pixels for the image.

The `Image` object is reset to a state similar to when it was first created so that if it is again rendered, the image data must be recreated or fetched again from its source.

getGraphics §1.24.4

`public abstract Graphics getGraphics()`

Creates a graphics context **(II-§1.20)** for drawing to an off-screen image. This method can only be called for off-screen images, which are created with the `createImage` method **(II-§1.10.7)** with two integer arguments.

RETURNS:

a graphics context to draw to the off-screen image.

getHeight §1.24.5

`public abstract int getHeight(ImageObserver observer)`

Determines the height of this image. If the height is not yet known, the observer is notified later.

PARAMETERS:

`observer`: an object waiting for the image to be loaded.

RETURNS:

the height of the image, or –1 if the height is not yet known.

SEE ALSO:

`getWidth` **(II-§1.24.8)**.

`ImageObserver` **(II-§2.11)**.

getProperty   §1.24.6

```
public abstract Object
getProperty(String name, ImageObserver observer)
```

Gets a property of this image by name.

Individual property names are defined by the various image formats. If a property is not defined for a particular image, this method returns the UndefinedProperty object.

If the properties for this image are not yet known, this method returns null, and the ImageObserver object is notified later.

The property name "comment" should be used to store an optional comment which can be presented to the application as a description of the image, its source, or its author.

PARAMETERS:

name: a property name.
observer: an object waiting for this image to be loaded.

RETURNS:

the value of the named property.

SEE ALSO:

ImageObserver **(II-§2.11)**.
UndefinedProperty **(II-§1.24.1)**.

getSource   §1.24.7

```
public abstract ImageProducer getSource()
```

RETURNS:

the image producer **(II-§2.12)** that produces the pixels for this image.

getWidth   §1.24.8

```
public abstract int getWidth(ImageObserver observer)
```

Determines the width of this image. If the width is not yet known, the observer is notified later.

PARAMETERS:

observer: an object waiting for the image to be loaded.

RETURNS:

the width of this image, or –1 if the width is not yet known.

SEE ALSO:

getHeight **(II-§1.24.5)**.
ImageObserver **(II-§2.11)**.

1.25 Class Insets

```
public class java.awt.Insets
    extends java.lang.Object (I-§1.12)
    implements java.lang.Cloneable (I-§1.22)
{
    // Fields
    public int bottom;                                      §1.25.1
    public int left;                                        §1.25.2
    public int right;                                       §1.25.3
    public int top;                                         §1.25.4

    // Constructors
    public Insets(int top, int left,                        §1.25.5
                  int bottom, int right);

    // Methods
    public Object clone();                                  §1.25.6
    public String toString();                               §1.25.7
}
```

The Insets object is a representation of the borders of a container. It specifies the space that a container must leave at each of its edges. The space can be a border, a blank space, or a title.

SEE ALSO:

LayoutManager (II-§1.43).

Container (II-§1.11).

Fields

bottom   §1.25.1

```
    public int bottom
```
   The inset from the bottom.

left   §1.25.2

```
    public int left
```
   The inset from the left.

right   §1.25.3

```
    public int right
```
   The inset from the right.

top   §1.25.4

    `public int top`

      The inset from the top.

Constructors

Insets   §1.25.5

    `public Insets(int top, int left, int bottom, int right)`

      Creates and initializes a new `Inset` with the specified top, left, bottom, and right insets.

    PARAMETERS:

    `top`: the inset from the top.
    `left`: the inset from the left.
    `bottom`: the inset from the bottom.
    `right`: the inset from the right.

Methods

clone   §1.25.6

    `public Object clone()`

    RETURNS:

    a copy of this inset.

    OVERRIDES:

    `clone` in class `Object` (**I-§1.12.2**).

toString   §1.25.7

    `public String toString()`

    RETURNS:

    a string representation of this inset.

    OVERRIDES:

    `toString` in class `Object` (**I-§1.12.9**).

1.26 Class Label

```
public class java.awt.Label
    extends java.awt.Component (II-§1.10)
{
    // Fields
    public final static int CENTER;                    §1.26.1
    public final static int LEFT;                       §1.26.2
    public final static int RIGHT;                      §1.26.3

    // Constructors
    public Label();                                     §1.26.4
    public Label(String label);                         §1.26.5
    public Label(String label, int alignment);          §1.26.6

    // Methods
    public void addNotify();                            §1.26.7
    public int getAlignment();                          §1.26.8
    public String getText();                            §1.26.9
    protected String paramString();                     §1.26.10
    public void setAlignment(int alignment);            §1.26.11
    public void setText(String label);                  §1.26.12
}
```

A label is a component for placing text in a container. The text can be changed by the application, but a user cannot edit it directly.[6]

For example, the code

```
setLayout(new FlowLayout(FlowLayout.CENTER,10,10));
add(new Label("Hi There!"));
add(new Label("Another Label"));
```

produces the following:

---

[6] In Java 1.0, the AWT does not send mouse, keyboard, or focus events to a label. In Java 1.1, the AWT sends to the label all mouse, keyboard, and focus events that occur over it.

Fields

CENTER   §1.26.1

```
public final static int CENTER = 1
```
Indicates that the label should be centered.

LEFT   §1.26.2

```
public final static int LEFT = 0
```
Indicates that the label should be left justified.

RIGHT   §1.26.3

```
public final static int RIGHT = 2
```
Indicates that the label should be right justified.

Constructors

Label   §1.26.4

```
public Label()
```
Constructs an empty label whose text is left justified.

Label   §1.26.5

```
public Label(String label)
```
Constructs a new label with the specified string of text left justified.

PARAMETERS:
label: the text that makes up the label.

Label   §1.26.6

```
public Label(String label, int alignment)
```
Constructs a new label with the specified string of text and the specified alignment.

The alignment value must be one of LEFT, RIGHT, or CENTER.

PARAMETERS:
label: the string that makes up the label.
alignment: the alignment value.

Methods

---

addNotify §1.26.7

    public void addNotify()

This method calls the `createLabel` method (**II-§1.41.12**) of this object's toolkit (**II-§1.10.20**) in order to create a `LabelPeer` (**II-§3.11**) for this label. This peer allows the application to change the look of a label without changing its functionality.

Most applications do not call this method directly.

OVERRIDES:

addNotify in class Component (**II-§1.10.2**).

getAlignment §1.26.8

    public int getAlignment()

RETURNS:

the current alignment of this label.

SEE ALSO:

setAlignment (**II-§1.26.11**).

getText §1.26.9

    public String getText()

RETURNS:

the text of this label.

SEE ALSO:

setText (**II-§1.26.12**).

paramString §1.26.10

    protected String paramString()

Returns the parameter string representing the state of this label. This string is useful for debugging.

RETURNS:

the parameter string of this label.

OVERRIDES:

paramString in class Component (**II-§1.10.51**).

setAlignment   §1.26.11

  `public void setAlignment(int alignment)`

    Sets the alignment for this label to the specified alignment.

  PARAMETERS:

  `alignment:` the alignment value.

  THROWS:

  `IllegalArgumentException` **(I-§1.32).**

  if an improper alignment was given.

  SEE ALSO:

  `getAlignment` **(II-§1.26.8).**

setText   §1.26.12

  `public void setText(String label)`

    Sets the text for this label to the specified text.

  PARAMETERS:

  `label:` the text that makes up the label.

  SEE ALSO:

  `getText` **(II-§1.26.9).**

1.27 Class List

```
public class java.awt.List
    extends java.awt.Component (II-§1.10)
{
    // Constructors
    public List();                                              §1.27.1
    public List(int rows, boolean multipleSelections);          §1.27.2

    // Methods
    public void addItem(String item);                           §1.27.3
    public void addItem(String item, int index);                §1.27.4
    public void addNotify();                                    §1.27.5
    public boolean allowsMultipleSelections();                  §1.27.6
    public void clear();                                        §1.27.7
    public int countItems();                                    §1.27.8
    public void delItem(int position);                          §1.27.9
    public void delItems(int start, int end);                   §1.27.10
    public void deselect(int index);                            §1.27.11
    public String getItem(int index);                           §1.27.12
    public int getRows();                                       §1.27.13
    public int getSelectedIndex();                              §1.27.14
    public int[] getSelectedIndexes();                          §1.27.15
    public String getSelectedItem();                            §1.27.16
    public String[] getSelectedItems();                         §1.27.17
    public int getVisibleIndex();                               §1.27.18
    public boolean isSelected(int index);                       §1.27.19
    public void makeVisible(int index);                         §1.27.20
    public Dimension minimumSize();                             §1.27.21
    public Dimension minimumSize(int rows);                     §1.27.22
    protected String paramString();                             §1.27.23
    public Dimension preferredSize();                           §1.27.24
    public Dimension preferredSize(int rows);                   §1.27.25
    public void removeNotify();                                 §1.27.26
    public void replaceItem(String newValue, int index);        §1.27.27
    public void select(int index);                              §1.27.28
    public void setMultipleSelections(boolean v);               §1.27.29
}
```

The List component presents the user with a scrolling list of text items. The list can be set up so that the user can choose either one item or multiple items.

For example, the code:

```
List l = new List(4, false);
l.addItem("Mercury");
l.addItem("Venus");
l.addItem("Earth");
l.addItem("JavaSoft");
```

```
l.addItem("Mars");
l.addItem("Jupiter");
l.addItem("Saturn");
l.addItem("Uranus");
l.addItem("Neptune");
l.addItem("Pluto");
add(l);
```

produces the following scrolling list:

Clicking[7] on an item that isn't selected selects it. Clicking on an item that is already selected deselects it. In the preceding example, since the second argument when creating the new scrolling list is `false`, only one item can be selected at a time from the scrolling list. Selecting any item causes any other selected item to be automatically deselected.

When an item is clicked and becomes selected, AWT sends a list select event (**II-§1.14.18**) to the scrolling list. When an item is clicked and becomes deselected, AWT sends a list deselect event (**II-§1.14.17**) to the scrolling list. The event's target is the scrolling list, and its object is an `Integer` (**I-§1.8**) giving the index of the item in the list.

When the user double-clicks on an item in a scrolling list, AWT sends an action event (**II-§1.14.11**) to the scrolling list after the list select or deselect event. The event's target is the scrolling list, and its object is the string label of the item selected or deselected.

When the user hits "return" inside a scrolling list, AWT also sends an action event (**II-§1.14.11**) to the scrolling list. The event's target is the scrolling list, and its object is the string label of the last item selected or deselected in the scrolling list.

---

7. In Java 1.0, the AWT does not send mouse, keyboard, or focus events to a scrolling list. In Java 1.1, the AWT sends to the scrolling list all mouse, keyboard, and focus events that occur over it.

If an application wants to perform some action based on an item being selected or deselected, it must override the `handleEvent` method of the scrolling list or of one of its containing windows. The code to perform that should be of the following form:

```
public boolean handleEvent(Event event) {
    switch(event.id) {
        case Event.LIST_SELECT:
            <do something if event.target is scrolling list>
        case Event.LIST_DESELECT:
            <do something if event.target is scrolling list>
        default:
            return super.handleEvent(event);
    }
}
```

If the application wants to perform some action based on the user double-clicking or hitting the return key, it should override the `action` method (**II-§1.10.1**) of the scrolling list or of one of its containing windows. Alternatively, it can override the `handleEvent` method as before and check to see if the event's `id` field is `Event.ACTION_EVENT`.

For multiple-selection scrolling lists, it is considered a better user interface to use an external event (such as clicking on a button) to trigger the action.

Constructors

List §1.27.1

`public List()`

Creates a new scrolling list. Initially there are no visible lines, and only one item can be selected from the list.

List §1.27.2

`public List(int rows, boolean multipleSelections)`

Creates a new scrolling list initialized to display the specified number of rows. If the `multipleSelections` argument is `true`, then the user can select multiple items at a time from the list. If it is `false`, only one item at a time can be selected.

PARAMETERS:

`rows`: the number of items to show.

`multipleSelections`: if `true`, then multiple selections are allowed; otherwise, only one item can be selected at a time.

Methods

---

addItem   **§1.27.3**

    `public void addItem(String item)`

      Adds the specified string to the end of this scrolling list.

    PARAMETERS:

    `item:` the string to be added.

addItem   **§1.27.4**

    `public void addItem(String item, int index)`

      Adds the specified string to this scrolling list at the specified position.

      The index argument is 0-based. If the index is -1, or greater than or equal to the number of items already in the list, then the item is added at the end of this list.

    PARAMETERS:

    `item:` the string to be added.
    `index:` the position at which to put in the item.

addNotify   **§1.27.5**

    `public void addNotify()`

      This method calls the `createList` method (**II-§1.41.13**) of this object's toolkit (**II-§1.10.20**) in order to create a `ListPeer` (**II-§3.12**) for this scrolling list. This peer allows the application to change the look of a scrolling list without changing its functionality.

      Most applications do not call this method directly.

    OVERRIDES:

    `addNotify` in class Component (**II-§1.10.2**).

allowsMultipleSelections   **§1.27.6**

    `public boolean allowsMultipleSelections()`

    RETURNS:

    `true` if this scrolling list allows multiple selections; `false` otherwise.

    SEE ALSO:

    `setMultipleSelections` (**II-§1.27.29**).

clear   **§1.27.7**

    `public void clear()`

      Removes all items from this scrolling list.

    SEE ALSO:

    `delItem` (**II-§1.27.9**).
    `delItems` (**II-§1.27.10**).

countItems §1.27.8

    `public int countItems()`

    RETURNS:

    the number of items in this list.

    SEE ALSO:

    `getItem` **(II-§1.27.12)**.

delItem §1.27.9

    `public void delItem(int position)`

    Deletes the item at the specified position from this scrolling list.

    PARAMETERS:

    `position`: the index of the item to delete.

delItems §1.27.10

    `public void delItems(int start, int end)`

    Deletes the items in the range $start \leq item \leq end$ from this scrolling list.

    PARAMETERS:

    `start`: the index of the first element to delete.
    `end`: the index of the last element to delete.

deselect §1.27.11

    `public void deselect(int index)`

    Deselects the item at the specified index of this scrolling list.

    If the item at the specified index is not selected, or if the index is out of range, then the operation is ignored.

    PARAMETERS:

    `index`: the position of the item to deselect.

    SEE ALSO:

    `select` **(II-§1.27.28)**.
    `getSelectedItem` **(II-§1.27.16)**.
    `isSelected` **(II-§1.27.19)**.

getItem §1.27.12

    `public String getItem(int index)`

    PARAMETERS:

    `index`: the position of the item.

    RETURNS:

    the string of this scrolling list at the specified index.

    SEE ALSO:

    `countItems` **(II-§1.27.8)**.

getRows   §1.27.13

```
public int getRows()
```
RETURNS:

the number of visible lines in this scrolling list.

getSelectedIndex   §1.27.14

```
public int getSelectedIndex()
```
RETURNS:

the index of the selected item on this scrolling list, or –1 if either no items are
selected or more than one item is selected.

SEE ALSO:

select (**II-§1.27.28**).
deselect (**II-§1.27.11**).
isSelected (**II-§1.27.19**).

getSelectedIndexes   §1.27.15

```
public int[] getSelectedIndexes()
```
RETURNS:

an array of the selected indexes of this scrolling list.

SEE ALSO:

select (**II-§1.27.28**).
deselect (**II-§1.27.11**).
isSelected (**II-§1.27.19**).

getSelectedItem   §1.27.16

```
public String getSelectedItem()
```
RETURNS:

the selected item on this scrolling list, or null if either no items are selected
or more than one item is selected.

SEE ALSO:

select (**II-§1.27.28**).
deselect (**II-§1.27.11**).
isSelected (**II-§1.27.19**).

getSelectedItems §1.27.17

`public String[] getSelectedItems()`

RETURNS:

an array of the selected items on this scrolling list.

SEE ALSO:

select **(II-§1.27.28).**
deselect **(II-§1.27.11).**
isSelected **(II-§1.27.19).**

getVisibleIndex §1.27.18

`public int getVisibleIndex()`

RETURNS:

the index of the item in this scrolling list that was last made visible by the makeVisible method **(II-§1.27.20).**

isSelected §1.27.19

`public boolean isSelected(int index)`

Determines if a specified item in this scrolling list is selected. No error occurs if the index argument is less than 0 or greater than or equal to the number of items in this scrolling list.

PARAMETERS:

index: the item to be checked.

RETURNS:

true if the item at the specified index has been selected; false otherwise.

SEE ALSO:

select **(II-§1.27.28).**
deselect **(II-§1.27.11).**
isSelected **(II-§1.27.19).**

makeVisible §1.27.20

`public void makeVisible(int index)`

Forces the item at the specified index in this scrolling list to be visible.

No error occurs if the index argument is less than 0 or greater than or equal to the number of items in this scrolling list.

PARAMETERS:

index: the position of the item.

SEE ALSO:

getVisibleIndex **(II-§1.27.18).**

minimumSize   §1.27.21

    `public Dimension minimumSize()`

Determines the minimum size of this scrolling list. If the application has specified the number of visible rows, and that number is greater than 0, the peer's `minimumSize` method (**II-§3.12.7**) is called with the number of rows in order to determine the minimum size.

If this scrolling list does not have a peer, or if the number of visible rows is less than or equal to 0, the superclass's `minimumSize` method (**II-§1.10.40**) is called to determine the minimum size.

RETURNS:

the minimum dimensions needed to display this scrolling list.

OVERRIDES:

`minimumSize` in class Component (**II-§1.10.40**).

minimumSize   §1.27.22

    `public Dimension minimumSize(int rows)`

Determines the minimum size of a scrolling list with the specified number of rows. This scrolling list's peer's `minimumSize` method (**II-§3.12.7**) is called with the number of rows in order to determine the minimum size.

If this scrolling list does not have a peer, the superclass's `minimumSize` method (**II-§1.10.40**) is called to determine the minimum size.

PARAMETERS:

`rows`: number of rows.

RETURNS:

the minimum dimensions needed to display the specified number of rows in a scrolling list.

paramString   §1.27.23

    `protected String paramString()`

Returns the parameter string representing the state of this scrolling list. This string is useful for debugging.

RETURNS:

the parameter string of this scrolling list.

OVERRIDES:

`paramString` in class Component (**II-§1.10.51**).

preferredSize §1.27.24

`public Dimension preferredSize()`

Determines the preferred size of this scrolling list. If the application has specified the number of visible rows, and that number is greater than 0, the peer's `preferredSize` method (**II-§3.12.8**) is called with the number of rows in order to determine the preferred size.

If this scrolling list does not have a peer, or if the number of visible rows is less than or equal to 0, the superclass's `preferredSize` method (**II-§1.10.40**) is called to determine the preferred size.

RETURNS:

the preferred dimensions for displaying this scrolling list.

OVERRIDES:

preferredSize in class Component (**II-§1.10.53**).

preferredSize §1.27.25

`public Dimension preferredSize(int rows)`

Determines the preferred size of a scrolling list with the specified number of rows. This scrolling list's peer's `preferredSize` method (**II-§3.12.8**) is called with the number of rows in order to determine the preferred size.

If this scrolling list does not have a peer, the superclass's `preferredSize` method (**II-§1.10.40**) is called to determine the preferred size.

PARAMETERS:

rows: number of rows.

RETURNS:

the preferred dimensions for displaying the specified number of rows.

removeNotify §1.27.26

`public void removeNotify()`

Notifies this scrolling list to destroy its peer.

OVERRIDES:

removeNotify in class Component (**II-§1.10.58**).

replaceItem §1.27.27

`public void replaceItem(String newValue, int index)`

Replaces the item at the given index in the scrolling list with the new string.

PARAMETERS:

newValue: the new value.
index: the position.

select   §1.27.28

```
public void select(int index)
```

Selects the item at the specified index in the scrolling list.

PARAMETERS:

index: the position of the item to select.

SEE ALSO:

getSelectedItem **(II-§1.27.16)**.
deselect **(II-§1.27.11)**.
isSelected **(II-§1.27.19)**.

setMultipleSelections   §1.27.29

```
public void setMultipleSelections(boolean v)
```

Sets whether this scrolling list allows multiple selections.

PARAMETERS:

v: if true, then multiple selections are allowed; otherwise, only one item
can be selected at a time.

SEE ALSO:

allowsMultipleSelections **(II-§1.27.6)**.

1.28 Class MediaTracker

```
public class java.awt.MediaTracker
    extends java.lang.Object (I-§1.12)
{
    // Fields
    public final static int ABORTED;                         §1.28.1
    public final static int COMPLETE;                        §1.28.2
    public final static int ERRORED;                         §1.28.3
    public final static int LOADING;                         §1.28.4

    // Constructors
    public MediaTracker(Component comp);                     §1.28.5

    // Methods
    public void addImage(Image image, int id);              §1.28.6
    public void addImage(Image image, int id, int w, int h);§1.28.7
    public boolean checkAll();                               §1.28.8
    public boolean checkAll(boolean load);                   §1.28.9
    public boolean checkID(int id);                          §1.28.10
    public boolean checkID(int id, boolean load);            §1.28.11
    public Object[] getErrorsAny();                          §1.28.12
    public Object[] getErrorsID(int id);                     §1.28.13
    public boolean isErrorAny();                             §1.28.14
    public boolean isErrorID(int id);                        §1.28.15
    public int statusAll(boolean load);                      §1.28.16
    public int statusID(int id, boolean load);               §1.28.17
    public void waitForAll();                                §1.28.18
    public boolean waitForAll(long ms);                      §1.28.19
    public void waitForID(int id);                           §1.28.20
    public boolean waitForID(int id, long ms);               §1.28.21
}
```

The MediaTracker class is a utility class to trace the status of a number of media objects. Media objects could include audio clips as well as images, though currently only images are supported.

To use the media tracker, create an instance of the MediaTracker class and then call the addImage method (II-§1.28.6) for each image to be tracked. In addition, each image can be assigned a unique identifier. The identifier controls the priority order in which the images are fetched, as well as identifying unique subsets of the images that can be waited on independently. Images with a lower ID are loaded in preference to those with a higher ID number.

Here is an example:

```java
import java.applet.Applet;
import java.awt.Color;
import java.awt.Image;
import java.awt.Graphics;
import java.awt.MediaTracker;
public class ImageBlaster extends Applet
implements Runnable {
    MediaTracker tracker;
    Image bg;
    Image anim[] = new Image[5];
    int index;
    Thread animator;
    // Get the images for the background (id == 0) and the
    // animation frames (id == 1) and add them to the
    // Media Tracker
    public void init() {
        tracker = new MediaTracker(this);
        bg = getImage(getDocumentBase(),
                        "images/background.gif");
        tracker.addImage(bg, 0);
        for (int i = 0; i   5; i++) {
            anim[i] = getImage(getDocumentBase(),
                            "images/anim"+i+".gif");
            tracker.addImage(anim[i], 1);
        }
     }

    // Start the animation thread.
    public void start() {
        animator = new Thread(this);
        animator.start();
    }
    // Stop the animation thread.
    public void stop() {
        animator.stop();
        animator = null;
    }
    // Run the animation thread.
    // First wait for the background image to fully load
    // and point.  Then wait for all of the animation
    // frames to finish loading.  Finally loop and
    // increment the animation frame index.
    public void run() {
        try {
            tracker.waitForID(0);
            tracker.waitForID(1);
        } catch (InterruptedException e) {
            return;
        }
```

```
            Thread me = Thread.currentThread();
            while (animator == me) {
                try {
                    Thread.sleep(100);
                } catch (InterruptedException e) {
                    break;
                }
                synchronized (this) {
                    index++;
                    if (index >= anim.length) {
                        index = 0;
                    }
                }
                repaint();
            }
        }

        // The background image fills our frame so we don't
        // need to clear the applet on repaints; just call the
        // paint method
        public void update(Graphics g) {
            paint(g);
        }
        // Paint a large red rectangle if there are any errors
        // loading the images.  Otherwise, always paint the
        // background so that it appears incrementally as it
        // is loading. Finally, only paint the current
        // animation frame if all of the frames (id == 1)
        // are done loading, so that we don't get partial
        // animations.
        public void paint(Graphics g) {
            if ((tracker.statusAll(false) &
                    MediaTracker.ERRORED) != 0) {
                g.setColor(Color.red);
                g.fillRect(0, 0, size().width, size().height);
                return;
            }
            g.drawImage(bg, 0, 0, this);
            if ((tracker.statusID(1, false) &
                    MediaTracker.COMPLETE) != 0) {
                g.drawImage(anim[index], 10, 10, this);
            }
        }
    }
}
```

Fields

ABORTED   §1.28.1

```
public final static int ABORTED = 2
```

Flag indicating that the download of some media was aborted.

SEE ALSO:

statusAll (II-§1.28.16).
statusID (II-§1.28.17).

COMPLETE   §1.28.2

```
public final static int COMPLETE = 8
```

Flag indicating that the download of media completed successfully.

SEE ALSO:

statusAll (II-§1.28.16).
statusID (II-§1.28.17).

ERRORED   §1.28.3

```
public final static int ERRORED = 4
```

Flag indicating that the download of some media encountered an error.

SEE ALSO:

statusAll (II-§1.28.16).
statusID (II-§1.28.17).

LOADING   §1.28.4

```
public final static int LOADING = 1
```

Flag indicating that some media is currently being loaded.

SEE ALSO:

statusAll (II-§1.28.16).
statusID (II-§1.28.17).

Constructors

MediaTracker   §1.28.5

```
public MediaTracker(Component comp)
```

Creates a media tracker to track images for a given component.

PARAMETERS:

comp: the component on which the images will eventually be drawn.

Methods

---

addImage   **§1.28.6**

> `public void addImage(Image image, int id)`

Adds an image to the list of images being tracked by this media tracker. The image will eventually be rendered at its default (unscaled) size.

PARAMETERS:

`image`: the image to be tracked.
`id`: the identifier used to later track this image.

addImage   **§1.28.7**

> `public void addImage(Image image, int id, int w, int h)`

Adds a scaled image to the list of images being tracked by this media tracker. The image will eventually be rendered at the indicated width and height.

PARAMETERS:

`image`: the image to be tracked.
`id`: the identifier used to later track this image.
`w`: the width at which the image will be rendered.
`h`: the height at which the image will be rendered.

checkAll   **§1.28.8**

> `public boolean checkAll()`

Checks to see if all images being tracked by this media tracker have finished loading.

This method does not start loading the images if they are not already loading.

If there is an error while loading or scaling an image, then that image is considered to have finished loading. Use the `isErrorAny` method **(II-§1.28.14)** or `isErrorID` method **(II-§1.28.15)** to check for errors.

RETURNS:

`true` if all images have finished loading, were aborted, or encountered an error; `false` otherwise.

SEE ALSO:

`checkID` **(II-§1.28.10)**.

checkAll   §1.28.9

```
public boolean checkAll(boolean load)
```

Checks to see if all images being tracked by this media tracker have finished loading.

If the load flag is `true`, then start loading any images that are not yet being loaded.

If there is an error while loading or scaling an image, then that image is considered to have finished loading. Use the `isErrorAny` method (**II-§1.28.14**) or `isErrorID` method (**II-§1.28.15**) to check for errors.

PARAMETERS:

`load`: if `true`, start loading any images that are not yet being loaded.

RETURNS:

`true` if all images have finished loading, were aborted, or encountered an error; `false` otherwise.

SEE ALSO:

`checkID` (**II-§1.28.11**).

checkID   §1.28.10

```
public boolean checkID(int id)
```

Checks to see if all images tracked by this media tracker that are tagged with the specified identifier have finished loading.

This method does not start loading the images if they are not already loading.

If there is an error while loading or scaling an image, then that image is considered to have finished loading. Use the `isErrorAny` method (**II-§1.28.14**) or `isErrorID` method (**II-§1.28.15**) to check for errors.

PARAMETERS:

`id`: the identifier of the images to check.

RETURNS:

`true` if all images have finished loading, were aborted, or encountered an error; `false` otherwise.

SEE ALSO:

`checkAll` (**II-§1.28.8**).

checkID §1.28.11

```
public boolean checkID(int id, boolean load)
```

Checks to see if all images tracked by this media tracker that are tagged with the specified identifier have finished loading.

If the load flag is `true`, then starts loading any images that are not yet being loaded.

If there is an error while loading or scaling an image, then that image is considered to have finished loading. Use the `isErrorAny` method (**II-§1.28.14**) or `isErrorID` method (**II-§1.28.15**) to check for errors.

PARAMETERS:

`id`: the identifier of the images to check.
`load`: if `true`, start loading any images that are not yet being loaded.

RETURNS:

`true` if all images have finished loading, were aborted, or encountered an error; `false` otherwise.

SEE ALSO:

`checkAll` (**II-§1.28.8**).

getErrorsAny §1.28.12

```
public Object[] getErrorsAny()
```

RETURNS:

an array of media objects tracked by this media tracker that have encountered an error, or `null` if there are none with errors.

SEE ALSO:

`isErrorAny` (**II-§1.28.14**).
`getErrorsID` (**II-§1.28.13**).

getErrorsID §1.28.13

```
public Object[] getErrorsID(int id)
```

PARAMETERS:

`id`: the identifier of the images to check.

RETURNS:

an array of media objects tracked by this media tracker with the specified identifier that have encountered an error, or `null` if there are none with errors.

SEE ALSO:

`isErrorID` (**II-§1.28.15**).
`getErrorsAny` (**II-§1.28.12**).

isErrorAny   §1.28.14

`public boolean isErrorAny()`

RETURNS:

true if any of the images tracked by this media tracker had an error during loading; `false` otherwise.

SEE ALSO:

`isErrorID` (**II-§1.28.15**).

`getErrorsAny` (**II-§1.28.12**).

isErrorID   §1.28.15

`public boolean isErrorID(int id)`

Checks the error status of all of the images tracked by this media tracker with the specified identifier.

PARAMETERS:

`id`: the identifier of the images to check.

RETURNS:

true if any of the images with the specified identifier had an error during loading; `false` otherwise.

SEE ALSO:

`isErrorAny` (**II-§1.28.14**).

`getErrorsID` (**II-§1.28.13**).

statusAll   §1.28.16

`public int statusAll(boolean load)`

Calculates and returns the bitwise inclusive **OR** of the status of all the media being tracked by this media tracker. The possible flags are specified by the following four constants:

♦ LOADING (**II-§1.28.4**)

♦ ABORTED (**II-§1.28.1**)

♦ ERRORED (**II-§1.28.3**)

♦ COMPLETE (**II-§1.28.2**)

An image that hasn't started loading has zero as its status.

If the load flag is `true`, then start loading any images that are not yet being loaded.

PARAMETERS:

`load`: if `true`, start loading any images that are not yet being loaded.

RETURNS:

the bitwise inclusive **OR** of the status of all of the media being tracked.

SEE ALSO:

`statusID` (**II-§1.28.17**).

statusID   §1.28.17

```
public int statusID(int id, boolean load)
```

Calculates and returns the bitwise inclusive **OR** of the status of all the media tracked by this media tracker with the specified identifier. The possible flags are as in the `statusAll` method (**II-§1.28.16**). An image that hasn't started loading has zero as its status.

If the load flag is `true`, then start loading any images that are not yet being loaded.

PARAMETERS:

`id`: the identifier of the images to check.

`load`: if `true`, start loading any images that are not yet being loaded.

RETURNS:

the bitwise inclusive **OR** of the status of all of the media being tracked.

waitForAll   §1.28.18

```
public void waitForAll()
throws InterruptedException
```

Starts loading all images tracked by this media tracker. This method waits until all the images being tracked have finished loading.

If there is an error while loading or scaling an image, then that image is considered to have finished loading. Use the `isErrorAny` method (**II-§1.28.14**) or `isErrorID` method (**II-§1.28.15**) to check for errors.

THROWS:

`InterruptedException` (**I-§1.37**).

if another thread has interrupted this thread.

SEE ALSO:

`waitForID` (**II-§1.28.20**).

waitForAll   **§1.28.19**

```
public boolean waitForAll(long ms)
throws InterruptedException
```

Starts loading all images tracked by this media tracker. This method waits until all the images being tracked have finished loading, or until the length of time specified in milliseconds by the ms argument has passed.

If there is an error while loading or scaling an image, then that image is considered to have finished loading. Use the isErrorAny method **(II-§1.28.14)** or isErrorID method **(II-§1.28.15)** to check for errors.

PARAMETERS:

ms: the number of milliseconds to wait for the loading to complete.

RETURNS:

true if all images were successfully loaded; false otherwise.

THROWS:

InterruptedException **(I-§1.37)**.
if another thread has interrupted this thread.

SEE ALSO:

waitForID **(II-§1.28.21)**.

waitForID   **§1.28.20**

```
public void waitForID(int id)
throws InterruptedException
```

Starts loading all images tracked by this media tracker with the specified identifier. This method waits until all the images with the specified identifier have finished loading.

If there is an error while loading or scaling an image, then that image is considered to have finished loading. Use the isErrorAny method **(II-§1.28.14)** or isErrorID method **(II-§1.28.15)** to check for errors.

PARAMETERS:

id: the identifier of the images to check.

THROWS:

InterruptedException **(I-§1.37)**.
if another thread has interrupted this thread.

SEE ALSO:

waitForAll **(II-§1.28.18)**.

waitForID §1.28.21

```
public boolean waitForID(int id, long ms)
throws InterruptedException
```

Starts loading all images tracked by this media tracker with the specified identifier. This method waits until all the images with the specified identifier have finished loading, or until the length of time specified in milliseconds by the ms argument has passed.

If there is an error while loading or scaling an image, then that image is considered to have finished loading. Use the isErrorAny method (**II-§1.28.14**) or isErrorID method (**II-§1.28.15**) to check for errors.

PARAMETERS:

id: the identifier of the images to check.
ms: the number of milliseconds to wait for the loading to complete.

RETURNS:

true if all images were successfully loaded; false otherwise.

THROWS:

InterruptedException (**I-§1.37**).
if another thread has interrupted this thread.

SEE ALSO:

waitForAll (**II-§1.28.19**).

1.29 Class Menu

```
public class java.awt.Menu
      extends java.awt.MenuItem (II-§1.32)
      implements java.awt.MenuContainer (II-§1.44)
{
      // Constructors
      public Menu(String label);                          §1.29.1
      public Menu(String label, boolean tearOff);         §1.29.2

      // Methods
      public MenuItem add(MenuItem mi);                   §1.29.3
      public void add(String label);                      §1.29.4
      public void addNotify();                            §1.29.5
      public void addSeparator();                         §1.29.6
      public int countItems();                            §1.29.7
      public MenuItem getItem(int index);                 §1.29.8
      public boolean isTearOff();                         §1.29.9
      public void remove(int index);                      §1.29.10
      public void remove(MenuComponent item);             §1.29.11
      public void removeNotify();                         §1.29.12
}
```

A menu is a pull-down component of a menu bar.

A menu can optionally be a *tear-off* menu. A tear-off menu can remain on the screen after the mouse button has been released. The mechanism for tearing off a menu is platform dependent.

Each item in a menu must belong to the `MenuItem` class (**II-§1.32**). This can be an instance of `MenuItem`, a submenu (an instance of `Menu`), or a check box (an instance of `CheckboxMenuItem` **[II-§1.7]**).

There is no event associated with clicking on a menu item to pull down the menu.

Constructors

Menu   **§1.29.1**

```
public Menu(String label)
```

Constructs a new menu with the specified label. This menu is not a tear-off menu.

PARAMETERS:

`label`: the menu's label in the menu bar.

Menu   **§1.29.2**

```
public Menu(String label, boolean tearOff)
```

Constructs a new menu with the specified label.

If the `tearOff` argument is true, the menu can be torn off; it can remain on the screen after the mouse button has been released.

PARAMETERS:

`label`: the menu's label in the menu bar.
`tearOff`: if `true`, the menu is a tear-off menu.

Methods

add   **§1.29.3**

```
public MenuItem add(MenuItem mi)
```

Adds the specified menu item to this menu.

If the menu item has been part of another menu, remove it from that menu.

PARAMETERS:

`mi`: the menu item to be added.

RETURNS:

the menu item added.

add §1.29.4

    public void add(String label)

Adds an item with the specified label to this menu. This method creates a menu item to hold the string.

PARAMETERS:

label: the text on the item.

addNotify §1.29.5

    public void addNotify()

This method calls the createMenu method (**II-§1.41.14**) of this object's toolkit (**II-§1.10.20**) in order to create a MenuPeer (**II-§3.16**) for this menu. This peer allows the application to change the look of a menu without changing its functionality.

Most applications do not call this method directly.

OVERRIDES:

addNotify in class MenuItem (**II-§1.32.2**).

addSeparator §1.29.6

    public void addSeparator()

Adds a separator line to this menu at the current position.

countItems §1.29.7

    public int countItems()

RETURNS:

the number of elements in this menu.

getItem §1.29.8

    public MenuItem getItem(int index)

PARAMETERS:

index: the position of the item to be returned.

RETURNS:

the item located at the specified index of this menu.

isTearOff §1.29.9

    public boolean isTearOff()

RETURNS:

true if this is a tear-off menu; false otherwise.

remove   §1.29.10

    `public void remove(int index)`

        Deletes the item at the specified index from this menu.

        PARAMETERS:

    `index`: an index in the menu.

remove   §1.29.11

    `public void remove(MenuComponent item)`

        Deletes the specified menu item from this menu. If the item is not part of the menu, nothing happens.

        PARAMETERS:

    `item`: the menu component to be removed.

removeNotify   §1.29.12

    `public void removeNotify()`

        Notifies the menu to destroy its peer.

        This menu also notifies each of its menu items to destroy their peers.

        OVERRIDES:

    `removeNotify` in class MenuComponent (**II-§1.31.7**).

1.30 Class MenuBar

```
public class java.awt.MenuBar
    extends java.awt.MenuComponent (II-§1.31)
    implements java.awt.MenuContainer (II-§1.44)
{
    // Constructors
    public MenuBar();                                       §1.30.1

    // Methods
    public Menu add(Menu m);                                §1.30.2
    public void addNotify();                                §1.30.3
    public int countMenus();                                §1.30.4
    public Menu getHelpMenu();                              §1.30.5
    public Menu getMenu(int i);                             §1.30.6
    public void remove(int index);                          §1.30.7
    public void remove(MenuComponent m);                    §1.30.8
    public void removeNotify();                             §1.30.9
    public void setHelpMenu(Menu m);                        §1.30.10
}
```

This class encapsulates the platform's concept of a menu bar bound to a frame.

In order to attach the menu bar to a frame, the `setMenuBar` method (**II-§1.19.28**) in class `Frame` must be called.

This is what a menu bar might look like:

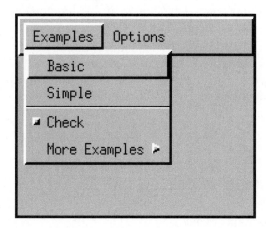

Constructors

MenuBar§1.30.1

> `public MenuBar()`
>> Creates a new menu bar.

Methods

add§1.30.2

> `public Menu add(Menu m)`
>> Adds the specified menu to this menu bar.

PARAMETERS:

m: the menu to be added.

RETURNS:

the menu added.

addNotify   §1.30.3

    `public void addNotify()`

This method calls the `createMenuBar` method (**II-§1.41.15**) of this object's toolkit (**II-§1.10.20**) in order to create a `MenuBarPeer` (**II-§3.13**) for this menu bar. This peer allows the application to change the look of a menu bar without changing its functionality.

Most applications do not call this method directly.

countMenus   §1.30.4

    `public int countMenus()`

RETURNS:

the number of menus on this menu bar.

getHelpMenu   §1.30.5

    `public Menu getHelpMenu()`

RETURNS:

the help menu on this menu bar.

getMenu   §1.30.6

    `public Menu getMenu(int i)`

PARAMETERS:

`i`: the position of the menu to be returned.

RETURNS:

the menu at the specified index of this menu bar.

remove   §1.30.7

    `public void remove(int index)`

Removes the menu located at the specified index from this menu bar.

PARAMETERS:

`index`: the position of the menu to be removed.

remove   §1.30.8

    `public void remove(MenuComponent m)`

Removes the specified menu component from this menu bar.

PARAMETERS:

`m`: the menu component to be removed.

removeNotify   §1.30.9
```
public void removeNotify()
```
Notifies this menu bar to destroy its peer. This menu bar also notifies each
of its menus to destroy their peers.

OVERRIDES:

removeNotify in class MenuComponent (II-§1.31.7).

setHelpMenu   §1.30.10
```
public void setHelpMenu(Menu m)
```
Sets the help menu on this menu bar to be the specified menu.

PARAMETERS:

m: the help menu.

1.31 Class MenuComponent

```
public abstract class java.awt.MenuComponent
    extends java.lang.Object (I-§1.12)
{
    // Constructors
    public MenuComponent();                            §1.31.1

    // Methods
    public Font getFont();                             §1.31.2
    public MenuContainer getParent();                  §1.31.3
    public MenuComponentPeer getPeer();                §1.31.4
    protected String paramString();                    §1.31.5
    public boolean postEvent(Event evt);               §1.31.6
    public void removeNotify();                        §1.31.7
    public void setFont(Font f);                       §1.31.8
    public String toString();                          §1.31.9
}
```

The abstract class MenuComponent is the superclass of all menu-related components.

Constructors

MenuComponent   §1.31.1
```
public MenuComponent()
```
The default constructor.

Methods

---

getFont   §1.31.2

```
public Font getFont()
```
RETURNS:

the font used in this menu component, if there is one; `null` otherwise.

getParent   §1.31.3

```
public MenuContainer getParent()
```
RETURNS:

the menu component containing this menu component; null if this is the out-
ermost component, the menu bar itself.

getPeer   §1.31.4

```
public MenuComponentPeer getPeer()
```
Returns this menu component's peer. Every menu component has a peer
associated with it. This peer allows the application to change the look of a
menu component without changing its functionality.

RETURNS:

the menu component's peer.

paramString   §1.31.5

```
protected String paramString()
```
Returns the parameter string representing the state of this menu component. This string is useful for debugging.

RETURNS:

the parameter string of this menu component.

postEvent   §1.31.6

```
public boolean postEvent(Event evt)
```
Posts an event to this menu component by calling its `handleEvent`
method. If `handleEvent` returns `false`, then posts the event to the menu
component's parent.

PARAMETERS:

`evt`: the event.

RETURNS:

`true` if this menu component or one of its parents handled the event; `false`
otherwise.

removeNotify §1.31.7

```
public void removeNotify()
```

Notifies this menu component to destroy its peer.

setFont §1.31.8

```
public void setFont(Font f)
```

Sets the font to be used for this menu component to the specified font. This font is also used by all subcomponents of the menu component, unless those subcomponents specify a different font.

PARAMETERS:

f: the font to be set.

toString §1.31.9

```
public String toString()
```

RETURNS:

a string representation of this menu component.

OVERRIDES:

toString in class Object (**I-§1.12.9**).

1.32 Class MenuItem

```
public class java.awt.MenuItem
    extends java.awt.MenuComponent (II-§1.31)
{
    // Constructors
    public MenuItem(String label);                  §1.32.1

    // Methods
    public void addNotify();                         §1.32.2
    public void disable();                           §1.32.3
    public void enable();                            §1.32.4
    public void enable(boolean cond);                §1.32.5
    public String getLabel();                        §1.32.6
    public boolean isEnabled();                      §1.32.7
    public String paramString();                     §1.32.8
    public void setLabel(String label);              §1.32.9
}
```

All items in a menu must belong to MenuItem class or a subclass.
The default menu item represents a simple labeled menu item.

The picture of a menu bar (page II-181) shows five menu items. The first two are simple menu items labeled "Basic" and "Simple". Following it is a separator (see §1.32.1). Next is a CheckboxMenuItem (II-§1.7) labeled "Check". Finally, there is a submenu labeled "More Examples", which is an instance of Menu (II-§1.29).

When a menu item is selected, the AWT sends an action event (II-§1.14.13) to the menu item's containing frame. The event's target is the menu item, and its object is the string label of the menu item. Note that the subclass Menu overrides this behavior and does not send any event to the frame until one of its subitems is selected.

Constructors

MenuItem   §1.32.1

> public MenuItem(String label)

Constructs a new menu item with the specified label.

The label "-" is reserved to mean a separator between menu items. By default, all menu items except for separators are enabled.

PARAMETERS:

label: the label for the menu item.

Methods

addNotify   §1.32.2

> public void addNotify()

This method calls the createMenuItem method (II-§1.41.16) of this object's toolkit (II-§1.10.20) in order to create a MenuItemPeer (II-§3.15) for this menu item. This peer allows the application to change the look of a menu item, without changing its functionality.

Most applications do not call this method directly.

disable   §1.32.3

> public void disable()

Disables this menu item. It can no longer be selected by the user.

enable   §1.32.4

> public void enable()

Enables this menu item; it can be selected by the user.

enable §1.32.5

    `public void enable(boolean cond)`

      Enables this menu item if the flag is `true`; otherwise, disables it.

    PARAMETERS:

    `cond`: if `true`, enables this menu item; otherwise, disables it.

    SEE ALSO:

    `enable` **(II-§1.32.4)**.

    `disable` **(II-§1.32.3)**.

getLabel §1.32.6

    `public String getLabel()`

    RETURNS:

    the label of this menu item, or `null` if this menu item has no label.

isEnabled §1.32.7

    `public boolean isEnabled()`

      Checks whether this menu item is enabled.

    RETURNS:

    `true` if this menu item is enabled; `false` otherwise.

paramString §1.32.8

    `public String paramString()`

      Returns the parameter string representing the state of this menu item. This string is useful for debugging.

    RETURNS:

    the parameter string of this menu item.

    OVERRIDES:

    `paramString` in class MenuComponent **(II-§1.31.5)**.

setLabel §1.32.9

    `public void setLabel(String label)`

      Changes this menu item's label to be the `label` argument.

    PARAMETERS:

    `label`: the new label, or `null` for no label.

1.33 Class Panel

```
public class java.awt.Panel
    extends java.awt.Container (II-§1.11)
{
    // Constructors
    public Panel();                                         §1.33.1

    // Methods
    public void addNotify();                                §1.33.2
}
```

A panel is the simplest container class. It provides space into which an application can attach any other component, including other panels.

The AWT sends the panel all mouse, keyboard, and focus events that occur over it.

The default layout manager for a Panel is the FlowLayout (II-§1.16) layout manager.

Constructors

Panel   §1.33.1

```
public Panel()
```

Creates a new panel. The default layout for a panel is FlowLayout (**II-§1.16**).

Methods

addNotify   §1.33.2

```
public void addNotify()
```

This method calls the createPanel method (**II-§1.41.17**) of this object's toolkit (**II-§1.10.20**) in order to create a PanelPeer (**II-§3.17**) for this panel. This peer allows the application to change the look of a panel without changing its functionality.

Most applications do not call this method directly.

OVERRIDES:

addNotify in class Container (**II-§1.11.4**).

1.34 Class Point

```
public class java.awt.Point
    extends java.lang.Object (I-§1.12)
{
    // Fields
    public int x;                                    §1.34.1
    public int y;                                    §1.34.2

    // Constructors
    public Point(int x, int y);                      §1.34.3

    // Methods
    public boolean equals(Object obj);               §1.34.4
    public int hashCode();                           §1.34.5
    public void move(int x, int y);                  §1.34.6
    public String toString();                        §1.34.7
    public void translate(int dx, int dy);           §1.34.8
}
```

A point represents an $\langle x, y \rangle$ coordinate.

Fields

x §1.34.1

```
public int x
```
> The x coordinate.

y §1.34.2

```
public int y
```
> The y coordinate.

Constructors

Point §1.34.3

```
public Point(int x, int y)
```
> Constructs and initializes a point to the specified $\langle x, y \rangle$ coordinate.

PARAMETERS:

x: the x coordinate.
y: the y coordinate.

Methods

equals   §1.34.4

```
public boolean equals(Object obj)
```

The result is true if and only if the argument is not null and is a Point object that has the same *x* and *y* coordinates as this object.

PARAMETERS:

obj: the object to compare with.

RETURNS:

true if the objects are the same; false otherwise.

OVERRIDES:

equals in class Object (**I-§1.12.3**).

hashCode   §1.34.5

```
public int hashCode()
```

RETURNS:

a hash code value for this point.

OVERRIDES:

hashCode in class Object (**I-§1.12.6**).

move   §1.34.6

```
public void move(int x, int y)
```

Modifies this point so that it now represents the $\langle x, y \rangle$ coordinates indicated.

PARAMETERS:

x: the new *x* coordinate.
y: the new *y* coordinate.

toString   §1.34.7

```
public String toString()
```

RETURNS:

a string representation of this point.

OVERRIDES:

toString in class Object (**I-§1.12.9**).

translate §1.34.8

```
public void translate(int dx, int dy)
```

Translates this point by dx to the right and dy downward so that it now represents the point $\langle x+dx, y+dy \rangle$, where it had been representing the point $\langle x, y \rangle$.

PARAMETERS:

dx: the amount to move this point to the right.
dy: the amount to move this point downward.

1.35 Class Polygon

```
public class java.awt.Polygon
        extends java.lang.Object (I-§1.12)
{
        // Fields
        public int npoints;                               §1.35.1
        public int xpoints[];                             §1.35.2
        public int ypoints[];                             §1.35.3

        // Constructors
        public Polygon();                                 §1.35.4
        public Polygon(int xpoints[], int ypoints[],      §1.35.5
                       int npoints);

        // Methods
        public void addPoint(int x, int y);               §1.35.6
        public Rectangle getBoundingBox();                §1.35.7
        public boolean inside(int x, int y);              §1.35.8
}
```

A polygon consists of a list of $\langle x, y \rangle$ coordinates, where each successive pair of coordinates defines a side of the polygon.

Fields

npoints §1.35.1

```
public int npoints
```

The total number of points.

xpoints §1.35.2

```
public int xpoints[]
```

The array of x coordinates.

ypoints   §1.35.3

  `public int ypoints[]`

   The array of *y* coordinates.

Constructors

Polygon   §1.35.4

  `public Polygon()`

   Creates an empty polygon.

Polygon   §1.35.5

  `public Polygon(int xpoints[], int ypoints[], int npoints)`

   Constructs and initializes a polygon from the specified parameters.

  PARAMETERS:

  `xpoints`: an array of *x* coordinates.
  `ypoints`: an array of *y* coordinates.
  `npoints`: the total number of points in the polygon.

Methods

addPoint   §1.35.6

  `public void addPoint(int x, int y)`

   Appends a point to this polygon.

   If an operation that calculates the bounding box of this polygon (`get-BoundingBox` [II-§1.35.7] or `inside` [II-§1.35.8]) has already been performed, this method updates the bounding box.

  PARAMETERS:

  `x`: the *x* coordinate of the point.
  `y`: the *y* coordinate of the point.

getBoundingBox   §1.35.7

  `public Rectangle getBoundingBox()`

  RETURNS:

  the smallest rectangle that contains this polygon.

inside §1.35.8

```
public boolean inside(int x, int y)
```

Determines if the specified point is inside this polygon. This method uses an even–odd insideness rule[8] (also known as an "alternating rule") to determine whether the point $\langle x, y \rangle$ is inside this polygon.

PARAMETERS:

x: the *x* coordinate of the point to be tested.
y: the *y* coordinate of the point to be tested.

RETURNS:

true if the point $\langle x, y \rangle$ is inside this polygon; false otherwise.

---

[8] This method is based on code by Hanpeter van Vliet (hvvliet@inter.nl.net).

1.36 Class Rectangle

```
public class java.awt.Rectangle
    extends java.lang.Object (I-§1.12)
{
    // Fields
    public int height;                                              §1.36.1
    public int width;                                               §1.36.2
    public int x;                                                   §1.36.3
    public int y;                                                   §1.36.4

    // Constructors
    public Rectangle();                                             §1.36.5
    public Rectangle(Dimension d);                                  §1.36.6
    public Rectangle(int width, int height);                        §1.36.7
    public Rectangle(int x, int y, int width, int height);          §1.36.8
    public Rectangle(Point p);                                      §1.36.9
    public Rectangle(Point p, Dimension d);                         §1.36.10

    // Methods
    public void add(int newx, int newy);                            §1.36.11
    public void add(Point pt);                                      §1.36.12
    public void add(Rectangle r);                                   §1.36.13
    public boolean equals(Object obj);                              §1.36.14
    public void grow(int h, int v);                                 §1.36.15
    public int hashCode();                                          §1.36.16
    public boolean inside(int x, int y);                            §1.36.17
    public Rectangle intersection(Rectangle r);                     §1.36.18
    public boolean intersects(Rectangle r);                         §1.36.19
    public boolean isEmpty();                                       §1.36.20
    public void move(int x, int y);                                 §1.36.21
    public void reshape(int x, int y, int width,                    §1.36.22
                        int height);
public void resize(int width, int height);                          §1.36.23
    public String toString();                                       §1.36.24
    public void translate(int dx, int dy);                          §1.36.25
    public Rectangle union(Rectangle r);                            §1.36.26
}
```

A rectangle specifies an area defined by its top left $\langle x, y \rangle$ coordinate, its width, and its height.

Fields

height §1.36.1

    `public int height`

        The height of the rectangle.

width §1.36.2

    `public int width`

        The width of the rectangle.

x §1.36.3

    `public int x`

        The x coordinate of the top left corner of the rectangle.

y §1.36.4

    `public int y`

        The y coordinate of the top left corner of the rectangle.

Constructors

Rectangle §1.36.5

    `public Rectangle()`

        Constructs a new rectangle whose top left corner is $\langle 0,0 \rangle$ and whose width and height are 0.

Rectangle §1.36.6

    `public Rectangle(Dimension d)`

        Constructs a new rectangle whose top left corner is $\langle 0,0 \rangle$ and whose width and height are specified by the dimension argument.

    PARAMETERS:

    `d`: the width and height.

Rectangle §1.36.7

    `public Rectangle(int width, int height)`

        Constructs a new rectangle whose top left corner is $\langle 0,0 \rangle$ and whose width and height are the specified arguments.

    PARAMETERS:

    `width`: the width of the rectangle.
    `height`: the height of the rectangle.

Rectangle   §1.36.8

```
public Rectangle(int x, int y, int width, int height)
```

Constructs a new rectangle whose top left corner is $\langle x, y \rangle$ and whose width and height are the specified arguments.

PARAMETERS:

x: the x coordinate.
y: the y coordinate.
width: the width of the rectangle.
height: the height of the rectangle.

Rectangle   §1.36.9

```
public Rectangle(Point p)
```

Constructs a new rectangle whose top left corner is the specified point argument and whose width and height are 0.

PARAMETERS:

p: the top left corner of the rectangle.

Rectangle   §1.36.10

```
public Rectangle(Point p, Dimension d)
```

Constructs a new rectangle whose top left corner is the specified point argument and whose width and height are specified by the dimension argument.

PARAMETERS:

p: the top left corner of the rectangle.
d: the width and height.

Methods

add   §1.36.11

```
public void add(int newx, int newy)
```

Adds the point $\langle newx, newy \rangle$ to this rectangle.

This rectangle is modified to be the smallest rectangle that contains both this rectangle and the point.

PARAMETERS:

newx: the x coordinate of the new point.
newy: the y coordinate of the new point.

add   §1.36.12

```
public void add(Point pt)
```

Adds the point to this rectangle.

This rectangle is modified to be the smallest rectangle that contains both this rectangle and the point.

PARAMETERS:

`pt`: a point.

add   §1.36.13

```
public void add(Rectangle r)
```

Adds the rectangle argument to this rectangle.

This rectangle is modified to be the smallest rectangle that contains both rectangles.

PARAMETERS:

`r`: a rectangle.

equals   §1.36.14

```
public boolean equals(Object obj)
```

The result is `true` if and only if the argument is not `null` and is a Rectangle object that has the same top left corner, width, and height as this rectangle.

PARAMETERS:

`obj`: the object to compare with.

RETURNS:

`true` if the objects are the same; `false` otherwise.

OVERRIDES:

`equals` in class `Object` (**I-§1.12.3**).

grow   §1.36.15

```
public void grow(int h, int v)
```

Modifies the rectangle so that it is h units larger on both the left and right side, and v units larger at both the top and bottom.

The new rectangle has $(x - h, y - v)$ as its top-left corner, a width of $x + 2h$, and a height of $y + 2v$.

PARAMETERS:

`h`: the horizontal expansion.
`v`: the vertical expansion.

hashCode   §1.36.16

    `public int hashCode()`

    RETURNS:

    a hash code value for this object.

    OVERRIDES:

    hashCode in class `Object` **(I-§1.12.6)**.

inside   §1.36.17

    `public boolean inside(int x, int y)`

      Checks if the specified point lies inside this rectangle.

    PARAMETERS:

    x: the *x* coordinate.

    y: the *y* coordinate.

    RETURNS:

    `true` if the point $\langle x, y \rangle$ is inside this rectangle; `false` otherwise.

intersection   §1.36.18

    `public Rectangle intersection(Rectangle r)`

    PARAMETERS:

    r: a rectangle.

    RETURNS:

    the largest rectangle contained in both the rectangle argument and in this
      rectangle.

intersects   §1.36.19

    `public boolean intersects(Rectangle r)`

      Determines if this rectangle and the rectangle argument intersect. Two
    rectangles insersect if their intersection is nonempty.

    PARAMETERS:

    r: a rectangle.

    RETURNS:

    `true` if the rectangle argument and this rectangle insersect; `false` otherwise.

isEmpty   §1.36.20

    `public boolean isEmpty()`

      Determines if this rectangle is empty. A rectangle is empty if its width or
    its height is less than or equal to 0.

    RETURNS:

    `true` if this rectangle is empty; `false` otherwise.

move   §1.36.21

```
public void move(int x, int y)
```

Moves this rectangle so that its new top left corner is the specified $\langle x, y \rangle$ coordinate.

PARAMETERS:

x: the new *x* coordinate.
y: the new *y* coordinate.

reshape   §1.36.22

```
public void reshape(int x, int y, int width, int height)
```

Reshapes this rectangle so that its new top left corner is the specified $\langle x, y \rangle$ coordinate and its new width and height are the specified arguments.

PARAMETERS:

x: the new *x* coordinate.
y: the new *y* coordinate.
width: the new width.
height: the new height.

resize   §1.36.23

```
public void resize(int width, int height)
```

Resizes this rectangle so that its new width and height are the indicated arguments.

PARAMETERS:

width: the new width.
height: the new height.

toString   §1.36.24

```
public String toString()
```

RETURNS:

a string representation of this rectangle.

OVERRIDES:

toString in class Object (**I-§1.12.9**).

translate   §1.36.25

```
public void translate(int dx, int dy)
```

Translates this rectangle by dx to the right and dy downward so that its top left corner is now point $\langle x + dx, y + dy \rangle$, where it had been the point $\langle x, y \rangle$.

PARAMETERS:

dx: the amount to move the rectangle to the right.
dy: the amount to move the rectangle downward.

union §1.36.26

```
public Rectangle union(Rectangle r)
```

Computes the union of this rectangle with the argument rectangle.

PARAMETERS:

r: a rectangle.

RETURNS:

the smallest rectangle containing both the rectangle argument and this rectangle.

1.37 Class Scrollbar

```
public class java.awt.Scrollbar
    extends java.awt.Component (II-§1.10)
{
    // Fields
    public final static int HORIZONTAL;                    §1.37.1
    public final static int VERTICAL;                      §1.37.2

    // Constructors
    public Scrollbar();                                    §1.37.3
    public Scrollbar(int orientation);                     §1.37.4
    public Scrollbar(int orientation, int value,           §1.37.5
                     int visible, int minimum, int maximum);

    // Methods
    public void addNotify();                               §1.37.6
    public int getLineIncrement();                         §1.37.7
    public int getMaximum();                               §1.37.8
    public int getMinimum();                               §1.37.9
    public int getOrientation();                           §1.37.10
    public int getPageIncrement();                         §1.37.11
    public int getValue();                                 §1.37.12
    public int getVisible();                               §1.37.13
    protected String paramString();                        §1.37.14
    public void setLineIncrement(int l);                   §1.37.15
    public void setPageIncrement(int l);                   §1.37.16
    public void setValue(int value);                       §1.37.17
    public void setValues(int value, int visible,          §1.37.18
                          int minimum, int maximum);
}
```

A scroll bar provides a convenient means of allowing a user to select from a range of values. For example, the following three scroll bars could be used to pick each of the red, green, and blue components of a color:

Each scroll bar was created with code like the following:

```
redSlider=new Scrollbar(Scrollbar.VERTICAL, 0, 1, 0, 255);
add(redSlider);
```

Alternatively, a scroll bar can represent a range of values. For example, if a scroll bar is used for scrolling through text, the width of the "bubble" can represent the amount of text visible. Here is an example of a scroll bar representing a range:

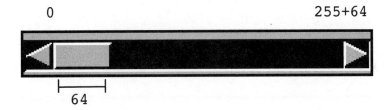

The value range represented by the bubble is the *visible* amount of the scroll bar.

The code to produce this scroll bar is

```
ranger = new Scrollbar(Scrollbar.HORIZONTAL, 0, 64, 0, 255);
add(ranger);
```

Note that the maximum value above, 255, is the maximum value for the "left side" of the scroll bar.

Whenever the user changes the value of the scroll bar, AWT sends one of the following five events to the application:

♦ A scroll absolute event **(I-§5.14.28)** if the user drags the bubble.

♦ A scroll line down **(I-§5.14.29)** event if the user clicks in the right arrow of a horizontal scroll bar or the bottom arrow of a vertical scroll bar.

♦ A scroll line up event **(II-§1.14.30)** if the user clicks in the left arrow of a horizontal scroll bar or the top arrow of a vertical scroll bar.

♦ A scroll page down **(I-§5.14.31)** event if the user clicks to the right of the bubble in a horizontal scroll bar or below the bubble in a vertical scroll bar.

♦ A scroll page up **(II-§1.14.32)** event if the user clicks to the left of the bubble in a horizontal scroll bar or above the bubble in a vertical scroll bar.

The event's target is the scroll bar, and its object is an `Integer` **(I-§1.8)** giving the value represented by the scroll bar.

If an application wants to perform some action when the value in a scroll bar is changed, it must override the `handleEvent` method of the scroll bar or of one of its containing windows. The code to perform that should be of the following form:

```
public boolean handleEvent(Event event) {
    if (event.target == scrollbar) {
        do something
        return true;
    } else {
        return super.handleEvent(event);
    }
}
```

Fields

HORIZONTAL   §1.37.1

```
public final static int HORIZONTAL = 0
```

Constant indicating to construct a horizontal scroll bar.

VERTICAL   §1.37.2

```
public final static int VERTICAL = 1
```

Constant indicating to construct a vertical scroll bar.

Constructors

Scrollbar   §1.37.3

```
public Scrollbar()
```

Constructs a new vertical scroll bar.

Scrollbar §1.37.4

```
public Scrollbar(int orientation)
```

Constructs a new scroll bar with the specified orientation.

The orientation argument must be one of the two values HORIZONTAL (**II-§1.37.1**) or VERTICAL (**II-§1.37.2**), indicating a horizontal or vertical scroll bar, respectively.

PARAMETERS:

orientation: indicates the orientation of the scroll bar.

THROWS:

IllegalArgumentException (**I-§1.32**)
when an illegal orientation is given.

Scrollbar §1.37.5

```
public Scrollbar(int orientation, int value, int visible,
                 int minimum, int maximum)
```

Constructs a new scroll bar with the specified orientation, initial value, page size, and minimum and maximum values.

The orientation argument must be one of the two values HORIZONTAL (**II-§1.37.1**), or VERTICAL (**II-§1.37.2**), indicating a horizontal or vertical scroll bar, respectively.

If the specified maximum value is less than the minimum value, it is changed to be the same as the minimum value. If the initial value is lower than the minimum value, it is changed to be the minimum value; if it is greater than the maximum value, it is changed to be the maximum value.

PARAMETERS:

orientation: indicates the orientation of the scroll bar.
value: the initial value of the scroll bar.
visible: the size represented by the bubble in the scroll bar; the scroll bar
    uses this value when paging up or down by a page.
minimum: the minimum value of the scroll bar.
maximum: the maximum value of the scroll bar.

Methods

---

addNotify   §1.37.6

`public void addNotify()`

This method calls the `createScrollbar` method (**II-§1.41.18**) of this object's toolkit (**II-§1.10.20**) in order to create a `ScrollbarPeer` (**II-§3.18**) for this button. This peer allows the application to change the look of a scroll bar without changing its functionality.

Most applications do not call this method directly.

OVERRIDES:

`addNotify` in class `Component` (**II-§1.10.2**).

getLineIncrement   §1.37.7

`public int getLineIncrement()`

Determines the line increment of this scroll bar, which is the amount that is added or subtracted from this scroll bar's value when the user hits the down or up gadget.

RETURNS:

the line increment of this scroll bar.

SEE ALSO:

`setLineIncrement` (**II-§1.37.15**).

getMaximum   §1.37.8

`public int getMaximum()`

RETURNS:

the maximum value of this scroll bar.

SEE ALSO:

`getMinimum` (**II-§1.37.9**).
`getValue` (**II-§1.37.12**).

getMinimum   §1.37.9

`public int getMinimum()`

RETURNS:

the minimum value of this scroll bar.

SEE ALSO:

`getMaximum` (**II-§1.37.8**).
`getValue` (**II-§1.37.12**).

getOrientation §1.37.10

    public int getOrientation()

Determines the orientation of this scroll bar. The value returned is either HORIZONTAL (**II-§1.37.1**) or VERTICAL (**II-§1.37.2**).

RETURNS:

the orientation of this scroll bar.

getPageIncrement §1.37.11

    public int getPageIncrement()

Determines the page increment of this scroll bar, which is the amount that is added to or subtracted from this scroll bar's value when the user hits the page down or page up gadget.

RETURNS:

the page increment for this scroll bar.

SEE ALSO:

getsetPageIncrement (**II-§1.37.16**).

getValue §1.37.12

    public int getValue()

RETURNS:

the current value of this scroll bar.

SEE ALSO:

getMinimum (**II-§1.37.9**).
getMaximum (**II-§1.37.8**).

getVisible §1.37.13

    public int getVisible()

Determines the "visible" amount of this scroll bar, which is the range of values represented by the width of the bubble in this scroll bar.

RETURNS:

the "visible" amount of this scroll bar.

paramString §1.37.14

    protected String paramString()

Returns the parameter string representing the state of this scroll bar. This string is useful for debugging.

RETURNS:

the parameter string of this scroll bar.

OVERRIDES:

paramString in class Component (**II-§1.10.51**).

setLineIncrement   §1.37.15

```
public void setLineIncrement(int l)
```

Sets the line increment of this scroll bar.

The line increment is the value that is added to or subtracted from the value of this scroll bar when the user hits the line down or line up gadget.

PARAMETERS:

l: the new line increment.

SEE ALSO:

getLineIncrement (**II-§1.37.7**).

setPageIncrement   §1.37.16

```
public void setPageIncrement(int l)
```

Sets the page increment of this scroll bar.

The page increment is the value that is added to or subtracted from the value of the scroll bar when the user hits the page down or page up gadget.

PARAMETERS:

l: the new page increment.

SEE ALSO:

getPageIncrement (**II-§1.37.11**).

setValue   §1.37.17

```
public void setValue(int value)
```

Sets the value of this scroll bar to the specified value. If the specified value is below this scroll bar's current minimum or above the current maximum, it becomes the minimum or maximum value, respectively.

PARAMETERS:

value: the new value of this scroll bar.

SEE ALSO:

getValue (**II-§1.37.12**).

setValues   §1.37.18

```
public void setValues(int value, int visible,
                      int minimum, int maximum)
```

Sets several parameters of this scroll bar simultaneously.

PARAMETERS:

value: the value of this scroll bar.
visible: the amount visible per page.
minimum: the minimum value of this scroll bar.
maximum: the maximum value of this scroll bar.

1.38 Class TextArea

```
public class java.awt.TextArea
    extends java.awt.TextComponent (II-§1.39)
{
    // Constructors
    public TextArea();                              §1.38.1
    public TextArea(int rows, int cols);            §1.38.2
    public TextArea(String text);                   §1.38.3
    public TextArea(String text, int rows, int cols); §1.38.4

    // Methods
    public void addNotify();                        §1.38.5
    public void appendText(String str);             §1.38.6
    public int getColumns();                        §1.38.7
    public int getRows();                           §1.38.8
    public void insertText(String str, int pos);    §1.38.9
    public Dimension minimumSize();                 §1.38.10
    public Dimension minimumSize(int rows, int cols); §1.38.11
    protected String paramString();                 §1.38.12
    public Dimension preferredSize();               §1.38.13
    public Dimension preferredSize(int rows, int cols); §1.38.14
    public void replaceText(String str, int start,  §1.38.15
                        int end);

}
```

A text area is a multiline area for displaying text. It can be set to allow editing or to be read-only.

For example, the following code:

```
new TextArea("Hello", 5, 40);
```

produces the text area shown below:

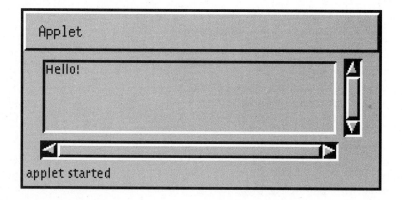

When the text area receives or loses the focus[9], AWT sends a "got focus" (**II-§1.14.12**) or "lost focus" (**II-§1.14.20**) event to the text area. An application should override the gotFocus method (**II-§1.10.21**) or the lostFocus method (**II-§1.10.39**) of the text area in order to cause some action to occur.

Most user interfaces use an external event (such as clicking on a button) to trigger an action on the text area.

Constructors

TextArea   §1.38.1

```
public TextArea()
```

Constructs a new text area.

TextArea   §1.38.2

```
public TextArea(int rows, int cols)
```

Constructs a new text area with the specified number of rows and columns.

PARAMETERS:

rows: the number of rows.
cols: the number of columns.

---

9. In Java 1.0, the AWT does not send mouse, keyboard, or focus events to a text area. In Java 1.1, the AWT sends the text area all mouse, keyboard, and focus events that occur over it.

TextArea §1.38.3

    `public TextArea(String text)`

    Constructs a new text area with the specified text displayed.

    PARAMETERS:

    `text`: the text to be displayed.

TextArea §1.38.4

    `public TextArea(String text, int rows, int cols)`

    Constructs a new text area with the specified text, and the specified number of rows and columns.

    PARAMETERS:

    `text`: the text to be displayed.
    `rows`: the number of rows.
    `cols`: the number of columns.

Methods

addNotify §1.38.5

    `public void addNotify()`

    This method calls the `createTextArea` method (**II-§1.41.19**) of this object's toolkit (**II-§1.10.20**) in order to create a `TextAreaPeer` (**II-§3.19**) for this text area. This peer allows the application to change the look of a text area without changing its functionality.

    Most applications do not call this method directly.

    OVERRIDES:

    `addNotify` in class Component (**II-§1.10.2**).

appendText §1.38.6

    `public void appendText(String str)`

    Appends the given text to this text area's current text.

    PARAMETERS:

    `str`: the text to append.

    SEE ALSO:

    `insertText` (**II-§1.38.9**).

getColumns §1.38.7

    `public int getColumns()`

    RETURNS:

    the number of columns in this text area.

getRows   §1.38.8

```
public int getRows()
```

RETURNS:

the number of rows in this text area.

insertText   §1.38.9

```
public void insertText(String str, int pos)
```

Inserts the specified text at the specified position in this text area.

PARAMETERS:

`str`: the text to insert.
`pos`: the position at which to insert the text.

SEE ALSO:

`setText` in class `TextComponent` (**II-§1.39.11**).
`replaceText` (**II-§1.38.15**).

minimumSize   §1.38.10

```
public Dimension minimumSize()
```

Determines the minimum size of this text area. If the application has specified both the number of rows and the number of columns for this text area, and both are greater than zero, then the text area's peer's `minimumSize` method (**II-§3.19.2**) is called with the number of rows and columns in order to determine the minimum size.

If the text area does not have a peer, or if the number of rows or number of columns specified by the application is less than or equal to zero, the superclass's `minimumSize` method (**II-§1.10.40**) is called to determine the minimum size.

RETURNS:

the minimum dimensions needed for this text area.

OVERRIDES:

`minimumSize` in class `Component` (**II-§1.10.40**).

minimumSize   §1.38.11

```
public Dimension minimumSize(int rows, int cols)
```

Determines the minimum size of a text area with the specified number of rows and columns. This text area's peer's `minimumSize` method (**II-§3.19.2**) is called with the number of rows and columns in order to determine the minimum size.

If this text area does not have a peer, the superclass's `minimumSize` method (**II-§1.10.40**) is called to determine the minimum size.

PARAMETERS:

`rows`: the number of rows.
`cols`: the number of columns.

RETURNS:

the minimum dimensions needed to display the text area with the specified number of rows and columns.

paramString   §1.38.12

```
protected String paramString()
```

Returns the parameter string representing the state of this text area. This string is useful for debugging.

RETURNS:

the parameter string of this text area.

OVERRIDES:

`paramString` in class `TextComponent` (**II-§1.39.6**).

preferredSize   §1.38.13

```
public Dimension preferredSize()
```

Determines the preferred size of this text area. If the application has specified both the number of rows and the number of columns for this text area, and both are greater than zero, then the text area's peer's `preferredSize` method (**II-§3.19.3**) is called with the number of rows and columns in order to determine the preferred size.

If this text area does not have a peer, or if the number of rows or number of columns specified by the application is less than or equal to zero, the superclass's `preferredSize` method (**II-§1.10.53**) is called to determine the preferred size.

RETURNS:

the preferred dimensions needed for this text area.

OVERRIDES:

`preferredSize` in class `Component` (**II-§1.10.53**).

preferredSize   §1.38.14

`public Dimension preferredSize(int rows, int cols)`

Determines the preferred size of a text area with the specified number of rows and columns. This text area's peer's `preferredSize` method (**II-§3.19.3**) is called with the number of rows and columns in order to determine the preferred size.

If this text area does not have a peer, the superclass's `preferredSize` method (**II-§1.10.53**) is called to determine the preferred size.

PARAMETERS:

`rows`: the number of rows.
`cols`: the number of columns.

RETURNS:

the preferred dimensions needed to display the text area with the specified number of rows and columns.

replaceText   §1.38.15

`public void replaceText(String str, int start, int end)`

Replaces the text in the text area from the `start` (inclusive) index to the end (exclusive) index with the new text specified.

PARAMETERS:

`str`: the replacement text.
`start`: the start position.
`end`: the end position.

SEE ALSO:

`insertText` (**II-§1.38.9**).

1.39 Class TextComponent

```
public class java.awt.TextComponent
    extends java.awt.Component (II-§1.10)
{
    // Methods
    public String getSelectedText();                          §1.39.1
    public int getSelectionEnd();                             §1.39.2
    public int getSelectionStart();                          §1.39.3
    public String getText();                                 §1.39.4
    public boolean isEditable();                             §1.39.5
    protected String paramString();                          §1.39.6
    public void removeNotify();                              §1.39.7
    public void select(int selStart, int selEnd);            §1.39.8
    public void selectAll();                                 §1.39.9
    public void setEditable(boolean t);                      §1.39.10
    public void setText(String t);                           §1.39.11
}
```

A text component is the superclass of any component that allows the editing of some text.

Methods

getSelectedText   §1.39.1

> public String getSelectedText()
>
> **RETURNS:**
>
> the selected text in this text component.
>
> **SEE ALSO:**
>
> setText (II-§1.39.11).

getSelectionEnd   §1.39.2

> public int getSelectionEnd()
>
> **RETURNS:**
>
> the selected text's end position in this text component.

getSelectionStart   §1.39.3

> public int getSelectionStart()
>
> **RETURNS:**
>
> the selected text's start position in this text component.

getText §1.39.4

```
public String getText()
```
RETURNS:

the text of this text component.

SEE ALSO:

setText (II-§1.39.11).

isEditable §1.39.5

```
public boolean isEditable()
```
RETURNS:

true if this text component is editable; false otherwise.

SEE ALSO:

setEditable (II-§1.39.10).

paramString §1.39.6

```
protected String paramString()
```
Returns the parameter string representing the state of this text component. This string is useful for debugging.

RETURNS:

the parameter string of this text component.

OVERRIDES:

paramString in class Component (II-§1.10.51).

removeNotify §1.39.7

```
public void removeNotify()
```
Notifies this text component to destroy its peer.

OVERRIDES:

removeNotify in class Component (II-§1.10.58).

select §1.39.8

```
public void select(int selStart, int selEnd)
```
Selects the text in this text component found from the specified start (inclusive) index to the specified end index (exclusive).

PARAMETERS:

selStart: the start position of the text to select.
selEnd: the end position of the text to select.

selectAll §1.39.9

```
public void selectAll()
```
Selects all the text in this text component.

setEditable §1.39.10

```
public void setEditable(boolean t)
```

If the `boolean` argument is `true`, this text component becomes user editable. If the flag is `false`, the user cannot change the text of this text component.

PARAMETERS:

`t`: a flag indicating whether the text component should become user editable.

SEE ALSO:

`isEditable` (**II-§1.39.5**).

setText §1.39.11

```
public void setText(String t)
```

Sets the text of this text component to be the specified text.

PARAMETERS:

`t`: the new text.

SEE ALSO:

`getText` (**II-§1.39.4**).

1.40 Class TextField

```
public class java.awt.TextField
    extends java.awt.TextComponent (II-§1.39)
{
    // Constructors
    public TextField();                              §1.40.1
    public TextField(int cols);                      §1.40.2
    public TextField(String text);                   §1.40.3
    public TextField(String text, int cols);         §1.40.4

    // Methods
    public void addNotify();                         §1.40.5
    public boolean echoCharIsSet();                  §1.40.6
    public int getColumns();                         §1.40.7
    public char getEchoChar();                       §1.40.8
    public Dimension minimumSize();                  §1.40.9
    public Dimension minimumSize(int cols);          §1.40.10
    protected String paramString();                  §1.40.11
    public Dimension preferredSize();                §1.40.12
    public Dimension preferredSize(int cols);        §1.40.13
    public void setEchoCharacter(char c);            §1.40.14
}
```

A text field is a component that presents the user with a single editable line of text.

For example, the following code:

```
TextField tf1, tf2, tf3, tf4;
// a blank text field
tf1 = new TextField();
// blank field of 20 columns
tf2 = new TextField(20);
// Predefined text displayed
tf3 = new TextField("Hello!");
// Predefined text in 30 columns
tf4 = new TextField("Hello", 30);
```

produces the text fields shown below:

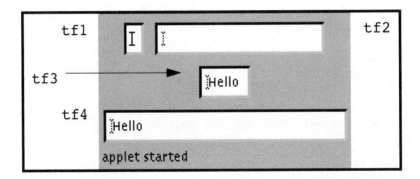

Every time the user types a key[10] in the text field, AWT sends a key press event (**II-§1.14.15**) and a key release event (**II-§1.14.16**) to the text field. These events' target field is the button, and their key field is the key typed.

In addition, whenever the user types the return key, AWT sends an action event (**II-§1.14.11**) to the text field. This event's target is the text field, and its object is the string contents of the text field; the string will not have a return character as its last character. An application should override the `action` method (**II-§1.10.1**) of the text field or of one of its containing windows in order to cause some action to occur.

[10.] In Java 1.0, the AWT does not send mouse or focus events to a text area. In Java 1.1, the AWT sends the text area all mouse, keyboard, and focus events that occur over it.

Constructors

TextField §1.40.1

    `public TextField()`

    Constructs a new text field.

TextField §1.40.2

    `public TextField(int cols)`

    Constructs a new text field the specified number of characters wide.

    PARAMETERS:

  `cols`: the number of characters.

TextField §1.40.3

    `public TextField(String text)`

    Constructs a new text field initialized with the specified text.

    PARAMETERS:

  `text`: the text to be displayed.

TextField §1.40.4

    `public TextField(String text, int cols)`

    Constructs a new text field initialized with the specified text and wide enough to hold the specified number of characters.

    PARAMETERS:

  `text`: the text to be displayed.
  `cols`: the number of characters.

Methods

addNotify §1.40.5

    `public void addNotify()`

    This method calls the `createTextField` method **(II-§1.41.20)** of this object's toolkit **(II-§1.10.20)** in order to create a `TextFieldPeer` **(II-§3.21)** for this text field. This peer allows the application to change the look of a text field without changing its functionality.

    Most applications do not call this method directly.

    OVERRIDES:

  `addNotify` in class `Component` **(II-§1.10.2)**.

echoCharIsSet   §1.40.6

> `public boolean echoCharIsSet()`
>
> **RETURNS:**
>
> `true` if this text field has a character set for echoing; `false` otherwise.
>
> **SEE ALSO:**
>
> `setEchoCharacter` (**II-§1.40.14**).
> `getEchoChar` (**II-§1.40.8**).

getColumns   §1.40.7

> `public int getColumns()`
>
> **RETURNS:**
>
> the number of columns in this text field.

getEchoChar   §1.40.8

> `public char getEchoChar()`
>
> **RETURNS:**
>
> the echo character for this text field.
>
> **SEE ALSO:**
>
> `setEchoCharacter` (**II-§1.40.14**).
> `echoCharIsSet` (**II-§1.40.6**).

minimumSize   §1.40.9

> `public Dimension minimumSize()`

Determines the minimum size of this text field. If the application has specified the number of columns for this text field, and that number is greater than zero, then this text field's peer's `minimumSize` method (**II-§3.21.1**) is called with the number of columns in order to determine the minimum size.

If this text field does not have a peer, or if the number of columns specified by the application is less than or equal to zero, the superclass's `minimumSize` method (**II-§1.10.40**) is called to determine the minimum size.

> **RETURNS:**
>
> the minimum dimensions needed for this text area.
>
> **OVERRIDES:**
>
> `minimumSize` in class `Component` (**II-§1.10.40**).

minimumSize §1.40.10

```
public Dimension minimumSize(int cols)
```

Determines the minimum size of a text field with the specified number of columns. This text field's peer's `minimumSize` method (**II-§3.21.1**) is called with the number of columns in order to determine the minimum size.

If this text field does not have a peer, the superclass's `minimumSize` method (**II-§1.10.40**) is called to determine the minimum size.

PARAMETERS:

`cols`: the number of columns.

RETURNS:

the minimum dimensions needed to display a text area with the specified number of columns.

paramString §1.40.11

```
protected String paramString()
```

Returns the parameter string representing the state of this text field. This string is useful for debugging.

RETURNS:

the parameter string of this text field.

OVERRIDES:

`paramString` in class `TextComponent` (**II-§1.39.6**).

preferredSize §1.40.12

```
public Dimension preferredSize()
```

Determines the preferred size of this text field. If the application has specified the number of columns for this text field, and that number is greater than zero, then this text field's peer's `preferredSize` method (**II-§3.21.2**) is called with the number of columns in order to determine the preferred size.

If this text field does not have a peer, or if the number of columns specified by the application is less than or equal to zero, the superclass's `preferredSize` method (**II-§1.10.53**) is called to determine the preferred size.

RETURNS:

the preferred dimensions needed for this text field.

OVERRIDES:

`preferredSize` in class `Component` (**II-§1.10.53**).

preferredSize   §1.40.13

`public Dimension preferredSize(int cols)`

Determines the preferred size of a text field with the specified number of columns. This text field's peer's `preferredSize` method (**II-§3.21.2**) is called with the number columns in order to determine the preferred size.

If this text field does not have a peer, the superclass's `preferredSize` method (**II-§1.10.53**) is called to determine the preferred size.

PARAMETERS:

`cols`: the number of columns.

RETURNS:

the preferred dimensions needed to display the text field with the specified number of columns.

setEchoCharacter   §1.40.14

`public void setEchoCharacter(char c)`

Sets the echo character for this text field. Any character that the user types in the text field is echoed in this text field as the echo character.

An echo character is useful for fields where the user input shouldn't be echoed to the screen, such as a text field for typing in a password.

PARAMETERS:

`c`: the echo character for this text field.

SEE ALSO:

`echoCharIsSet` (**II-§1.40.6**).

`getEchoChar` (**II-§1.40.8**).

1.41 Class Toolkit

```
public abstract class java.awt.Toolkit
    extends java.lang.Object (I-§1.12)
{
    // Constructors
    public Toolkit();                                     §1.41.1

    // Methods
    public abstract int                                   §1.41.2
        checkImage(Image image, int width, int height,
                    ImageObserver observer);
    protected abstract ButtonPeer                         §1.41.3
        createButton(Button target);
    protected abstract CanvasPeer                         §1.41.4
        createCanvas(Canvas target);
    protected abstract CheckboxPeer                       §1.41.5
        createCheckbox(Checkbox target);
    protected abstract CheckboxMenuItemPeer               §1.41.6
        createCheckboxMenuItem(CheckboxMenuItem target);
    protected abstract ChoicePeer                         §1.41.7
        createChoice(Choice target);
    protected abstract DialogPeer                         §1.41.8
        createDialog(Dialog target);
    protected abstract FileDialogPeer                     §1.41.9
        createFileDialog(FileDialog target);
    protected abstract FramePeer                          §1.41.10
        createFrame(Frame target);
    public abstract Image                                 §1.41.11
        createImage(ImageProducer producer);
    protected abstract LabelPeer                          §1.41.12
        createLabel(Label target);
    protected abstract ListPeer createList(List target);  §1.41.13
    protected abstract MenuPeer createMenu(Menu target);  §1.41.14
    protected abstract MenuBarPeer                        §1.41.15
        createMenuBar(MenuBar target);
    protected abstract MenuItemPeer                       §1.41.16
        createMenuItem(MenuItem target);
    protected abstract PanelPeer                          §1.41.17
        createPanel(Panel target);
    protected abstract ScrollbarPeer                      §1.41.18
        createScrollbar(Scrollbar target);
    protected abstract TextAreaPeer                       §1.41.19
        createTextArea(TextArea target);
    protected abstract TextFieldPeer                      §1.41.20
        createTextField(TextField target);
    protected abstract WindowPeer                         §1.41.21
        createWindow(Window target);
    public abstract ColorModel getColorModel();           §1.41.22
```

```
public static Toolkit getDefaultToolkit();          §1.41.23
public abstract String[] getFontList();             §1.41.24
public abstract FontMetrics                         §1.41.25
    getFontMetrics(Font font);
public abstract Image getImage(String filename);    §1.41.26
public abstract Image getImage(URL url);            §1.41.27
public abstract int getScreenResolution();          §1.41.28
public abstract Dimension getScreenSize();          §1.41.29
public abstract boolean                             §1.41.30
    prepareImage(Image image, int width, int height,
                ImageObserver observer);
public abstract void sync();                         §1.41.31
}
```

This class is the abstract superclass of all actual implementations of the Abstract Window Toolkit. Subclasses of the class are used to bind the various components to particular native toolkit implementations.

Most applications should not call any of the methods in this class directly. These methods are called by the addNotify methods of the various components in the Abstract Window Toolkit.

Constructors

Toolkit   §1.41.1

```
public Toolkit()
```

The default constructor for a toolkit.

Methods

---

checkImage §1.41.2

```
public abstract int
checkImage(Image image, int width, int height,
        ImageObserver observer)
```

If the width and height arguments are both –1, this method returns the status of the construction of a screen representation of the specified image in this toolkit. Otherwise, this method returns the status of the construction of a scaled representation of the specified image at the specified width and height.

This method does not cause the image to begin loading. An application must use the prepareImage **(II-§1.41.30)** method to force the loading of an image.

This toolkit method is used by the checkImage methods **(II-§1.10.4, §1.10.5)** of Component.

Information on the flags returned by this method can be found in II-§2.11.

PARAMETERS:
image: the image whose status is being checked.
width: the width of the scaled version whose status is being checked.
height: the height of the scaled version whose status is being checked.
observer: the ImageObserver object to be notified as the image is being prepared.

RETURNS:

the bitwise inclusive **OR** of the ImageObserver flags **(II-§2.11)** indicating what information about the image is available.

createButton §1.41.3

```
protected abstract ButtonPeer createButton(Button target)
```
PARAMETERS:
target: the button to be implemented.

RETURNS:
this toolkit's implementation of a Button **(II-§1.2)**.

createCanvas §1.41.4

```
protected abstract CanvasPeer createCanvas(Canvas target)
```
PARAMETERS:
target: the canvas to be implemented.

RETURNS:
this toolkit's implementation of a Canvas **(II-§1.3)**.

createCheckbox   §1.41.5

    protected abstract CheckboxPeer
    createCheckbox(Checkbox target)

PARAMETERS:

target: the check box to be implemented.

RETURNS:

this toolkit's implementation of a Checkbox (**II-§1.5**).

createCheckboxMenuItem   §1.41.6

    protected abstract CheckboxMenuItemPeer
    createCheckboxMenuItem(CheckboxMenuItem target)

PARAMETERS:

target: the check box menu item to be implemented.

RETURNS:

this toolkit's implementation of a CheckboxMenuItem (**II-§1.7**).

createChoice   §1.41.7

    protected abstract ChoicePeer createChoice(Choice target)

PARAMETERS:

target: the choice list to be implemented.

RETURNS:

this toolkit's implementation of a Choice (**II-§1.8**).

createDialog   §1.41.8

    protected abstract DialogPeer createDialog(Dialog target)

PARAMETERS:

target: the dialog window to be implemented.

RETURNS:

this toolkit's implementation of a Dialog (**II-§1.12**).

createFileDialog   §1.41.9

    protected abstract FileDialogPeer
    createFileDialog(FileDialog target)

PARAMETERS:

target: the file dialog window to be implemented.

RETURNS:

this toolkit's implementation of a FileDialog (**II-§1.15**).

createFrame §1.41.10

protected abstract FramePeer createFrame(Frame target)

PARAMETERS:

target: the frame to be implemented.

RETURNS:

this toolkit's implementation of a Frame (**II-§1.19**).

createImage §1.41.11

public abstract Image createImage(ImageProducer producer)

PARAMETERS:

target: the image to be implemented.

RETURNS:

this toolkit's implementation of an Image (**II-§1.24**).

createLabel §1.41.12

protected abstract LabelPeer createLabel(Label target)

PARAMETERS:

target: the label to be implemented.

RETURNS:

this toolkit's implementation of a Label (**II-§1.26**).

createList §1.41.13

protected abstract ListPeer createList(List target)

PARAMETERS:

target: the scrolling list to be implemented.

RETURNS:

this toolkit's implementation of a List (**II-§1.27**).

createMenu §1.41.14

protected abstract MenuPeer createMenu(Menu target)

PARAMETERS:

target: the menu to be implemented.

RETURNS:

this toolkit's implementation of a Menu (**II-§1.29**).

createMenuBar   §1.41.15

```
protected abstract MenuBarPeer
createMenuBar(MenuBar target)
```

PARAMETERS:

`target`: the menu bar to be implemented.

RETURNS:

this toolkit's implementation of a `MenuBar` (**II-§1.30**).

createMenuItem   §1.41.16

```
protected abstract MenuItemPeer
createMenuItem(MenuItem target)
```

PARAMETERS:

`target`: the menu item to be implemented.

RETURNS:

this toolkit's implementation of a `MenuItem` (**II-§1.32**).

createPanel   §1.41.17

```
protected abstract PanelPeer createPanel(Panel target)
```

PARAMETERS:

`target`: the panel to be implemented.

RETURNS:

this toolkit's implementation of a `Panel` (**II-§1.33**).

createScrollbar   §1.41.18

```
protected abstract ScrollbarPeer
createScrollbar(Scrollbar target)
```

PARAMETERS:

`target`: the scroll bar to be implemented.

RETURNS:

this toolkit's implementation of a `ScrollBar` (**II-§1.37**).

createTextArea   §1.41.19

```
protected abstract TextAreaPeer
createTextArea(TextArea target)
```

PARAMETERS:

`target`: the text area to be implemented.

RETURNS:

this toolkit's implementation of a `TextArea` (**II-§1.38**).

createTextField §1.41.20

```
protected abstract TextFieldPeer
createTextField(TextField target)
```

PARAMETERS:

target: the text field to be implemented.

RETURNS:

this toolkit's implementation of a TextField (**II-§1.40**).

createWindow §1.41.21

```
protected abstract WindowPeer createWindow(Window target)
```

PARAMETERS:

target: the window to be implemented.

RETURNS:

this toolkit's implementation of a Window (**II-§1.42**).

getColorModel §1.41.22

```
public abstract ColorModel getColorModel()
```

Determines the color model of this toolkit's screen.

The ColorModel (**II-§2.1**) is an abstract class that encapsulates how to translate between pixel values of an image and its red, green, blue, and alpha components.

This toolkit method is used by the getColorModel method (**II-§1.10.13**) of Component.

RETURNS:

the color model of this toolkit's screen.

getDefaultToolkit §1.41.23

```
public static Toolkit getDefaultToolkit()
```

Gets the default toolkit.

If there is a system property named "awt.toolkit", that property is treated as the name of a class that is a subclass of Toolkit.

If the system property does not exist, then the default toolkit used is the class named "sun.awt.motif.MToolkit", which is a motif implementation of the Abstract Window Toolkit.

RETURNS:

the default toolkit.

THROWS:

AWTError (**II-§1.46**).

if a toolkit could not be found or could not be instantiated.

getFontList   §1.41.24

    `public abstract String[] getFontList()`

    RETURNS:

    the names of the available fonts in this toolkit.

getFontMetrics   §1.41.25

    `public abstract FontMetrics getFontMetrics(Font font)`

    PARAMETERS:

    `font`: a font.

    RETURNS:

    the screen metrics of the font argument in this toolkit.

getImage   §1.41.26

    `public abstract Image getImage(String filename)`

    PARAMETERS:

    `filename`: a file containing pixel data in a recognized file format.

    RETURNS:

    an image which gets its pixel data from the specified file.

getImage   §1.41.27

    `public abstract Image getImage(URL url)`

    PARAMETERS:

    `url`: a URL which specifies an image.

    RETURNS:

    an image which gets its pixel data from the specified URL.

getScreenResolution   §1.41.28

    `public abstract int getScreenResolution()`

    RETURNS:

    this toolkit's screen resolution in dots-per-inch.

getScreenSize   §1.41.29

    `public abstract Dimension getScreenSize()`

    RETURNS:

    the size of this toolkit's screen in pixels.

prepareImage §1.41.30

```
public abstract boolean
prepareImage(Image image, int width, int height,
             ImageObserver observer)
```

Prepares an image for rendering. If the width and height arguments are both −1, this method prepares the image for rendering on the default screen; otherwise, this method prepares an image for rendering on the default screen at the specified width and height.

The image data is downloaded asynchronously in another thread, and an appropriately scaled screen representation of the image is generated.

This toolkit method is used by the `prepareImage` methods (**II-§1.10.54**, **§1.10.55**) of Component.

Information on the flags returned by this method can be found in **II-§2.11**.

PARAMETERS:

`image`: the image for which to prepare a screen representation.
`width`: the width of the desired screen representation.
`height`: the height of the desired screen representation.
`observer`: the ImageObserver object to be notified as the image is being prepared.

RETURNS:

`true` if the image has already been fully prepared; `false` otherwise.

sync §1.41.31

```
public abstract void sync()
```

Synchronizes this toolkit's graphics state. Some window systems may do buffering of graphics events. This method ensures that the display is up-to-date.

1.42 Class Window

```
public class java.awt.Window
    extends java.awt.Container (II-§1.11)
{
    // Constructors
    public Window(Frame parent);                              §1.42.1

    // Methods
    public void addNotify();                                  §1.42.2
    public void dispose();                                    §1.42.3
    public Toolkit getToolkit();                              §1.42.4
    public final String getWarningString();                  §1.42.5
    public void pack();                                       §1.42.6
    public void show();                                       §1.42.7
    public void toBack();                                     §1.42.8
    public void toFront();                                    §1.42.9
}
```

A Window is a top-level window; it has no borders and no menu bar. It could be used, for example, to implement a pop-up menu. The AWT sends the window all mouse, keyboard, and focus events that occur over it.

The default layout for a window is BorderLayout (II-§1.1).

Constructors

Window   **§1.42.1**

```
public Window(Frame parent)
```

Constructs a new invisible window.

The window behaves as a modal dialog in that it will block input to other application windows when shown.

Use the show method (II-§1.42.7) to cause the window to become visible.

PARAMETERS:

parent: the main application frame.

Methods

---

addNotify §1.42.2

    public void addNotify()

This method calls the createWindow method (**II-§1.41.21**) of this object's toolkit (**II-§1.10.20**) in order to create a WindowPeer (**II-§3.22**) for this window. This peer allows the application to change the look of a window without changing its functionality.

Most applications do not call this method directly.

OVERRIDES:

addNotify in class Container (**II-§1.11.4**).

dispose §1.42.3

    public void dispose()

Disposes of this window and any resources used by this window.

getToolkit §1.42.4

    public Toolkit getToolkit()

Determines the toolkit of this window.

The implementation of getToolkit in class Window returns the default toolkit (**II-§1.41.23**). However, subclasses of Window can override this method in order to create their own toolkits.

RETURNS:

the toolkit of this window.

OVERRIDES:

getToolkit in class Component (**II-§1.10.20**).

getWarningString §1.42.5

    public final String getWarningString()

Returns the warning string that is displayed with this window. If this window is insecure, the warning string is displayed somewhere in the visible area of the window. A window is insecure if there is a security manager, and its checkTopLevelWindow method (**I-§1.15.22**) returns false when passed this window as an argument.

If the window is secure, then the getWarningString method returns null. If the window is insecure, this methods checks for a system property awt.appletWarning and returns the string value of that property. If there is no such property, the default warning string is used instead. The default warning string is "Warning: Applet Window".

RETURNS:

the warning string for this window.

pack   §1.42.6

    public void pack()

    Causes the subcomponents of this window to be laid out at their preferred
size.

show   §1.42.7

    public void show()

    If this window is not yet visible, makes it visible. If this window is already
visible, then brings it to the front (**II-§1.42.9**).

    OVERRIDES:

    show in class Component (**II-§1.10.70**).

    SEE ALSO:

    hide in class Component (**II-§1.10.23**).

toBack   §1.42.8

    public void toBack()

    Sends this window to the back.

toFront   §1.42.9

    public void toFront()

    Brings this window to the front.

1.43 Interface LayoutManager

```
public interface java.awt.LayoutManager
{
    // Methods
    public abstract void addLayoutComponent(String name,     §1.43.1
                                            Component comp);
    public abstract void layoutContainer(Container parent); §1.43.2
    public abstract Dimension                                §1.43.3
        minimumLayoutSize(Container parent);
    public abstract Dimension                                §1.43.4
        preferredLayoutSize(Container parent);
    public abstract void                                     §1.43.5
        removeLayoutComponent(Component comp);
}
```

    The LayoutManager interface specifies the methods that all layout managers
must implement.

    A layout manager is a class for laying out the components of a Container
(**II-§1.11**).

Methods

addLayoutComponent   §1.43.1

```
public abstract void
addLayoutComponent(String name, Component comp)
```

Adds the specified component to this layout using the indicated tag.

Most applications do not call this method directly. This method is called when a component is added to a container using the add(String, Component) method (**II-§1.11.3**).

PARAMETERS:

name: a tag understood by this layout manager.

comp: the component to be added.

layoutContainer   §1.43.2

```
public abstract void layoutContainer(Container parent)
```

Lays out the container argument using this layout.

This method may reshape the components in the specified target container in order to satisfy the constraints of this layout manager.

Most applications do not call this method directly. This method is called when a container calls its layout method (**II-§1.11.11**).

PARAMETERS:

parent: the container in which to do the layout.

minimumLayoutSize   §1.43.3

```
public abstract Dimension
minimumLayoutSize(Container parent)
```

Determines the minimum size of the container argument using this layout manager. Most applications do not call this method directly. This method is called when a container calls its layout method (**II-§1.11.11**).

PARAMETERS:

parent: the container in which to do the layout.

RETURNS:

the minimum dimensions needed to lay out the subcomponents of the specified container.

SEE ALSO:

preferredLayoutSize (II-§1.43.4).

preferredLayoutSize   §1.43.4

```
public abstract Dimension
preferredLayoutSize(Container parent)
```

Determines the preferred size of the container argument using this layout manager. Most applications do not call this method directly. This method is called when a container calls its `preferredSize` method (**II-§1.11.17**).

PARAMETERS:

parent: the container in which to do the layout.

RETURNS:

the preferred dimensions to lay out the subcomponents of the specified container.

SEE ALSO:

`minimumLayoutSize` (II-§1.43.3).

removeLayoutComponent   §1.43.5

```
public abstract void
removeLayoutComponent(Component comp)
```

Removes the specified component from this layout.

Most applications do not call this method directly. This method is called when a container calls its `remove` (**II-§1.11.19**) or `removeAll` (**II-§1.11.20**) methods.

PARAMETERS:

comp: the component to be removed.

1.44 Interface MenuContainer

```
public interface java.awt.MenuContainer
{
    // Methods
    public abstract Font getFont();                          §1.44.1
    public abstract boolean postEvent(Event evt);           §1.44.2
    public abstract void remove(MenuComponent comp);        §1.44.3
}
```

The `MenuContainer` interface specifies the methods that all menu-related containers must implement. Note that menu containers are not required to be full-fledged `Container` objects (**II-§1.11**).

Methods

getFont   §1.44.1

> `public abstract Font getFont()`
>
> **RETURNS:**
>
> the font used in this menu component, if there is one; `null` otherwise.

postEvent   §1.44.2

> `public abstract boolean postEvent(Event evt)`
>
> > Posts an event to this menu container.
>
> **PARAMETERS:**
>
> `evt`: the event.
>
> **RETURNS:**
>
> `true` if this menu component or one of its parents handled the event; `false` otherwise.

remove   §1.44.3

> `public abstract void remove(MenuComponent comp)`
>
> > Removes the specified menu component from this menu container.
>
> **PARAMETERS:**
>
> `m`: the menu component to be removed.

1.45 Class AWTException

```
public class java.awt.AWTException
    extends java.lang.Exception (I-§1.30)
{
    // Constructors
    public AWTException(String msg);                    §1.45.1
}
```

> Thrown when an Abstract Window Toolkit exception has occurred.

Constructors

AWTException   §1.45.1

> `public AWTException(String msg)`
>
> > Constructs an `AWTException` with the specified detail message.
>
> **PARAMETERS:**
>
> `msg`: the detail message.

1.46 Class AWTError

```
public class java.awt.AWTError
    extends java.lang.Error (I-§1.48)
{
    // Constructors
    public AWTError(String msg);                        §1.46.1
}
```

Thrown when a serious Abstract Window Toolkit error has occurred.

Constructors

AWTError   §1.46.1

    public AWTError(String msg)

      Constructs an AWTException with the specified detail message.

      PARAMETERS:

    msg: the detail message.

CHAPTER 2

Package java.awt.image

THE java.awt.image package contains classes and interfaces used by applications that perform sophisticated image processing. For most applications, the classes and interfaces in the java.awt package should be sufficient.

The classes and interfaces in this package can be divided into several groups:

◆ **Color**: The ColorModel (II-§2.1) class is an abstract class that provides the basic framework for translating from a pixel value to its alpha, red, green, and blue components. The subclasses of ColorModel include Direct-ColorModel (II-§2.3) and IndexColorModel (II-§2.6).

◆ **Image Producers**: The ImageProducer (II-§2.12) interface provides a flexible model whereby an object can be constructed, fetched, or created again as necessary. The MemoryImageSource (II-§2.7) class is the simplest image producer, in which the image comes from an array of pixels. A specialized image producer is the FilteredImageSource (II-§2.4), which takes an image producer and an image filter and produces a new image that is the original image transformed by the filter.

The createImage method (II-§1.10.6) can be used to create an Image (II-§1.24) object from an image producer.

◆ **Image Consumers**: The ImageConsumer (II-§2.10) interface is the set of methods used by the image producer to deliver the actual contents of an image to other objects. The PixelGrabber (II-§2.8) is one implementation of a consumer, which copies the image into a buffer. In addition, all image filters are image consumers.

◆ **Image Filters**: The ImageFilter (II-§2.5) class is an abstract class that provides the basic framework for transforming images. Two basic image filters are the CropImageFilter (II-§2.2), which crops an image, and the RGBImageFilter (II-§2.9), which modifies the colors in the image

♦ **Image Observers**: The `ImageObserver` interface **(II-§2.11)** allows objects to express an interest in being informed of the status of an image as it is being created. All the GUI components of `java.awt` that are subclasses of Component **(II-§1.10)** implement this interface.

2.1 Class ColorModel

```
public abstract class java.awt.image.ColorModel
    extends java.lang.Object (I-§1.12)
{
    // Fields
    protected int pixel_bits;                                    §2.1.1

    // Constructors
    public ColorModel(int bits);                                 §2.1.2

    // Methods
    public abstract int getAlpha(int pixel);                     §2.1.3
    public abstract int getBlue(int pixel);                      §2.1.4
    public abstract int getGreen(int pixel);                     §2.1.5
    public int getPixelSize();                                   §2.1.6
    public abstract int getRed(int pixel);                       §2.1.7
    public int getRGB(int pixel);                                §2.1.8
    public static ColorModel getRGBdefault();                    §2.1.9
}
```

This abstract class is the superclass for all classes that encapsulate methods for translating from pixel values to their alpha (transparency), red, green, and blue components.

The `java.awt.image` classes `IndexColorModel` **(II-§2.6)** and `DirectColor-Model` **(II-§2.3)** are subclasses of this class.

Fields

pixel_bits   §2.1.1

> `protected int pixel_bits`
>
> The number of bits per pixel.

Constructors

ColorModel §2.1.2

```
public ColorModel(int bits)
```

Constructs a ColorModel which describes a pixel with the specified number of bits.

PARAMETERS:

bits: the number of bits per pixel.

Methods

getAlpha §2.1.3

```
public abstract int getAlpha(int pixel)
```

Determines the alpha transparency of a pixel in this color model. The value ranges from 0 to 255. The value 0 indicates that the pixel is completely transparent. The value 255 indicates that the pixel is opaque.

PARAMETERS:

pixel: a pixel value.

RETURNS:

the alpha transparency represented by the pixel value.

getBlue §2.1.4

```
public abstract int getBlue(int pixel)
```

Determines the blue component of a pixel in this color model. The value ranges from 0 to 255. The value 0 indicates no contribution from this primary color. The value 255 indicates the maximum intensity of this color component.

PARAMETERS:

pixel: a pixel value.

RETURNS:

the blue color component represented by the pixel value.

getGreen   §2.1.5

```
public abstract int getGreen(int pixel)
```

Determines the green component of a pixel in this color model. The value ranges from 0 to 255. The value 0 indicates no contribution from this primary color. The value 255 indicates the maximum intensity of this color component.

PARAMETERS:

pixel: a pixel value.

RETURNS:

The green color component ranging from 0 to 255.

getPixelSize   §2.1.6

```
public int getPixelSize()
```

RETURNS:

the number of bits per pixel in this color model.

getRed   §2.1.7

```
public abstract int getRed(int pixel)
```

Determines the red component of a pixel in this color model. The value ranges from 0 to 255. The value 0 indicates no contribution from this primary color. The value 255 indicates the maximum intensity of this color component.

PARAMETERS:

pixel: a pixel value.

RETURNS:

the red color component ranging from 0 to 255.

getRGB   §2.1.8

```
public int getRGB(int pixel)
```

Calculates a single integer representing the alpha, red, green, and blue components of a pixel in this color model. The components are each scaled to be a value between 0 and 255 . The integer returned is the number such that bits 24–31 are the alpha value, bits 16–23 are the red value, bits 8–15 are the green value, and bits 0–7 are the blue value.

PARAMETERS:

pixel: a pixel value.

RETURNS:

an integer representing this color in RGB format.

SEE ALSO:

getRGBdefault (II-§2.1.9).

getRGBdefault   §2.1.9

```
public static ColorModel getRGBdefault()
```

Returns the default Abstract Window Toolkit color model.

The Abstract Window Toolkit represents each pixel as a 32-bit integer. Bits 24–31 are the alpha transparency, bits 16–23 are the red value, bits 8–15 are the green value, and bits 0–7 are the blue value.

This method returns a `ColorModel` object which describes that pixel format and can be used to extract alpha, red, green, and blue values from such color values.

RETURNS:

the default Abstract Window Toolkit color model.

2.2 Class CropImageFilter

```
public class java.awt.image.CropImageFilter
    extends java.awt.image.ImageFilter (II-§2.5)
{
    // Constructors
    public CropImageFilter(int x, int y, int w, int h);      §2.2.1

    // Methods
    public void setDimensions(int w, int h);                 §2.2.2
    public void setPixels(int x, int y, int w, int h,        §2.2.3
                    ColorModel model, byte pixels[],
                     int off, int scansize);
    public void setPixels(int x, int y, int w, int h,        §2.2.4
                    ColorModel model, int pixels[],
                     int off, int scansize);
    public void setProperties(Hashtable props);              §2.2.5
}
```

The cropped image filter is an image filter for cropping images. This class extends the basic `ImageFilter` class **(II-§2.5)** to extract a given rectangular region of an existing image and provides a source for new image containing only the extracted region.

This class is meant to be used in conjunction with a `FilteredImageSource` **(II-§2.4)** to produce cropped versions of existing images.

Constructors

CropImageFilter   §2.2.1

```
public CropImageFilter(int x, int y, int w, int h)
```

Constructs a cropped image filter that extracts the absolute rectangular region of pixels from its source Image as specified by the x, y, w, and h parameters.

PARAMETERS:

x: the *x* location of the top of the rectangle to be extracted.
y: the *y* location of the top of the rectangle to be extracted.
w: the width of the rectangle to be extracted.
h: the height of the rectangle to be extracted.

Methods

---

setDimensions   §2.2.2

```
public void setDimensions(int w, int h)
```

The image producer calls the setDimensions of the image consumer to tell it the width and height of the image.

The setDimensions method of CroppedImageFilter ignores its arguments. It calls the setDimensions method (**II-§2.10.12**) of its image consumer with the width and height arguments of the constructor (**II-§2.2.1**).

PARAMETERS:

width: the width of the image.
height: the height of the image.

OVERRIDES:

setDimensions in class ImageFilter (**II-§2.5.8**).

setPixels   §2.2.3

```
public void
setPixels(int x, int y, int w, int h, ColorModel model,
          byte pixels[], int off, int scansize)
```

The image producer calls the setPixels method of the image consumer one or more times to deliver the pixels of the image. For more information on this method and its arguments, see **II-§2.10.14** on page II-289.

The setPixels method of CroppedImageFilter determines if the specified rectangle intersects its cropping region. If so, it calls the setPixels method (**II-§2.10.14**) after modifying the x, y, w, h, and offset arguments to reflect only the intersecting region.

PARAMETERS:

x: the left coordinate of the rectangle.
y: the top coordinate of the rectangle.
w: the width of the rectangle.
h: the height of the rectangle.
model: the color model for bits.
pixels: the array of bits.
off: the offset for the first element.
scansize: the number of elements per row.

OVERRIDES:

setPixels in class ImageFilter (**II-§2.5.10**).

setPixels   §2.2.4

```
public void
setPixels(int x, int y, int w, int h, ColorModel model,
          int pixels[], int off, int scansize)
```

The image producer calls the `setPixels` method of the image consumer one or more times to deliver the pixels of the image. For more information on this method and its arguments, see **II-§2.10.15** on page II-289.

The `setPixels` method of `CroppedImageFilter` determines if the specified rectangle intersects its cropping region. If so, it calls the `setPixels` method (**II-§2.10.15**) after modifying the x, y, w, h, and `offset` arguments to reflect only the intersecting region.

PARAMETERS:

x: the left coordinate of the rectangle.
y: the top coordinate of the rectangle.
w: the width of the rectangle.
h: the height of the rectangle.
model: the color model for bits.
pixels: the array of bits.
off: the offset for the first element.
scansize: the number of elements per row.

OVERRIDES:

`setPixels` in class `ImageFilter` (**II-§2.5.11**).

setProperties   §2.2.5

```
public void setProperties(Hashtable props)
```

The image producer calls the `setProperties` method of the image consumer to let it know of additional properties of the image. For more information on this method and its arguments, see **II-§2.10.16** on page II-290.

The `setProperties` method of `CroppedImageFilter` adds the property `"croprect"` with the value

```
new Rectangle(x, y, width, height)
```

to the table of properties, and then calls the `setProperties` method of its image consumer (**II-§2.10.16**) with the modified properties table.

PARAMETERS:

props: a hashtable that maps image properties to their value.

OVERRIDES:

`setProperties` in class `ImageFilter` (**II-§2.5.12**).

2.3 Class DirectColorModel

```
public class java.awt.image.DirectColorModel
    extends java.awt.image.ColorModel (II-§2.1)
{
    // Constructors
    public DirectColorModel(int bits, int rmask,        §2.3.1
                            int gmask, int bmask);
    public DirectColorModel(int bits, int rmask, int gmask, §2.3.2
                            int bmask, int amask);
    // Methods
    public final int getAlpha(int pixel);               §2.3.3
    public final int getAlphaMask();                    §2.3.4
    public final int getBlue(int pixel);                §2.3.5
    public final int getBlueMask();                     §2.3.6
    public final int getGreen(int pixel);               §2.3.7
    public final int getGreenMask();                    §2.3.8
    public final int getRed(int pixel);                 §2.3.9
    public final int getRedMask();                      §2.3.10
    public final int getRGB(int pixel);                 §2.3.11
}
```

The direct color model is a color model (**II-§2.1**) which specifies a translation from pixel values to alpha, red, green, and blue components using the actual bits of the pixel value. This color model is similar to an X11 TrueColor visual.

Many of the methods in this class are final. The underlying native graphics code makes assumptions about the layout and operation of this class, and those assumptions are reflected in the implementations of those final methods. Applications can subclass this class for other reasons, but they cannot override or modify the behavior of the final methods.

Constructors

DirectColorModel   §2.3.1

```
public DirectColorModel(int bits, int rmask,
                        int gmask, int bmask)
```

Constructs a direct color model in which each of the given masks specify which bits in the pixels contain the red, green, and blue components.

Pixels described by this color model all have alpha components of 255, indicating that they are fully opaque.

Each of the bit masks must be contiguous and must be smaller than 2^{bits}.

PARAMETERS:

bits: the number of bits in a pixel.
rmask: the bits in the pixel representing the red component.
gmask: the bits in the pixel representing the green component.
bmask: the bits in the pixel representing the blue component.

DirectColorModel   §2.3.2

```
public
DirectColorModel(int bits, int rmask, int gmask,
                 int bmask, int amask)
```

Constructs a direct color model in which each of the given masks specify which bits in the pixels contain the alpha, red, green, and blue components.

Each of the bit masks must be contiguous, and must be smaller than 2^{bits}.

PARAMETERS:

bits: the number of bits in a pixel.
rmask: the bits in the pixel representing the red component.
gmask: the bits in the pixel representing the green component.
bmask: the bits in the pixel representing the blue component.
amask: the bits in the pixel representing the alpha component.

Methods

getAlpha   §2.3.3

```
public final int getAlpha(int pixel)
```

Determines the alpha transparency of a pixel in this color model. The value ranges from 0 to 255. The value 0 indicates that the pixel is completely transparent. The value 255 indicates that the pixel is opaque.

PARAMETERS:

pixel: a pixel value.

RETURNS:

the alpha transparency represented by the pixel value.

getAlphaMask   §2.3.4

```
public final int getAlphaMask()
```
RETURNS:

a mask indicating which bits in a pixel contain the alpha transparency component in this color model.

getBlue   §2.3.5

```
public final int getBlue(int pixel)
```
Determines the blue component of a pixel in this color model. The value ranges from 0 to 255. The value 0 indicates no contribution from this primary color. The value 255 indicates the maximum intensity of this color component.

PARAMETERS:

`pixel`: a pixel value.

RETURNS:

the blue color component represented by the pixel value.

OVERRIDES:

`getBlue` in class `ColorModel` (**II-§2.1.4**).

getBlueMask   §2.3.6

```
public final int getBlueMask()
```
RETURNS:

a mask indicating which bits in a pixel contain the blue color component in this color model.

getGreen   §2.3.7

```
public final int getGreen(int pixel)
```
Determines the green component of a pixel in this color model. The value ranges from 0 to 255. The value 0 indicates no contribution from this primary color. The value 255 indicates the maximum intensity of this color component.

PARAMETERS:

`pixel`: a pixel value.

RETURNS:

the blue color component represented by the pixel value.

OVERRIDES:

`getGreen` in class `ColorModel` (**II-§2.1.5**).

getGreenMask   §2.3.8

```
public final int getGreenMask()
```

RETURNS:

a mask indicating which bits in a pixel contain the green color component in this color model.

getRed   §2.3.9

```
public final int getRed(int pixel)
```

Determines the red component of a pixel in this color model. The value ranges from 0 to 255. The value 0 indicates no contribution from this primary color. The value 255 indicates the maximum intensity of this color component.

PARAMETERS:

pixel: a pixel value.

RETURNS:

the red color component represented by the pixel value.

OVERRIDES:

getRed in class ColorModel (**II-§2.1.7**).

getRedMask   §2.3.10

```
public final int getRedMask()
```

RETURNS:

a mask indicating which bits in a pixel contain the red color component in this color model.

getRGB   §2.3.11

```
public final int getRGB(int pixel)
```

Calculates a single integer representing the alpha, red, green, and blue components of the pixel in this color model. The components are each scaled to be a value between 0 and 255. The integer returned is the number such that bits 24–31 are the alpha value, bits 16–23 are the red value, bits 8–15 are the green value, and bits 0–7 are the blue value.

This format is the pixel format of the default RGB color model (**II-§2.1.9**).

PARAMETERS:

pixel: a pixel value.

RETURNS:

an integer representing this color in RGB format.

OVERRIDES:

getRGB in class ColorModel (**II-§2.1.8**).

2.4 Class FilteredImageSource

```
public class java.awt.image.FilteredImageSource
    extends java.lang.Object (I-§1.12)
    implements java.awt.image.ImageProducer (II-§2.12)
{
    // Constructors
    public FilteredImageSource(ImageProducer orig,            §2.4.1
                                ImageFilter imgf);

    // Methods
    public void addConsumer(ImageConsumer ic);               §2.4.2
    public boolean isConsumer(ImageConsumer ic);             §2.4.3
    public void removeConsumer(ImageConsumer ic);            §2.4.4
    public void                                              §2.4.5
        requestTopDownLeftRightResend(ImageConsumer ic);
    public void startProduction(ImageConsumer ic);          §2.4.6
}
```

A filtered image source is an implementation of the image producer interface (**II-§2.12**) which takes an existing image and an image filter (**II-§2.5**) and uses them to produce a new filtered version of the original image.

Here is an example which filters an image by swapping the red and blue components:

```
Image src = getImage("doc:///demo/images/duke/T1.gif");
// see comments in II-§2.9 for an implementation of
RedBlueSwapFilter

ImageFilter colorfilter = new RedBlueSwapFilter();
Image img = createImage(new FilteredImageSource(src.getSource
),                                               (colorfilter));
```

Constructors

FilteredImageSource   §2.4.1

    `public`

    `FilteredImageSource(ImageProducer orig, ImageFilter imgf)`

    Constructs a new image producer from an existing image producer and an image filter (**II-§2.5**).

    PARAMETERS:

    `orig`: an existing image producer.

    `imgf`: an image filter.

Methods

addConsumer   §2.4.2

    `public void addConsumer(ImageConsumer ic)`

    Registers the image consumer (**II-§2.10**) argument as wanting the image produced by this image producer. For more information on this method and its arguments, see **II-§2.12.1** on page II-294.

    The `addConsumer` method of `FilteredImageSource` calls its image filter's `getFilterInstance` method (**II-§2.5.4**) to create a new filter instance for the image consumer argument. The resulting filter instance is then passed as an argument to the image producer's `addConsumer` method (**II-§2.12.1**).

    PARAMETERS:

    `ic`: an image consumer.

isConsumer   §2.4.3

    `public boolean isConsumer(ImageConsumer ic)`

    PARAMETERS:

    `ic`: an image consumer.

    RETURNS:

    `true` if the specified image consumer argument (**II-§2.10**) is currently registered with this image producer as one of its consumers; `false` otherwise.

removeConsumer   §2.4.4

```
public void removeConsumer(ImageConsumer ic)
```

Removes the specified image consumer (**II-§2.10**) object from the list of consumers registered to receive the image data from this image producer. For more information on this method and its arguments, see **II-§2.12.3** on page II-295.

The `removeConsumer` method of `FilteredImageSource` calls its image producer's `removeConsumer` method (**II-§2.12.3**) with the image filter than was created when this image consumer was first registered (**II-§2.4.2**, **§2.4.6**).

PARAMETERS:

ic: an image consumer.

requestTopDownLeftRightResend   §2.4.5

```
public void
requestTopDownLeftRightResend(ImageConsumer ic)
```

An image consumer sends this message to request that the image producer attempt to resend the image data one more time in top-down, left-to-right order. For more information on this method and its arguments, see **II-§2.12.4** on page II-295.

The `requestTopDownLeftRightResend` method of `FilteredImage-Source` calls its image producer's `requestTopDownLeftRightResend` method (**II-§2.12.4**) with the image filter than was created when this image consumer was first registered (**II-§2.4.2**, **§2.4.6**).

PARAMETERS:

ic: an image consumer.

startProduction   §2.4.6

```
public void startProduction(ImageConsumer ic)
```

Registers the image consumer (**II-§2.10**) argument as wanting the image produced by this image producer. In addition, this method forces the image producer to start an immediate reconstruction of the image data. For more information on this method and its arguments, see **II-§2.12.5** on page II-295.

The `startProduction` method of `FilteredImageSource` calls its image filter's `getFilterInstance` method (**II-§2.5.4**) to create a new filter instance for the image consumer argument. The resulting filter instance is then passed as an argument to the image producer's `startProduction` method (**II-§2.12.5**).

PARAMETERS:

ic: an image consumer.

2.5 Class ImageFilter

```
public class java.awt.image.ImageFilter
    extends java.lang.Object (I-§1.12)
    implements java.awt.image.ImageConsumer (II-§2.10),
               java.lang.Cloneable (I-§1.22)
{
    // Fields
    protected ImageConsumer consumer;                       §2.5.1

    // Constructors
    public ImageFilter();                                   §2.5.2

    // Methods
    public Object clone();                                  §2.5.3
    public ImageFilter                                      §2.5.4
               getFilterInstance(ImageConsumer ic);
    public void imageComplete(int status);                 §2.5.5
    public void resendTopDownLeftRight(ImageProducer ip);  §2.5.6
    public void setColorModel(ColorModel model);           §2.5.7
    public void setDimensions(int width, int height);      §2.5.8
    public void setHints(int hints);                       §2.5.9
    public void setPixels(int x, int y, int w, int h,      §2.5.10
                    ColorModel model, byte pixels[],
                    int off, int scansize);
    public void setPixels(int x, int y, int w, int h,      §2.5.11
                    ColorModel model, int pixels[],
                    int off, int scansize);
    public void setProperties(Hashtable props);            §2.5.12
}
```

This class is the superclass of all classes that are meant to filter the data delivered from an ImageProducer (II-§2.12) to an ImageConsumer (II-§2.10).

This class and its subclasses are meant to be used in conjunction with a FilteredImageSource (II-§2.4) object to produce filtered versions of existing images.

The image filter implemented by this class is the "null filter," which has no effect on the data passing through. Filters should subclass this class and override the methods in order to modify the data as necessary.

Fields

---

consumer §2.5.1

```
protected ImageConsumer consumer
```

The image consumer **(II-§2.10)** of the particular image data stream for which this image filter is filtering data.

The field is not initialized by the constructor, but by the call to the get-FilterInstance method **(II-§2.5.4)**, when the FilteredImageSource **(II-§2.4)** is creating a unique instance of this object for a particular image data stream.

Constructors

ImageFilter §2.5.2

```
public ImageFilter()
```

The default constructor for this method.

Methods

---

clone §2.5.3

```
public Object clone()
```

RETURNS:

a clone of this object.

OVERRIDES:

clone in class Object **(I-§1.12.2)**.

getFilterInstance §2.5.4

```
public ImageFilter getFilterInstance(ImageConsumer ic)
```

Creates an image filter which filters the image for the specified image consumer.

The getFilterInstance method of ImageFilter clones the object and sets its consumer field to the image consumer argument. Subclasses can override this method if they require more setup than this.

PARAMETERS:

ic: the image consumer.

RETURNS:

a unique instance of an image filter object which actually performs the filtering for the specified image consumer **(II-§2.10)**.

imageComplete   §2.5.5

```
public void imageComplete(int status)
```

The image producer calls the imageComplete method when it has completed an image or it has encountered an error in producing or loading the image. For more information on this method and its status argument, see **II-§2.10.10** on page II-286.

The imageComplete method of ImageFilter calls the imageComplete method (**II-§2.10.10**) of the image consumer with the identical argument.

PARAMETERS:

status: the status of the image.

resendTopDownLeftRight   §2.5.6

```
public void resendTopDownLeftRight(ImageProducer ip)
```

An image consumer calls the resendTopDownLeftRight of its producer to request that the pixel data be resent in that order. For more information on this method, see **II-§2.12.4** on page II-295.

An image filter can respond to this request in one of three ways:

♦ The filter can forward this request to the image producer (**II-§2.12.4**) using itself as the requesting image consumer. This is the default behavior provided by the resendTopDownLeftRight method of ImageFilter.

♦ The filter can resend the pixels in the right order on its own (presumably because the generated pixels have been saved in some sort of buffer).

♦ The filter can ignore this request.

PARAMETERS:

ip: the image producer that is feeding this instance of the filter.

setColorModel   §2.5.7

```
public void setColorModel(ColorModel model)
```

The image producer calls the setColorModel method to specify the color model for the majority of the subsequent setPixels method calls. For more information on this method and its model argument, see **II-§2.10.11** on page II-287.

The setColorModel method of ImageFilter calls the setColorModel method (**II-§2.10.11**) of the image consumer with the identical argument.

PARAMETERS:

model: a color map used in subsequent setPixel calls.

setDimensions §2.5.8

```
public void setDimensions(int width, int height)
```

The image producer calls the `setDimensions` of the image consumer to tell it the width and height of the image.

The `setDimensions` method of `ImageFilter` calls the `setDimensions` method (**II-§2.10.12**) of its image consumer with the identical arguments.

PARAMETERS:

`width`: the width of the image.
`height`: the height of the image.

setHints §2.5.9

```
public void setHints(int hints)
```

The image producer calls the `setHints` method of the image consumer to indicate the order in which the bits are to be delivered. For more information on the hints passed to the image consumer, see **II-§2.10.13** on page II-288.

The `setHints` method of `ImageFilter` calls the `setHints` method (**II-§2.10.13**) of its image consumer with the identical argument.

PARAMETERS:

`hints`: hints about the order in which the bits are to be delivered.

setPixels §2.5.10

```
public void
setPixels(int x, int y, int w, int h, ColorModel model,
          byte pixels[], int off, int scansize)
```

The image producer calls the `setPixels` method of the image consumer one or more times to deliver the pixels of the image. For more information on this method and its arguments, see **II-§2.10.14** on page II-289.

The `setPixels` method of `ImageFilter` calls the `setPixels` method (**II-§2.10.14**) of its image consumer with the identical arguments.

PARAMETERS:

`x`: the left coordinate of the rectangle.
`y`: the top coordinate of the rectangle.
`w`: the width of the rectangle.
`h`: the height of the rectangle.
`model`: the color model for bits.
`pixels`: the array of bits.
`off`: the offset for the first element.
`scansize`: the number of elements per row.

setPixels   §2.5.11

```
public void
setPixels(int x, int y, int w, int h, ColorModel model,
          int pixels[], int off, int scansize)
```

The image producer calls the setPixels method of the image consumer one or more times to deliver the pixels of the image. For more information on this method and its arguments, see **II-§2.10.15** on page II-289.

The setPixels method of ImageFilter calls the setPixels method (**II-§2.10.15**) of its image consumer with the identical arguments.

PARAMETERS:

x: the left coordinate of the rectangle.
y: the top coordinate of the rectangle.
w: the width of the rectangle.
h: the height of the rectangle.
model: the color model for bits.
pixels: the array of bits.
off: the offset for the first element.
scansize: the number of elements per row.

setProperties   §2.5.12

```
public void setProperties(Hashtable props)
```

The image producer calls the setProperties method of the image consumer to let it know of additional properties of the image. For more information on this method and its arguments, see **II-§2.10.16** on page II-290.

The setProperties method of ImageFilter calls the setProperties method §2.10.16 of its image consumer with the properties argument after modifying it slightly:

♦ If the hashtable has no key "filters", a string representation of the current filter is added to the hashtable under the key "filter".

♦ If such a key is already in the hashtable, a string representation of the current filter is appended to the property (which must be a String) already stored under that key, and this value is stored back in the hashtable.

PARAMETERS:

props: a hashtable that maps image properties to their value.

2.6 Class IndexColorModel

```
public class java.awt.image.IndexColorModel
    extends java.awt.image.ColorModel (II-§2.1)
{
    // Constructors
    public IndexColorModel(int bits, int size,              §2.6.1
                           byte r[], byte g[], byte b[]);
    public IndexColorModel(int bits, int size,              §2.6.2
                           byte r[], byte g[],
                           byte b[], byte a[]);
    public IndexColorModel(int bits, int size,              §2.6.3
                           byte r[], byte g[],
                           byte b[], int trans);
    public IndexColorModel(int bits, int size,              §2.6.4
                           byte cmap[], int start,
                           boolean hasalpha);
    public IndexColorModel(int bits, int size,              §2.6.5
                           byte cmap[], int start,
                           boolean hasalpha, int trans);

    // Methods
    public final int getAlpha(int pixel);                   §2.6.6
    public final void getAlphas(byte a[]);                  §2.6.7
    public final int getBlue(int pixel);                    §2.6.8
    public final void getBlues(byte b[]);                   §2.6.9
    public final int getGreen(int pixel);                   §2.6.10
    public final void getGreens(byte g[]);                  §2.6.11
    public final int getMapSize();                          §2.6.12
    public final int getRed(int pixel);                     §2.6.13
    public final void getReds(byte r[]);                    §2.6.14
    public final int getRGB(int pixel);                     §2.6.15
    public final int getTransparentPixel();                 §2.6.16
}
```

The index color model class specifies a color model (**II-§2.1**) in which a pixel value is converted into alpha, red, green, and blue components by using the pixel value as an index into a color map. Each entry in the color map gives the alpha, red, green, and blue component for the corresponding pixel.

An optional *transparent* pixel can be specified. This pixel is completely transparent, independent of the alpha value recorded for that pixel value.

The maximum size of the color map is 256 entries.

This color model is similar to an X11 PseudoColor visual.

Many of the methods in this class are final. The underlying native graphics code makes assumptions about the layout and operation of this class, and those assumptions are reflected in the implementations of those final methods. Applications can subclass this class for other reasons, but they cannot override or modify the behavior of the final methods.

Constructors

IndexColorModel §2.6.1

```
public IndexColorModel(int bits, int size, byte r[],
                       byte g[], byte b[])
```

Constructs an index color model from the given arrays of red, green, and blue components.

Pixels described by this color model all have alpha components of 255 (fully opaque).

Each of the three arrays must have at least size elements, and it must be the case that $size < 2^{bits}$. These first size elements of the arrays are the red, green, and blue values for pixels in the range $0 \le i < size$. Pixels in the range $size \le i < 2^{bits}$ have red, green, and blue values of 0.

PARAMETERS:

bits: the number of bits in a pixel.
size: the size of the color component arrays.
r: an array of red color components.
g: an array of green color components.
b: an array of blue color components.

IndexColorModel §2.6.2

```
public IndexColorModel(int bits, int size, byte r[],
                       byte g[], byte b[], byte a[])
```

Constructs an index color model from the given arrays of red, green, blue, and alpha components.

Each of the four arrays must have at least size elements, and it must be the case that $size < 2^{bits}$. These first size elements of the arrays are the red, green, and blue values for pixels in the range $0 \le i < size$. Pixels in the range $size \le i < 2^{bits}$ have red, green, blue, and alpha values of 0.

PARAMETERS:

bits: the number of bits in a pixel.
size: a lower bound on the size of each of the arrays.
r: an array of red color components.
g: an array of green color components.
b: an array of blue color components.
a: an array of alpha value components.

IndexColorModel §2.6.3

```
public
IndexColorModel(int bits, int size, byte r[],
                byte g[], byte b[], int trans)
```

Constructs an index color model from the given arrays of red, green, and blue components.

Pixels described by this color model all have alpha components of 255 (fully opaque), except for the transparent pixel.

Each of the three arrays must have at least `size` elements, and it must be the case that $size < 2^{bits}$. These first size elements of the arrays are the red, green, and blue values for pixels in the range $0 \le i < size$. Pixels in the range $size \le i < 2^{bits}$ have red, green, and blue values of 0.

PARAMETERS:

`bits`: the number of bits in a pixel.
`size`: the size of the color component arrays.
`r`: an array of red color components.
`g`: an array of green color components.
`b`: an array of blue color components.
`trans`: the index of the transparent pixel.

IndexColorModel §2.6.4

```
public
IndexColorModel(int bits, int size, byte cmap[],
                int start, boolean hasalpha)
```

Constructs an index color model from a single array of packed red, green, blue, and optional alpha components.

If the `hasalpha` argument is `false`, then the `cmap` array must have length of at least $start + 3 \times size$. The red, green, and blue components for a pixel i in the range $0 \le i < size$ are in the three elements of the `cmap` array starting at cmap[$start + 3i$]. Its alpha component is 255 (fully opaque).

If the `hasalpha` argument is `true`, then the `cmap` array must have length of at least $start + 4 \times size$. The red, green, blue, and alpha components for a pixel i in the range $0 \le i < size$ are in the four elements of the `cmap` array starting at cmap[$start + 4i$].

Pixels in the range $size \le i < 2^{bits}$ have red, green, and blue values of 0. Their alpha component is 0 if `hasalpha` is `true`, and 255 otherwise.

PARAMETERS:

`bits`: the number of bits in a pixel.
`size`: the size of the color component arrays.
`cmap`: an array of color components.
`start`: the starting offset of the first color component.
`hasalpha`: if true, the alpha values are contained in the `cmap` array.

IndexColorModel   §2.6.5

```
public IndexColorModel(int bits, int size,
                       byte cmap[], int start,
                       boolean hasalpha, int trans)
```

Constructs an index color model from a single array of packed red, green, blue, and optional alpha values.

The color model is constructed the same way as described in **II-§2.6.4**. In addition, the specified transparent index represents a pixel which is considered entirely transparent regardless of any alpha value specified for it. The array must have enough values in it to fill all of the needed component arrays of the specified size.

PARAMETERS:

bits: the number of bits in a pixel.
size: the size of the color component arrays.
cmap: an array of color components.
start: the starting offset of the first color component.
hasalpha: if true, the alpha values are in the cmap array.
trans: the index of the fully transparent pixel.

Methods

getAlpha   §2.6.6

```
public final int getAlpha(int pixel)
```

Determines the alpha transparency value of the pixel in this color model. The value ranges from 0 to 255. The value 0 indicates that the pixel is completely transparent. The value 255 indicates that the pixel is opaque.

PARAMETERS:

pixel: a pixel value.

RETURNS:

the alpha transparency represented by the pixel value.

OVERRIDES:

getAlpha in class ColorModel (**II-§2.1.3**).

getAlphas   §2.6.7

```
public final void getAlphas(byte a[])
```

Copies the array of alpha transparency values from this color model into the given array.

Only the initial entries of the array as specified by the getMapSize method (**II-§2.6.12**) are written.

PARAMETERS:

a: an array into which to place the results.

getBlue §2.6.8

```
public final int getBlue(int pixel)
```

Determines the blue component of the pixel in this color model. The value ranges from 0 to 255. The value 0 indicates no contribution from this primary color. The value 255 indicates the maximum intensity of this color component.

PARAMETERS:

`pixel`: a pixel value.

RETURNS:

the blue color component represented by the pixel value.

OVERRIDES:

getBlue in class ColorModel (**II-§2.1.4**).

getBlues §2.6.9

```
public final void getBlues(byte b[])
```

Copies the array of blue color components from this color model into the given array.

Only the initial entries of the array as specified by the getMapSize method (**II-§2.6.12**) are written.

PARAMETERS:

b: an array into which to place the results.

getGreen §2.6.10

```
public final int getGreen(int pixel)
```

Determines the green component of the pixel in this color model. The value ranges from 0 to 255. The value 0 indicates no contribution from this primary color. The value 255 indicates the maximum intensity of this color component.

PARAMETERS:

`pixel`: a pixel value.

RETURNS:

the blue color component represented by the pixel value.

OVERRIDES:

getGreen in class ColorModel (**II-§2.1.5**).

getGreens   §2.6.11

```
public final void getGreens(byte g[])
```

Copies the array of green color components from this color model into the given array.

Only the initial entries of the array as specified by the `getMapSize` method **(II-§2.6.12)** are written.

PARAMETERS:

g: an array into which to place the results.

getMapSize   §2.6.12

```
public final int getMapSize()
```

RETURNS:

the value of the `size` argument when creating this index color model.

getRed   §2.6.13

```
public final int getRed(int pixel)
```

Determines the red component of the pixel in this color model. The value ranges from 0 to 255. The value 0 indicates no contribution from this primary color. The value 255 indicates the maximum intensity of this color component.

PARAMETERS:

pixel: a pixel value.

RETURNS:

the red color component represented by the pixel value.

OVERRIDES:

getRed in class `ColorModel` **(II-§2.1.7)**.

getReds   §2.6.14

```
public final void getReds(byte r[])
```

Copies the array of red color components from this color model into the given array.

Only the initial entries of the array as specified by the `getMapSize` method **(II-§2.6.12)** are written.

PARAMETERS:

a: an array into which to place the results.

getRGB §2.6.15

```
public final int getRGB(int pixel)
```

Calculates a single integer representing the alpha, red, green, and blue components of the pixel in this color model. The components are each scaled to be a value between 0 and 255 . The integer returned is the number such that bits 24–31 are the alpha value, bits 16–23 are the red value, bits 8–15 are the green value, and bits 0–7 are the blue value.

This format is the format used by the default RGB color model (**II-§2.1.9**).

PARAMETERS:

`pixel`: a pixel value.

RETURNS:

an integer representing this color in RGB format.

OVERRIDES:

getRGB in class `ColorModel` (**II-§2.1.8**).

getTransparentPixel §2.6.16

```
public final int getTransparentPixel()
```

RETURNS:

the index of the transparent pixel in this color model, or –1 if there is no transparent pixel.

2.7 Class MemoryImageSource

```
public class java.awt.image.MemoryImageSource
    extends java.lang.Object (I-§1.12)
    implements java.awt.image.ImageProducer (II-§2.12)
{
    // Constructors
    public MemoryImageSource(int w, int h, ColorModel cm,    §2.7.1
                             byte pix[], int off,
                             int scan);
public MemoryImageSource(int w, int h, ColorModel cm,        §2.7.2
                             byte pix[], int off, int scan,
                             Hashtable props);
    public MemoryImageSource(int w, int h, ColorModel cm,    §2.7.3
                             int pix[], int off, int scan);
    public MemoryImageSource(int w, int h, ColorModel cm,    §2.7.4
                             int pix[], int off, int scan,
                             Hashtable props);
    public MemoryImageSource(int w, int h, int pix[],        §2.7.5
                             int off, int scan);
    public MemoryImageSource(int w, int h, int pix[],        §2.7.6
                             int off, int scan,
                             Hashtable props);

    // Methods
    public void addConsumer(ImageConsumer ic);              §2.7.7
    public boolean isConsumer(ImageConsumer ic);            §2.7.8
    public void removeConsumer(ImageConsumer ic);           §2.7.9
    public void                                             §2.7.10
        requestTopDownLeftRightResend(ImageConsumer ic);
    public void startProduction(ImageConsumer ic);          §2.7.11
}
```

A memory image source is an implementation of the image producer interface (II-§2.12). It uses an array to produce pixel values for the image.

Here is an example which calculates a 100×100 image representing a fade from black to blue along the *x* axis and from black to red along the *y* axis:

```
int w = 100;
int h = 100;
int pix[] = new int[w * h];
int index = 0;
for (int y = 0; y < h; y++) {
    int red = (y * 255) / (h - 1);
    for (int x = 0; x < w; x++) {
        int blue = (x * 255) / (w - 1);
        pix[index++] = (255 << 24) | (red << 16) | blue;
```

```
        }
    }
    Image img = createImage(new MemoryImageSource(w, h, pix, 0, w));
```

An application can use the method `createImage` in class `Component` (**II-§1.10.6**) to create an `Image` from a `MemoryImageSource`.

Constructors

MemoryImageSource   §2.7.1

```
    public
    MemoryImageSource(int w, int h, ColorModel cm,
                      byte pix[], int off, int scan)
```

Constructs an image producer (**II-§2.12**) object which uses an array of bytes to produce data for the image object. The pixel at coordinate $\langle i, j \rangle$ is stored in the pixel array at index $j \times \mathsf{scan} + i + \mathsf{offset}$.

PARAMETERS:
w: the width of the image.
h: the height of the image.
cm: the color model used for the pixels.
pix: the array of pixel values.
off: the offset of the first pixel in the array.
scan: the number of pixels in the array per line.

MemoryImageSource   §2.7.2

```
    public MemoryImageSource(int w, int h, ColorModel cm,
                             byte pix[], int off, int scan,
                             Hashtable props)
```

Constructs an image producer (**II-§2.12**) object which uses an array of bytes to produce data for the image object. The pixel at coordinate $\langle i, j \rangle$ is stored in the pixel array at index $j \times \mathsf{scan} + i + \mathsf{offset}$.

In addition, the image has the properties indicated in the hashtable argument.

PARAMETERS:
w: the width of the image.
h: the height of the image.
cm: the color model used for the pixels.
pix: the array of pixel values.
off: the offset of the first pixel in the array.
scan: the number of pixels in the array per line.
props: a hashtable of properties.

MemoryImageSource   §2.7.3

```
public MemoryImageSource(int w, int h, ColorModel cm,
                         int pix[], int off, int scan)
```

Constructs an image producer (II-§2.12) object which uses an array of integers to produce data for the image object. The pixel at coordinate $\langle i, j \rangle$ is stored in the pixel array at index $j \times \text{scan} + i + \text{offset}$.

PARAMETERS:

w: the width of the image.
h: the height of the image.
cm: the color model used for the pixels.
pix: the array of pixel values.
off: the offset of the first pixel in the array.
scan: the number of pixels in the array per line.

MemoryImageSource   §2.7.4

```
public MemoryImageSource(int w, int h, ColorModel cm,
                         int pix[], int off, int scan,
                         Hashtable props)
```

Constructs an image producer (II-§2.12) object which uses an array of integers to produce data for the image object. The pixel at coordinate $\langle i, j \rangle$ is stored in the pixel array at index $j \times \text{scan} + i + \text{offset}$.

In addition, the image has the properties indicated in the hashtable argument.

PARAMETERS:

w: the width of the image.
h: the height of the image.
cm: the color model used for the pixels.
pix: the array of pixel values.
off: the offset of the first pixel in the array.
scan: the number of pixels in the array per line.
props: a hashtable of properties.

MemoryImageSource §2.7.5

```
public MemoryImageSource(int w, int h, int pix[],
                         int off, int scan)
```

Constructs an image producer (**II-§2.12**) object which uses an array of integers to produce data for the image object. The pixel at coordinate $\langle i, j \rangle$ is stored in the pixel array at index $j \times$ scan $+ i +$ offset .

The resulting image uses the default RGB color model (**II-§2.1.9**).

PARAMETERS:

w: the width of the image.
h: the height of the image.
pix: the array of pixel values.
off: the offset of the first pixel in the array.
scan: the number of pixels in the array per line.

MemoryImageSource §2.7.6

```
public MemoryImageSource(int w, int h, int pix[], int off,
                         int scan, Hashtable props)
```

Constructs an image producer (**II-§2.12**) object which uses an array of integers to produce data for the image object. The pixel at coordinate $\langle i, j \rangle$ is stored in the pixel array at index $j \times$ scan $+ i +$ offset . The resulting image uses the default RGB color model (**II-§2.1.9**).

In addition, the image has the properties indicated in the hashtable argument.

PARAMETERS:

w: the width of the image.
h: the height of the image.
cm: the color model used for the pixels.
pix: the array of pixel values.
off: the offset of the first pixel in the array.
scan: the number of pixels in the array per line.
props: a hashtable of properties.

Methods

addConsumer   §2.7.7

```
public void addConsumer(ImageConsumer ic)
```

Registers the image consumer (**II-§2.10**) argument as wanting the image produced by this image producer. For more information on this method and its arguments, see **II-§2.12.1** on page II-294.

The addConsumer method of MemoryImageSource, since it already has the image data, immediately delivers the data to the image consumer.

PARAMETERS:

ic: an image consumer.

isConsumer   §2.7.8

```
public boolean isConsumer(ImageConsumer ic)
```

Determines if the image consumer argument is registered with this image producer as a consumer. Because the memory image source delivers data immediately to its image consumer, the memory image source can have at most one consumer at a time.

PARAMETERS:

ic: an image consumer.

RETURNS:

true if the specified image consumer argument (**II-§2.10**) is currently registered with this image producer as one of its consumers; false otherwise.

removeConsumer   §2.7.9

```
public void removeConsumer(ImageConsumer ic)
```

Removes the specified image consumer (**II-§2.10**) object from the list of consumers registered to receive the image data. For more information on this method and its arguments, see **II-§2.12.3** on page II-295.

PARAMETERS:

ic: an image consumer.

requestTopDownLeftRightResend   §2.7.10

    public void requestTopDownLeftRightResend(ImageConsumer ic)

An image consumer sends this message to request that the image producer attempt to resend the image data one more time in top-down, left-to-right order. For more information on this method and its arguments, see **II-§2.12.4** on page II-295.

The requestTopDownLeftRightResend method of memoryImageSource ignores this request, since it always sends its data in that order.

PARAMETERS:

ic: an image consumer.

startProduction   §2.7.11

    public void startProduction(ImageConsumer ic)

Registers the image consumer (**II-§2.10**) argument as wanting the image produced by this image producer. In addition, this method forces the image producer to start an immediate reconstruction of the image data. For more information on this method and its arguments, see **II-§2.12.5** on page II-295.

The addConsumer method of MemoryImageSource, since it already has the image data, immediately delivers the data to the image consumer.

PARAMETERS:

ic: an image consumer.

2.8 Class PixelGrabber

```
public class java.awt.image.PixelGrabber
    extends java.lang.Object (I-§1.12)
    implements java.awt.image.ImageConsumer (II-§2.10)
{
    // Constructors
    public PixelGrabber(Image img, int x, int y,            §2.8.1
                        int w, int h, int pix[],
                        int off, int scansize);
    public PixelGrabber(ImageProducer ip, int x,            §2.8.2
                        int y, int w, int h,
                        int pix[], int off,
                        int scansize);

    // Methods
    public boolean grabPixels();                            §2.8.3
    public boolean grabPixels(long ms);                     §2.8.4
    public void imageComplete(int status);                  §2.8.5
    public void setColorModel(ColorModel model);            §2.8.6
    public void setDimensions(int width, int height)        §2.8.7
    public void setHints(int hints);                        §2.8.8
    public void setPixels(int srcX, int srcY, int srcW,     §2.8.9
                          int srcH, ColorModel model,
                          byte pixels[], int srcOff,
                          int srcScan);
    public void setPixels(int srcX, int srcY, int srcW,     §2.8.10
                          int srcH, ColorModel model,
                          int pixels[], int srcOff,
                          int srcScan);
    public void setProperties(Hashtable props);             §2.8.11
    public int status();                                    §2.8.12
}
```

The pixel grabber implements an image consumer which can be attached to an image or image producer object to retrieve a subset of the pixels in that image. Pixels are stored in the array in the default RGB color model (**II-§2.1.9**).

For example:

```
    public void handleSinglePixel(int x, int y, int pixel) {
        int alpha = (pixel >> 24) & 0xff;
        int red   = (pixel >> 16) & 0xff;
        int green = (pixel >>  8) & 0xff;
        int blue  = (pixel      ) & 0xff;
        // Deal with the pixel as necessary...
    }

    public void GetPixels(Image img, int x, int y, int w, int h) {
```

```
    int[] pixels = new int[w * h];
    PixelGrabber pg =
        new PixelGrabber(img, x, y, w, h, pixels, 0, w);
    try {
        pg.grabPixels();
    } catch (InterruptedException e) {
        System.err.println("interrupted waiting for pixels!");
        return;
    }
    if ((pg.status() & ImageObserver.ABORT) != 0) {
        System.err.println("image fetch aborted or errored");
        return;
    }
    for (int j = 0; j < h; j++) {
        for (int i = 0; i < w; i++) {
            // look at the pixel
            handleSinglePixel(x+i, y+j, pixels[j * w + i]);
        }
    }

}
```

Most applications need to call only the grabPixel methods (**II-§2.8.3, §2.8.4**) and the status method (**II-§2.8.12**) of this class. The remaining methods are part of the ImageConsumer interface and allow the pixel grabber to receive the image from the image producer.

Constructors

PixelGrabber   §2.8.1

```
public PixelGrabber(Image img, int x, int y, int w, int h,
                    int pix[], int off, int scansize)
```

Creates a new pixel grabber object to grab the rectangular section of pixels from the specified image into the specified array.

The pixels are stored in the array in the default RGB color model (**II-§2.1.9**). The pixel data for the coordinate $\langle i, j \rangle$, where $\langle i, j \rangle$ is inside the indicated rectangle, is stored in the array at index

$$(j - \mathsf{y}) \times \mathsf{scan} + (i - \mathsf{x}) + \mathsf{offset}$$

of the pixel array.

The x and y arguments indicate the upper left corner of the rectangle of pixels to retrieve from the image, relative to the default (unscaled) size of the image.

PARAMETERS:

img: the image from which to retrieve pixels.

x: the x coordinate of the upper left corner.

y: the y coordinate of the upper left corner.

w: the width of the rectangle to retrieve.

h: the height of the rectangle to retrieve.

pix: the array of integers into which to place the RGB pixels retrieved from the image.

off: the offset into the array to store the first pixel.

scansize: the distance from the start of one row of pixels to the start of the next row in the array.

PixelGrabber   §2.8.2

```
public PixelGrabber(ImageProducer ip, int x, int y,
                    int w, int h, int pix[],
                    int off, int scansize)
```

Creates a new pixel grabber object to grab the rectangular section of pixels from the specified image producer into the specified array.

The pixels are stored in the array in the default RGB color model (**II-§2.1.9**). The pixel data for the coordinate $\langle i, j \rangle$, where $\langle i, j \rangle$ is inside the indicated rectangle, is stored in the array at the index

$$(j - y) \times \texttt{scan} + (i - x) + \texttt{offset}$$

of the pixel array.

The x and y arguments indicate the upper left corner of the rectangle of pixels to retrieve from the image, relative to the default (unscaled) size of the image.

PARAMETERS:

ip: the image producer.
x: the x coordinate of the upper left corner.
y: the y coordinate of the upper left corner.
w: the width of the rectangle to retrieve.
h: the height of the rectangle to retrieve.
pix: the array of integers into which to place the RGB pixels retrieved from the image.
off: the offset into the array to store the first pixel.
scansize: the distance from the start of one row of pixels to the start of the next row in the array.

Methods

grabPixels   §2.8.3

```
public boolean grabPixels()
throws InterruptedException
```

Requests the image or image producer to start delivering pixels to this image consumer. It waits for all of the pixels in the rectangle of interest to be delivered.

RETURNS:

true if the pixels were successfully grabbed; false on abort or error.

THROWS:

InterruptedException (**I-§1.37**)
if another thread has interrupted this thread.

grabPixels   §2.8.4

```
public boolean grabPixels(long ms)
throws InterruptedException
```

Requests the image or image producer to start delivering pixels to this image consumer. It waits for all of the pixels in the rectangle of interest to be delivered, or until the specified timeout has elapsed.

PARAMETERS:

ms: the number of milliseconds to wait for the pixels.

RETURNS:

true if the pixels were successfully grabbed; false on abort, error, or time-out.

THROWS:

InterruptedException **(I-§1.37)**
if another thread has interrupted this thread.

imageComplete   §2.8.5

```
public void imageComplete(int status)
```

The image producer calls the imageComplete method when it has completed an image or it has errored in producing or loading the image. For more information on this method and its status argument, see **II-§2.10.10** on page II-286.

The imageComplete method of PixelGrabber notifies all processes waiting for the pixels to wake up. It uses the value of the status flag to determine whether the image was successfully retrieved or not.

PARAMETERS:

status: the status of the image.

setColorModel   §2.8.6

```
public void setColorModel(ColorModel model)
```

The image producer calls the setColorModel method to specify the color model for the majority of the subsequent setPixels method calls. For more information on this method and its model argument, see **II-§2.10.11** on page II-287.

The setColorModel method of PixelGrabber ignores this call.

PARAMETERS:

model: a color map used in subsequent setPixel calls.

setDimensions   §2.8.7

```
public void setDimensions(int width, int height)
```

The image producer calls the setDimensions of the image consumer to tell it the width and height of the image.

The setDimensions method of PixelGrabber ignores the dimensions.

PARAMETERS:

width: the width of the image.
height: the height of the image.

setHints   §2.8.8

```
public void setHints(int hints)
```

The image producer calls the setHints method of the image consumer to indicate the order in which the bits will be delivered. For more information on the hints passed to the image consumer, see **II-§2.10.13** on page II-288.

The setHints method of PixelGrabber ignores the hints.

PARAMETERS:

hints: hints about the order in which the bits will be delivered.

setPixels   §2.8.9

```
public void
setPixels(int srcX, int srcY, int srcW, int srcH,
          ColorModel model, byte pixels[],
          int srcOff, int srcScan)
```

The image producer calls the setPixels method of the image consumer one or more times to deliver the pixels of the image. For more information on this method and its arguments, see **II-§2.10.14** on page II-289.

The setPixels method of PixelGrabber places the bits, if appropriate, into the array of bits passed to it by a call to the grabPixels method **(II-§2.8.3)**.

PARAMETERS:

x: the left coordinate of the rectangle.
y: the top coordinate of the rectangle.
w: the width of the rectangle.
h: the height of the rectangle.
model: the color model for bits.
pixels: the array of bits.
off: the offset for the first element.
scansize: the number of elements per row.

setPixels §2.8.10

```
public void
setPixels(int srcX, int srcY, int srcW, int srcH,
        ColorModel model, int pixels[],
        int srcOff, int srcScan)
```

The image producer calls the `setPixels` method of the image consumer one or more times to deliver the pixels of the image. For more information on this method and its arguments, see **II-§2.10.15** on page II-289.

The `setPixels` method of `PixelGrabber` places the bits, if appropriate, into the array of bits passed to it by a call to the `grabPixels` method **(II-§2.8.3)**.

PARAMETERS:

`x`: the left coordinate of the rectangle.
`y`: the top coordinate of the rectangle.
`w`: the width of the rectangle.
`h`: the height of the rectangle.
`model`: the color model for bits.
`pixels`: the array of bits.
`off`: the offset for the first element.
`scansize`: the number of elements per row.

setProperties §2.8.11

```
public void setProperties(Hashtable props)
```

The image producer calls the `setProperties` method of the image consumer to let it know of additional properties of the image. For more information on this method and its arguments, see **II-§2.10.16** on page II-290.

The `setProperties` method of `PixelGrabber` does nothing.

PARAMETERS:

`props`: a hashtable that maps image properties to their value.

status §2.8.12

```
public int status()
```

Returns the bitwise inclusive **OR** of the appropriate `ImageObserver` interface **(II-§2.11)** flags.

RETURNS:

the status of the pixels.

2.9 Class **RGBImageFilter**

```
public abstract class java.awt.image.RGBImageFilter
    extends java.awt.image.ImageFilter (II-§2.5)
{
    // Fields
    protected boolean canFilterIndexColorModel;           §2.9.1
    protected ColorModel newmodel;                        §2.9.2
    protected ColorModel origmodel;                       §2.9.3

    // Constructors
    public RGBImageFilter();                              §2.9.4

    // Methods
    public IndexColorModel                               §2.9.5
        filterIndexColorModel(IndexColorModel icm);
    public abstract int filterRGB(int x, int y, int rgb); §2.9.6
    public void filterRGBPixels(int x, int y, int w,      §2.9.7
                                int h, int pixels[],
                                int off, int scansize);
    public void setColorModel(ColorModel model);          §2.9.8
    public void setPixels(int x, int y, int w, int h,     §2.9.9
                    ColorModel model, byte pixels[],
                    int off, int scansize);
    public void setPixels(int x, int y, int w, int h,     §2.9.10
                    ColorModel model, int pixels[],
                    int off, int scansize);
    public void substituteColorModel(ColorModel oldcm,    §2.9.11
                                ColorModel newcm);
}
```

This class provides an easy way to create an image filter (**II-§2.5**) which modifies the pixels of the original image by converting them one at a time into the default RGB color model (**II-§2.1.9**).

Objects of this class are meant to be used in conjunction with a filtered image source (**II-§2.4**) object to produce filtered versions of existing images.

This class is an abstract class. It provides the calls needed to channel all the pixel data through a single method which converts pixels, one at a'time, into the default RGB color model, regardless of the color model being used by the image producer. The only method which needs to be defined to create a usable image filter is the `filterRGB` method.

Here is an example of a filter which swaps the red and blue components of an image:

```
class RedBlueSwapFilter extends RGBImageFilter {
    public RedBlueSwapFilter() {
        // The filter's operation does not depend on the
        // pixel's location, so IndexColorModels can be
        // filtered directly.
        canFilterIndexColorModel = true;
    }
    public int filterRGB(int x, int y, int rgb) {
        return ((rgb & 0xff00ff00)
            | ((rgb & 0xff0000) >> 16)
            | ((rgb & 0xff) << 16));
    }
}
```

Fields

canFilterIndexColorModel §2.9.1

protected boolean canFilterIndexColorModel

Setting this value to true indicates that the the value returned by the filterRGB method (**II-§2.9.6**) is independent of the x and y arguments and depends only on the rgb argument.

Subclasses of RGBImageFilter should set this field to true in their constructor if their filterRGB method does not depend on the coordinate of the pixel being filtered. Filtering the color-map entries of an indexed color map can be much faster than filtering every pixel.

The default value is false.

SEE ALSO:

substituteColorModel (**II-§2.9.11**).
IndexColorModel (**II-§2.6**).

newmodel §2.9.2

protected ColorModel newmodel

This field is used to remember the newcm argument passed to the substituteColorModel (**II-§2.9.11**) method.

origmodel §2.9.3

protected ColorModel origmodel

This field is used to remember the oldcm argument passed to the substituteColorModel (**II-§2.9.11**) method.

Constructors

RGBImageFilter §2.9.4

```
public RGBImageFilter()
```
The default constructor.

Methods

filterIndexColorModel §2.9.5

```
public IndexColorModel
filterIndexColorModel(IndexColorModel icm)
```

Filters an index color model (**II-§2.6**) object by running each entry in its color table through the filterRGB method (**II-§2.9.6**). The call to filterRGB has the x and y arguments set to –1 as a flag to indicate that a color table entry is being filtered rather than an actual pixel value.

PARAMETERS:

icm: the index color model object to be filtered.

RETURNS:

a new index color model with the filtered colors.

filterRGB §2.9.6

```
public abstract int filterRGB(int x, int y, int rgb)
```

Specifies a method to convert a single input pixel, whose value is specified in the default RGB color model (**II-§2.1.9**), to a new pixel value also in the default RGB color model. Subclasses of RGBImageFilter must provide an implementation of this method.

If the value of the field canFilterIndexColorModel (**II-§2.9.1**) is true, then the value returned by this method must not depend on the *x* and *y* coordinates.

If the x and y arguments are both –1, this method is being called by the filterIndexColorModel method (**II-§2.9.5**).

PARAMETERS:

x: the *x* coordinate of the pixel.
y: the *y* coordinate of the pixel.
rgb: the value of the pixel, in the default RGB color model.

RETURNS:

the new value of the pixel, in the default RGB color model.

SEE ALSO:

filterRGBPixels (**II-§2.9.7**).

filterRGBPixels   §2.9.7

```
public void
filterRGBPixels(int x, int y, int w, int h,
                int pixels[], int off, int scansize)
```

Filters a buffer of pixels in the default RGB color model (**II-§2.1.9**) by passing them one by one through the `filterRGB` method (**II-§2.9.6**).

The `setPixels` method (**II-§2.10.15**) of the filter's consumer (**II-§2.5.1**) is then called with the resulting buffer, and the color model argument is set to the default RGB color model.

Only pixels that fall within the specified rectangle are modified. The value of the pixel at coordinate $\langle i, j \rangle$ is stored in the pixel array at index $j \times \mathsf{scan} + i + \mathsf{offset}$.

PARAMETERS:

x: the left coordinate of the rectangle.
y: the top coordinate of the rectangle.
w: the width of the rectangle.
h: the height of the rectangle.
model: the color model for bits.
pixels: the array of bits.
off: the offset for the first element.
scansize: the number of elements per row.

setColorModel §2.9.8

    public void setColorModel(ColorModel model)

The image producer calls the `setColorModel` method to specify the color model for the majority of the subsequent `setPixels` method calls. For more information on this method and its `model` argument, see **II-§2.10.11** on page II-287.

The `setColorModel` method of `RGBImageFilter` determines if the color model argument is an index color model **(II-§2.6)** and if the `canFilter-IndexColorModel` field **(II-§2.9.1)** is `true`.

If both conditions are `true`, the method creates a new color model by calling the `filterIndexColorModel` method **(II-§2.9.5)** on the model argument. The original color model and the newly created color model are then passed as arguments to the `substituteColorModel` method **(II-§2.9.11)**. In addition, the `setColorModel` method **(II-§2.9.8)** of the filter's consumer **(II-§2.5.1)** is called with the newly created color model.

If either condition is `false`, the method calls the `setColorModel` method **(II-§2.10.11)** of its consumer **(II-§2.5.1)** with the default RGB color map **(II-§2.1.9)**.

PARAMETERS:

`model`: a color map used in subsequent `setPixel` calls.

OVERRIDES:

`setColorModel` in class `ImageFilter` **(II-§2.5.7)**.

setPixels   **§2.9.9**

```
public void
setPixels(int x, int y, int w, int h, ColorModel model,
          byte pixels[], int off, int scansize)
```

The image producer calls the setPixels method of the image consumer one or more times to deliver the pixels of the image. For more information on this method and its arguments, see **II-§2.10.14** on page II-289.

The setPixels method of RGBImageFilter looks to see if the color model is the same one that has already been converted and remembered for substitution by a previous call to the substituteColorModel (**II-§2.9.11**) method.

If so, it calls the setPixels method (**II-§2.10.14**) of its consumer (**II-§2.5.1**), changing the color model argument to be the alternative color model.

Otherwise, the method converts the buffer of byte pixels to the default RGB color model (**II-§2.1.9**) and passes the converted buffer to the filter-RGBPixels (**II-§2.9.7**) method to be converted one by one.

PARAMETERS:

x: the left coordinate of the rectangle.
y: the top coordinate of the rectangle.
w: the width of the rectangle.
h: the height of the rectangle.
model: the color model for bits.
pixels: the array of bits.
off: the offset for the first element.
scansize: the number of elements per row.

OVERRIDES:

setPixels in class ImageFilter (**II-§2.5.10**).

setPixels   §2.9.10

```
public void
setPixels(int x, int y, int w, int h, ColorModel model,
          int pixels[], int off, int scansize)
```

The image producer calls the setPixels method of the image consumer one or more times to deliver the pixels of the image. For more information on this method and its arguments, see **II-§2.10.15** on page II-289.

The setPixels method of RGBImageFilter looks to see if the color model is the same one that has already been converted and remembered for substitution by a previous call to the substituteColorModel (**II-§2.9.11**) method.

If so, it calls the setPixels method (**II-§2.10.14**) of the filter's consumer (**II-§2.5.1**), changing the color model argument to be the alternative color model.

Otherwise, the method converts the buffer of byte pixels to the default RGB color model (**II-§2.1.9**) and passes the converted buffer to the filter-RGBPixels (**II-§2.9.7**) method to be converted one by one.

PARAMETERS:

x: the left coordinate of the rectangle.
y: the top coordinate of the rectangle.
w: the width of the rectangle.
h: the height of the rectangle.
model: the color model for bits.
pixels: the array of bits.
off: the offset for the first element.
scansize: the number of elements per row.

OVERRIDES:

setPixels in class ImageFilter (**II-§2.5.11**).

substituteColorModel   §2.9.11

```
public void substituteColorModel(ColorModel oldcm,
                                 ColorModel newcm)
```

Registers two color model objects for substitution: if the oldcm is the color model during any subsequent call to either of the setPixels methods (**II-§2.9.9, §2.9.10**), the newcm argument is substituted and the pixels are passed through unmodified.

PARAMETERS:

oldcm: the ColorModel object to be replaced on the fly.
newcm: the ColorModel object to replace oldcm on the fly.

2.10 Interface ImageConsumer

```
public interface java.awt.image.ImageConsumer
{
    // status value for the imageComplete method
    public final static int IMAGEABORTED;                §2.10.1
    public final static int IMAGEERROR;                  §2.10.2
    public final static int SINGLEFRAMEDONE;             §2.10.3
    public final static int STATICIMAGEDONE;             §2.10.4

    // hints used by the setHints method
    public final static int COMPLETESCANLINES;           §2.10.5
    public final static int RANDOMPIXELORDER;            §2.10.6
    public final static int SINGLEFRAME;                 §2.10.7
    public final static int SINGLEPASS;                  §2.10.8
    public final static int TOPDOWNLEFTRIGHT;            §2.10.9

    // Methods
    public abstract void imageComplete(int status);      §2.10.10
    public abstract void setColorModel(ColorModel model); §2.10.11
    public abstract void                                 §2.10.12
        setDimensions(int width, int height);
    public abstract void setHints(int hintflags);        §2.10.13
    public abstract void                                 §2.10.14
        setPixels(int x, int y, int w, int h,
                  ColorModel model, byte pixels[],
                  int off, int scansize);
    public abstract void                                 §2.10.15
        setPixels(int x, int y, int w, int h,
                  ColorModel model, int pixels[],
                  int off, int scansize);
    public abstract void setProperties(Hashtable props); §2.10.16
}
```

The image consumer interface specifies the methods that all image consumers must implement. An image consumer is an object interested in data produced by the image producers (**II-§2.12**).

When a consumer is added to an image producer, the producer delivers all the data about the image using the method calls defined in this interface.

Fields

IMAGEABORTED §2.10.1

> `public final static int IMAGEABORTED = 4`

Argument to the `imageComplete` method **(II-§2.10.10)** indicating that the image creation process was deliberately aborted.

IMAGEERROR §2.10.2

> `public final static int IMAGEERROR = 1`

Argument to the `imageComplete` method **(II-§2.10.10)** indicating that an error was encountered while producing the image.

SINGLEFRAMEDONE §2.10.3

> `public final static int SINGLEFRAMEDONE = 2`

Argument to the `imageComplete` method **(II-§2.10.10)** indicating that one frame of the image is complete but there are more frames to be delivered.

STATICIMAGEDONE §2.10.4

> `public final static int STATICIMAGEDONE = 3`

Argument to the `imageComplete` method **(II-§2.10.10)** indicating that the image is complete and there are no more pixels or frames to be delivered.

COMPLETESCANLINES §2.10.5

> `public final static int COMPLETESCANLINES = 4`

Flag in the `setHints` method **(II-§2.10.13)** indicating that the pixels will be delivered in (multiples of) complete scanlines at a time.

RANDOMPIXELORDER §2.10.6

> `public final static int RANDOMPIXELORDER = 1`

Flag in the `setHints` method **(II-§2.10.13)** indicating that the pixels will be delivered in a random order.

The image consumer should not use any optimizations that depend on the order of pixel delivery. If the image producer does not call the `setHints` method, the image consumer should assume that the bits are being delivered in a random order.

SINGLEFRAME   §2.10.7

`public final static int SINGLEFRAME = 8`

Flag in the `setHints` method (**II-§2.10.13**) indicating that the image contains a single static image. The pixels will be defined in calls to the `set-Pixels` methods; the image producer then calls the `imageComplete` method (**II-§2.10.10**) with the `STATICIMAGEDONE` flag (**II-§2.10.4**), after which no more image data is delivered.

Examples of image types that do not meet these criteria include the output of a video feed, or the representation of a 3-D rendering being manipulated by the user. The end of each frame of those types of images is indicated by the image producer calling the `imageComplete` method (**II-§2.10.10**) with the `SINGLEFRAMEDONE` flag (**II-§2.10.4**).

SINGLEPASS   §2.10.8

`public final static int SINGLEPASS = 8`

Flag in the `setHints` method (**II-§2.10.13**) indicating that each pixel will be delivered only once.

An image type that does not meet this criterion is a progressive JPEG image, which defines pixels in multiple passes, each more refined than the one previous.

TOPDOWNLEFTRIGHT = 2   §2.10.9

`public final static int TOPDOWNLEFTRIGHT`

Flag in the `setHints` method (**II-§2.10.13**) indicating that the pixels will be delivered in a top-down, left-to-right order.

Methods

imageComplete   §2.10.10

`public abstract void imageComplete(int status)`

The image producer calls the `imageComplete` method when one of the following conditions has occurred:

◆ It has delivered all the pixels that the source image contains.

◆ A single frame of a multiframe animation has been completed.

◆ An error in loading or producing the image has occurred.

◆ The image production was explicitly aborted by the application.

The image consumer should remove itself from the list of consumers registered with the image producer (**II-§2.12.3**), unless it is interested in subsequent frames.

The status is one of the following values:

IMAGEERROR (**II-§2.10.2**)
SINGLEFRAMEDONE (**II-§2.10.7**)
STATICIMAGEDONE (**II-§2.10.4**)
IMAGEABORTED (**II-§2.10.1**)

PARAMETERS:
`status`: the status of the image.

setColorModel §2.10.11

```
public abstract void setColorModel(ColorModel model)
```

The image producer calls the `setColorModel` method to specify the color model (**II-§2.1**) for the majority of the subsequent `setPixels` method calls.

Each set of pixels delivered using the `setPixels` method includes its own color model, so the image consumer should not assume that the model argument is the color model argument in every subsequent `setPixels` method call.

A notable case where multiple `ColorModel` objects may be seen is a filtered image where for each set of pixels that it filters, the filter determines whether the pixels can be sent on untouched, using the original color model, or should be modified (filtered) and passed on using a color model more convenient for the filtering process.

PARAMETERS:
`model`: a color map used in subsequent `setPixel` calls.

setDimensions §2.10.12

```
public abstract void
setDimensions(int width, int height)
```

The image producer calls the `setDimensions` of the image consumer to indicate the width and height of the image.

PARAMETERS:
`width`: the width of the image.
`height`: the height of the image.

setHints   §2.10.13

```
public abstract void setHints(int hintflags)
```

The image producer calls the setHints method of the image consumer to indicate the order in which the bits will be delivered.

The image producer is allowed to deliver the pixels in any order, but the image consumer may be able to scale or convert the pixels more efficiently or with higher quality if it knows some information about how the pixels will be presented.

The image producer should call the setHints method before any calls to the image consumer's setPixels method.

The hintflags argument is a bit mask of hints about the manner in which the pixels are delivered.

The possible hint flags are these:

COMPLETESCANLINES (II-§2.10.5)
RANDOMPIXELORDER (II-§2.10.5)
SINGLEFRAME (II-§2.10.5)
SINGLEPASS (II-§2.10.5)
TOPDOWNLEFTRIGHT (II-§2.10.5)

PARAMETERS:

hints: hints about the order in which the bits will be delivered.

setPixels §2.10.14

```
public abstract void
setPixels(int x, int y, int w, int h, ColorModel model,
         byte pixels[], int off, int scansize)
```

The image producer calls the setPixels method of the image consumer one or more times to deliver the pixels of the image. Each call specifies the location and size of the rectangle of source pixels contained in the array of pixels.

The specified color model object should be used to convert the pixels into their corresponding color and alpha components. The pixel at coordinate $\langle i, j \rangle$ is stored in the pixel array at index

$$(j - y) \times \mathsf{scan} + (i - x) + \mathsf{offset}$$

The pixels delivered using this method are all stored as bytes.

PARAMETERS:

x: the left coordinate of the rectangle.
y: the top coordinate of the rectangle.
w: the width of the rectangle.
h: the height of the rectangle.
model: the color model for bits.
pixels: the array of bits.
off: the offset for the first element.
scansize: the number of elements per row

setPixels §2.10.15

```
public abstract void
setPixels(int x, int y, int w, int h, ColorModel model,
         int pixels[], int off, int scansize)
```

The image producer calls the setPixels method of the image consumer one or more times to deliver the pixels of the image. Each call specifies the location and size of the rectangle of source pixels that are contained in the array of pixels.

The specified color model object should be used to convert the pixels into their corresponding color and alpha components. The pixel at coordinate $\langle i, j \rangle$ is stored in the pixel array at index

$$(j - y) \times \mathsf{scan} + (i - x) + \mathsf{offset}$$

The pixels delivered using this method are all stored as integers.

PARAMETERS:

x: the left coordinate of the rectangle.
y: the top coordinate of the rectangle.
w: the width of the rectangle.
h: the height of the rectangle.
model: the color model for bits.
pixels: the array of bits.
off: the offset for the first element.

setProperties   §2.10.16

```
public abstract void setProperties(Hashtable props)
```

 The image producer calls the `setProperties` method of the image consumer to indicate additional properties of the image.

 All keys to the hashtable are strings. The corresponding values depend on the string.

PARAMETERS:

`props`: a hashtable of properties.

SEE ALSO:

`getProperty` in class Image (II-§1.24.6).

2.11 Interface ImageObserver

```
public interface java.awt.image.ImageObserver
{
    // flags for the infoflags argument to imageUpdate
    public final static int ABORT;                     §2.11.1
    public final static int ALLBITS;                   §2.11.2
    public final static int ERROR;                     §2.11.3
    public final static int FRAMEBITS;                 §2.11.4
    public final static int HEIGHT;                    §2.11.5
    public final static int PROPERTIES;                §2.11.6
    public final static int SOMEBITS;                  §2.11.7
    public final static int WIDTH;                     §2.11.8

    // Methods
    public abstract boolean                            §2.11.9
        imageUpdate(Image img, int infoflags,
                    int x, int y, int width, int height);
}
```

 The image observer interface specifies the methods that all image observers must implement.

 An image observer is interested in receiving asynchronous notifications about the image as the image is being constructed.

Fields

ABORT   §2.11.1

```
public final static int ABORT = 128
```

This flag in the `infoflags` argument to `imageUpdate` (**II-§2.11.9**) indicates that the image was aborted before production was complete.

No more information will become available without further action to trigger another image production sequence.

If the ERROR flag was not also set in this image update, then accessing any of the data in the image restarts the production again, possibly from the beginning.

ALLBITS   §2.11.2

```
public final static int ALLBITS = 32
```

This flag in the `infoflags` argument to `imageUpdate` (**II-§2.11.9**) indicates that a static image is now complete and can be drawn in its final form.

The `x`, `y`, `width`, and `height` arguments to the `imageUpdate` method should be ignored when this flag is set in the `status`.

SEE ALSO:

`drawImage` in class `Graphics` (**II-§1.20.12**).

ERROR   §2.11.3

```
public final static int ERROR = 64
```

This flag in the `infoflags` argument to `imageUpdate` (**II-§2.11.9**) indicates that an image which was being tracked asynchronously has encountered an error. No further information will become available, and drawing the image will fail.

Whenever this flag is set, the ABORT flag must also be set.

FRAMEBITS   §2.11.4

```
public final static int FRAMEBITS = 16
```

This flag in the `infoflags` argument to `imageUpdate` (**II-§2.11.9**) indicates that another complete frame of a multiframe image can now be drawn.

The `x`, `y`, `width`, and `height` arguments to the `imageUpdate` method should be ignored when this flag is set in the `status`.

SEE ALSO:

`drawImage` in class `Graphics` (**II-§1.20.12**).

HEIGHT   §2.11.5

```
public final static int HEIGHT = 2
```

This flag in the infoflags argument to imageUpdate (II-§2.11.9) indicates that the height of the base image is now available and can be taken from the height argument to the imageUpdate method.

SEE ALSO:

getHeight in class Image (II-§1.24.5).

PROPERTIES   §2.11.6

```
public final static int PROPERTIES = 4
```

This flag in the infoflags argument to imageUpdate (II-§2.11.9) indicates that the properties of the image are now available.

SEE ALSO:

getProperty in class Image (II-§1.24.6).

SOMEBITS   §2.11.7

```
public final static int SOMEBITS = 8
```

This flag in the infoflags argument to imageUpdate (II-§2.11.9) indicates that the pixels needed for drawing a scaled variation of the image are now available.

The bounding box of the new pixels can be taken from the x, y, width, and height arguments to the imageUpdate method.

SEE ALSO:

drawImage in class Graphics (II-§1.20.12).

WIDTH   §2.11.8

```
public final static int WIDTH
```

This flag in the infoflags argument to imageUpdate (II-§2.11.9) indicates that the width of the base image is now available and can be taken from the width argument to the imageUpdate method.

SEE ALSO:

getWidth in class Image (II-§1.24.8).

Methods

---

imageUpdate §2.11.9

```
public abstract boolean
imageUpdate(Image img, int infoflags, int x, int y,
            int width, int height)
```

This image observer method is called when previously requested information about an image becomes available.

Asynchronous interfaces are method calls such as `getWidth` **(II-§1.24.8)**, `getHeight` **(II-§1.24.5)**, and `drawImage` **(II-§1.20.12)**, which take an image observer as an argument. These methods register the caller as being interested in information either about the image or about an output version of the image.

This method should return `true` if further calls to `imageUpdate` are needed by this image observer, and `false` if it needs no more information.

The infoflags argument should be bitwise inclusive **OR** of the following flags:

```
WIDTH (II-§2.11.8)
HEIGHT (II-§2.11.5)
PROPERTIES (II-§2.11.6)
SOMEBITS (II-§2.11.7)
FRAMEBITS (II-§2.11.4)
ALLBITS (II-§2.11.2)
ERROR (II-§2.11.3)
ABORT (II-§2.11.1)
```

The interpretation of the `x`, `y`, `width`, and `height` arguments depends on the `infoflags` argument.

PARAMETERS:
`img`: the image being observed.
`infoflags`: the **OR** of the above flags.
`x`: an *x* coordinate.
`y`: a *y* coordinate.
`width`: the width.
`height`: the height.

RETURNS:
`true` if further calls to `imageUpdate` are needed by this image observer; `false` otherwise.

2.12 Interface ImageProducer

```
public interface java.awt.image.ImageProducer
{
    // Methods
    public abstract void addConsumer(ImageConsumer ic);       §2.12.1
    public abstract boolean isConsumer(ImageConsumer ic);     §2.12.2
    public abstract void removeConsumer(ImageConsumer ic);    §2.12.3
    public abstract void                                      §2.12.4
        requestTopDownLeftRightResend(ImageConsumer ic);
    public abstract void startProduction                      §2.12.5
        (ImageConsumer ic);
}
```

The image producer interface specifies the methods that all image producers must implement. Every image contains an image producer which can reconstruct the image whenever it is needed by an image consumer (**II-§2.10**).

Methods

addConsumer   §2.12.1

```
public abstract void addConsumer(ImageConsumer ic)
```

Registers the image consumer argument as wanting information about this image.

The image producer may, at its discretion, start delivering the image data immediately, or it may wait until the next image reconstruction is forced by a call to the startProduction method (**II-§2.12.5**).

PARAMETERS:

ic: an image consumer.

isConsumer   §2.12.2

```
public abstract boolean isConsumer(ImageConsumer ic)
```

PARAMETERS:

ic: an image consumer.

RETURNS:

true if the specified image consumer argument is currently registered with this image producer as one of its consumers; false otherwise.

removeConsumer   §2.12.3

```
public abstract void removeConsumer(ImageConsumer ic)
```

Removes the specified image consumer object from the list of consumers registered to receive the image data. It is not an error to remove a consumer that is not registered.

The image producer should stop sending data to this consumer as soon as it is feasible.

PARAMETERS:

ic: an image consumer.

requestTopDownLeftRightResend   §2.12.4

```
public abstract void
requestTopDownLeftRightResend(ImageConsumer ic)
```

An image consumer invokes this method to request that the image producer attempt to resend the image data one more time in top-down, left-to-right order.

If the data cannot be resent in that order, the image producer ignores this call.

If the data can be resent in that order, the image producer should respond by executing the following minimum set of image consumer method calls.

```
ic.setHints(TOPDOWNLEFTRIGHT | otherhints );
    ic.setPixels(...); // As many times as needed
    ic.imageComplete();
```

An image consumer might call this method so that it can use a higher-quality conversion algorithm which depends on receiving the pixels in order.

PARAMETERS:

ic: an image consumer.

SEE ALSO:

setHints in class ImageConsumer **(II-§2.10.13)**.

startProduction   §2.12.5

```
public abstract void startProduction(ImageConsumer ic)
```

Registers the image consumer argument as wanting information about this image.

In addition, this method forces the image producer to start an immediate reconstruction of the image data. The data will be delivered both to this image consumer and to any other image consumers which may have already been registered with the producer using the addConsumer method **(II-§2.12.1)**.

PARAMETERS:

ic: an image consumer.

CHAPTER 3

Package java.awt.peer

THE java.awt.peer package contains interfaces used to connect AWT components to their window system–specific implementations (such as Motif widgets). Unless an application is creating a window system–specific implementation of the AWT, it should not need to use the interfaces in the java.awt.peer package.

Each of the interfaces in this package has a corresponding component in the java.awt package. An application can modify the appearance or implementation of a component without changing its functionality by creating its own toolkit (**II-§1.41**).

3.1 Interface ButtonPeer

```
public interface java.awt.peer.ButtonPeer
    extends java.awt.peer.ComponentPeer (II-§3.6)
{
    // Methods
    public abstract void setLabel(String label);        §3.1.1
}
```

The button peer interface specifies the methods that all implementations of Abstract Window Toolkit buttons must define.

Methods

setLabel   §3.1.1

    public abstract void setLabel(String label)

      Changes the button's label to be the String argument.

    PARAMETERS:

    label: the new label, or null for no label.

3.2 Interface CanvasPeer

```
public interface java.awt.peer.CanvasPeer
    extends java.awt.peer.ComponentPeer (II-§3.6)
{
}
```

The canvas peer interface specifies the methods that all implementations of Abstract Window Toolkit canvases must define.

In general, canvas implementations only need to implement methods required of all component peers.

3.3 Interface CheckboxMenuItemPeer

```
public interface java.awt.peer.CheckboxMenuItemPeer
    extends java.awt.peer.MenuItemPeer (II-§3.15)
{
    //Methods
    public abstract void setState(boolean t);                    §3.3.1
}
```

The check box menu peer interface specifies the methods that all implementations of Abstract Window Toolkit check box menus must define.

Methods

setState   §3.3.1

```
    public abstract void setState(boolean t)
```

Sets the check box to the specifed boolean state: true indicates "on"; false indicates "off."

PARAMETERS:

state: the boolean state.

3.4 Interface CheckboxPeer

```
public interface java.awt.peer.CheckboxPeer
     extends java.awt.peer.ComponentPeer (II-§3.6)
{
     // Methods
     public abstract void setCheckboxGroup(CheckboxGroup g); §3.4.1
     public abstract void setLabel(String label);              §3.4.2
     public abstract void setState(boolean state);             §3.4.3
}
```

The check box peer interface specifies the methods that all implementations of Abstract Window Toolkit check boxes must define.

Methods

setCheckboxGroup   §3.4.1

   public abstract void setCheckboxGroup(CheckboxGroup g)

   Sets the group of the check box to be the specified CheckboxGroup.

   PARAMETERS:

   g: the new check box group, or null to remove the check box from any
      check box group.

setLabel   §3.4.2

   public abstract void setLabel(String label)

   Changes the check box's label to be the string argument.

   PARAMETERS:

   label: the new label, or null for no label.

setState   §3.4.3

   public abstract void setState(boolean state)

   Sets the check box to the specified boolean state: true indicates "on";
   false indicates "off."

   PARAMETERS:

   state: the boolean state.

3.5 Interface ChoicePeer

```
public interface java.awt.peer.ChoicePeer
    extends java.awt.peer.ComponentPeer (II-§3.6)
{
    // Methods
    public abstract void addItem(String item, int index);   §3.5.1
    public abstract void select(int index);                 §3.5.2
}
```

The choice menu peer interface specifies the methods that all implementations of Abstract Window Toolkit choice menus must define.

Methods

addItem   §3.5.1

    `public abstract void addItem(String item, int index)`

      Adds an item to the choice menu at the specified position.

    PARAMETERS:
    `item`: the string item.
    `index`: the position.

select   §3.5.2

    `public abstract void select(int index)`

      Sets the selected item to be the item at the specified position.

    PARAMETERS:
    `index`: the selected item position.

3.6 Interface ComponentPeer

```
public interface java.awt.peer.ComponentPeer
{
    // Methods
    public abstract int                                      §3.6.1
        checkImage(Image img, int w, int h,
                    ImageObserver o);
    public abstract Image                                    §3.6.2
        createImage(ImageProducer producer);
    public abstract Image                                    §3.6.3
        createImage(int width, int height);
    public abstract void disable();                          §3.6.4
    public abstract void dispose();                          §3.6.5
    public abstract void enable();                           §3.6.6
    public abstract ColorModel getColorModel();             §3.6.7
    public abstract FontMetrics getFontMetrics(Font font);  §3.6.8
    public abstract Graphics getGraphics();                 §3.6.9
    public abstract Toolkit getToolkit();                   §3.6.10
    public abstract boolean handleEvent(Event e);           §3.6.11
    public abstract void hide();                            §3.6.12
    public abstract Dimension minimumSize();                §3.6.13
    public abstract void nextFocus();                       §3.6.14
    public abstract void paint(Graphics g);                 §3.6.15
    public abstract Dimension preferredSize();              §3.6.16
    public abstract boolean                                 §3.6.17
        prepareImage(Image img, int w, int h,
                    ImageObserver o);
    public abstract void print(Graphics g);                 §3.6.18
    public abstract void repaint(long tm, int x, int y,     §3.6.19
                                  int width, int height);
    public abstract void requestFocus();                    §3.6.21
    public abstract void reshape(int x, int y, int width,   §3.6.22
                                  int height);
    public abstract void setBackground(Color c);            §3.6.23
    public abstract void setFont(Font f);                   §3.6.24
    public abstract void setForeground(Color c);            §3.6.25
    public abstract void show();                            §3.6.26
}
```

The component peer interface specifies the methods that all implementations of Abstract Window Toolkit components must define.

Methods

---

checkImage   §3.6.1

```
public abstract int
checkImage(Image img, int w, int h, ImageObserver o)
```

Returns the status of the construction of a scaled screen representation of the specified image.

This method does not cause the image to begin loading. An application must use the prepareImage (II-§3.6.17) method to force the loading of an image.

Information on the flags returned by this method can be found in II-§2.11.

PARAMETERS:

img: the image whose status is being checked.
w: the width of the scaled version whose status is being checked.
h: the height of the scaled version whose status is being checked.
o: the ImageObserver object to be notified as the image is being prepared.

RETURNS:

the bitwise inclusive **OR** of the ImageObserver (II-§2.11) flags for the data that is currently available.

SEE ALSO:

prepareImage (II-§3.6.17).

createImage   §3.6.2

```
public abstract Image createImage(ImageProducer producer)
```

Creates an image from the specified image producer.

PARAMETERS:

producer: the image producer.

RETURNS:

the image produced.

createImage   §3.6.3

```
public abstract Image createImage(int width, int height)
```

Creates an off-screen drawable image to be used for double buffering.

PARAMETERS:

width: the specified width.
height: the specified height.

RETURNS:

an off-screen drawable image.

disable §3.6.4

    `public abstract void disable()`

    Makes the component insensitive to user input.

    SEE ALSO:

    `enable` **(II-§3.6.6)**.

dispose §3.6.5

    `public abstract void dispose()`

    Disposes of the component peer and any resources used by it.

enable §3.6.6

    `public abstract void enable()`

    Makes the component sensitive to user input. This is the default.

    SEE ALSO:

    `disable` **(II-§3.6.4)**.

getColorModel §3.6.7

    `public abstract ColorModel getColorModel()`

    Gets the component's color model **(II-§2.1)**, which is an abstract class that encapsulates how to translate between pixel values of an image and its red, green, blue, and alpha components.

    RETURNS:

    the color model of the component.

getFontMetrics §3.6.8

    `public abstract FontMetrics getFontMetrics(Font font)`

    PARAMETERS:

    `font`: the font.

    RETURNS:

    the font metrics for this component; if the component is not currently on the screen, this method returns `null`.

getGraphics §3.6.9

    `public abstract Graphics getGraphics()`

    RETURNS:

    the graphics context of this component; this method returns `null` if the component is not currently on the screen.

    SEE ALSO:

    `paint` **(II-§3.6.15)**.

getToolkit §3.6.10

```
public abstract Toolkit getToolkit()
```
RETURNS:

the toolkit that the component peer is part of.

handleEvent §3.6.11

```
public abstract boolean handleEvent(Event e)
```
This method is called when any event occurs inside the component.

The method must return `true` to indicate that it has successfully handled the action, or `false` if the event that triggered the action should be passed up to the component's containing object.

PARAMETERS:

e: the event.

RETURNS:

`false` if the event is to be given to the component's containing object; `true` if the event has been handled and no further action is necessary.

hide §3.6.12

```
public abstract void hide()
```
Hides the component.

SEE ALSO:

show (II-§3.6.26).

minimumSize §3.6.13

```
public abstract Dimension minimumSize()
```
RETURNS:

the minimum size of this component.

SEE ALSO:

preferredSize (II-§3.6.16).

nextFocus §3.6.14

```
public abstract void nextFocus()
```
Moves the focus to the next component.

paint   **§3.6.15**

    `public abstract void paint(Graphics g)`

    Paints the component.

    The $\langle 0,0 \rangle$ coordinate of the graphics context is the top left corner of the component. The clipping region of the graphics context is the bounding rectangle of the component.

    PARAMETERS:

    `g`: the graphics context to use for painting.

preferredSize   **§3.6.16**

    `public abstract Dimension preferredSize()`

    RETURNS:

    the preferred size of this component.

    SEE ALSO:

    `minimumSize` (**II-§3.6.13**).

prepareImage   **§3.6.17**

    `public abstract boolean`
    `prepareImage(Image img, int w, int h, ImageObserver o)`

    Prepares an image for rendering on this component at the specified width and height.

    The image data is downloaded asynchronously in another thread, and an appropriately scaled screen representation of the image is generated.

    PARAMETERS:

    `image`: the image for which to prepare a screen representation.
    `width`: the width of the desired screen representation.
    `height`: the height of the desired screen representation.
    `observer`: the `ImageObserver` object to be notified as the image is being prepared.

    RETURNS:

    `true` if the image has already been fully prepared; `false` otherwise.

    SEE ALSO:

    `ImageObserver` (**II-§2.11**).

print   §3.6.18

```
public abstract void print(Graphics g)
```

Prints this component.

The $\langle 0, 0 \rangle$ coordinate of the graphics context is the top left corner of the component. The clipping region of the graphics context is the bounding rectangle of the component.

SEE ALSO:

paint **(II-§3.6.15).**

repaint   §3.6.19

```
public abstract void repaint(long tm, int x, int y,
                             int width, int height)
```

Repaints the specified rectangle of the component.

PARAMETERS:

x: the x coordinate.
y: the y coordinate.
width: the width.
height: the height.   §3.6.20

SEE ALSO:

paint **(II-§3.6.15).**

requestFocus   §3.6.21

```
public abstract void requestFocus()
```

Requests the input focus.

reshape   §3.6.22

```
public abstract void
reshape(int x, int y, int width, int height)
```

Reshapes the component to the specified bounding rectangle.

PARAMETERS:

x: the x coordinate.
y: the y coordinate.
width: the width of the component.
height: the height of the component.

setBackground   §3.6.23

```
public abstract void setBackground(Color c)
```

Sets the background color for the component.

PARAMETERS:

c: the color.

setFont §3.6.24

    `public abstract void setFont(Font f)`

      Sets the font of the component.

    PARAMETERS:

    `f`: the font.

setForeground §3.6.25

    `public abstract void setForeground(Color c)`

      Sets the foreground color for the component.

    PARAMETERS:

    `c`: the color.

show §3.6.26

    `public abstract void show()`

      Shows the component: if the component had been made invisible by a call to the `hide` method (**II-§3.6.12**), makes the component visible again.

3.7 Interface ContainerPeer

```
public interface java.awt.peer.ContainerPeer
    extends java.awt.peer.ComponentPeer (II-§3.6)
{
    // Methods
    public abstract Insets insets();                      §3.7.1
}
```

    The container peer interface specifies the methods that all implementations of Abstract Window Toolkit containers must define.

Methods

insets §3.7.1

    `public abstract Insets insets()`

      Determines the insets of the container, which indicate the size of the border of the container.

      A `Frame`, for example, has a top inset that corresponds to the height of the frame's title bar.

3.8 Interface DialogPeer

```
public interface java.awt.peer.DialogPeer
    extends java.awt.peer.WindowPeer (II-§3.22)
{
    // Methods
    public abstract void setResizable(boolean resizable);   §3.8.1
    public abstract void setTitle(String title);            §3.8.2
}
```

The dialog window peer interface specifies the methods that all implementations of Abstract Window Toolkit dialog windows must define.

Methods

setResizable   §3.8.1

    public abstract void setResizable(boolean resizable)
Sets the resizable flag.

PARAMETERS:
resizable: true if the dialog window is resizable; false otherwise.

setTitle   §3.8.2

    public abstract void setTitle(String title)
Sets the title of the dialog window.

PARAMETERS:
title: the new title.

3.9 Interface FileDialogPeer

```
public interface java.awt.peer.FileDialogPeer
    extends java.awt.peer.DialogPeer (II-§3.8)
{
    // Methods
    public abstract void setDirectory(String dir);          §3.9.1
    public abstract void setFile(String file);              §3.9.2
    public abstract void                                    §3.9.3
        setFilenameFilter(FilenameFilter filter);
}
```

The file dialog window peer interface specifies the methods that all implementations of Abstract Window Toolkit file dialog windows must define.

Methods

---

setDirectory §3.9.1

    `public abstract void setDirectory(String dir)`

    Sets the directory of the file dialog window to the specified directory.

    PARAMETERS:

    `dir`: the specific directory.

setFile §3.9.2

    `public abstract void setFile(String file)`

    Sets the selected file for the file dialog window to the specified file.

    PARAMETERS:

    `file`: the file being set.

setFilenameFilter §3.9.3

    `public abstract void`
    `setFilenameFilter(FilenameFilter filter)`

    Sets the filename filter (**I-§2.26**) for this file dialog window to the specified filter.

    PARAMETERS:

    `filter`: the specified filter.

3.10 Interface FramePeer

```
public interface java.awt.peer.FramePeer
    extends java.awt.peer.WindowPeer (II-§3.22)
{
    // Methods
    public abstract void setCursor(int cursorType);        §3.10.1
    public abstract void setIconImage(Image im);           §3.10.2
    public abstract void setMenuBar(MenuBar mb);           §3.10.3
    public abstract void setResizable(boolean resizable);  §3.10.4
    public abstract void setTitle(String title);           §3.10.5
}
```

The frame peer interface specifies the methods that all implementations of Abstract Window Toolkit frames must define.

Methods

setCursor   §3.10.1

```
public abstract void setCursor(int cursorType)
```

Sets the cursor image to be one of the predefined cursors.

PARAMETERS:

cursorType: one of the predefined cursor constants defined above.

setIconImage   §3.10.2

```
public abstract void setIconImage(Image im)
```

Sets the image to display when this frame is iconized.
Note that not all platforms support the concept of iconizing a window.

PARAMETERS:

image: the icon image to be displayed.

setMenuBar   §3.10.3

```
public abstract void setMenuBar(MenuBar mb)
```

Sets the menu bar of this frame to the specified menu bar.

PARAMETERS:

mb: the new menu bar.

setResizable   §3.10.4

```
public abstract void setResizable(boolean resizable)
```

Determines whether this frame should be resizable.

PARAMETERS:

resizable: true if the frame should be resizable; false otherwise.

setTitle   §3.10.5

```
public abstract void setTitle(String title)
```

Sets the title of this frame to the specified title.

PARAMETERS:

title: the new title of this frame, or null to delete the title.

3.11 Interface LabelPeer

```
public interface java.awt.peer.LabelPeer
    extends java.awt.peer.ComponentPeer (II-§3.6)
{
    // Methods
    public abstract void setAlignment(int alignment);        §3.11.1
    public abstract void setText(String label);              §3.11.2
}
```

The label peer interface specifies the methods that all implementations of Abstract Window Toolkit labels must define.

Methods

setAlignment   §3.11.1

```
    public abstract void setAlignment(int alignment)
```
Sets the alignment for this label to the specified alignment.

PARAMETERS:

alignment: the alignment value.

setText   §3.11.2

```
    public abstract void setText(String label)
```
Sets the text for this label to the specified text.

PARAMETERS:

label: the text that makes up the label.

3.12 Interface ListPeer

```
public interface java.awt.peer.ListPeer
    extends java.awt.peer.ComponentPeer (II-§3.6)
{
    // Methods
    public abstract void addItem(String item, int index);      §3.12.1
    public abstract void clear();                              §3.12.2
    public abstract void delItems(int start, int end)         §3.12.3
    public abstract void deselect(int index);                 §3.12.4
    public abstract int[] getSelectedIndexes();               §3.12.5
    public abstract void makeVisible(int index);              §3.12.6
    public abstract Dimension minimumSize(int v);             §3.12.7
    public abstract Dimension preferredSize(int v);           §3.12.8
    public abstract void select(int index);                   §3.12.9
    public abstract void setMultipleSelections(boolean v);    §3.12.10
}
```

The scrolling list peer interface specifies the methods that all implementations of Abstract Window Toolkit scrolling lists must define.

Methods

addItem   §3.12.1

```
public abstract void addItem(String item, int index)
```

Adds the specified string to the scrolling list at the specified position.

The index argument is 0-based. If the index is –1, or greater than or equal to the number of items already in the list, then the item is added at the end of the list.

PARAMETERS:

item: the string to be added.
index: the position at which to put in the item.

clear   §3.12.2

```
public abstract void clear()
```

Removes all items from the scrolling list.

SEE ALSO:

delItems (II-§3.12.3).

delItems   §3.12.3

    `public abstract void delItems(int start, int end)`

      Deletes the items in the range $\text{start} \leq item \leq \text{end}$ from the scrolling list.

PARAMETERS:

`start`: the index of the first element to delete.
`end`: the index of the last element to delete.

deselect   §3.12.4

    `public abstract void deselect(int index)`

      Deselects the item at the specified index.

PARAMETERS:

`index`: the position of the item to deselect.

SEE ALSO:

`select` **(II-§3.12.9)**.

getSelectedIndexes   §3.12.5

    `public abstract int[] getSelectedIndexes()`

RETURNS:

an array of the selected indexes on the scrolling list.

SEE ALSO:

`select` **(II-§3.12.9)**.
`deselect` **(II-§3.12.4)**.

makeVisible   §3.12.6

    `public abstract void makeVisible(int index)`

      Forces the item at the specified index to be visible.

minimumSize   §3.12.7

    `public abstract Dimension minimumSize(int v)`

PARAMETERS:

`rows`: number of rows.

RETURNS:

the minimum dimensions needed to display the specified number of rows in a scrolling list.

preferredSize   §3.12.8

> `public abstract Dimension preferredSize(int v)`

> **PARAMETERS:**

> `rows`: number of rows.

> **RETURNS:**

> the preferred dimensions needed to display the specified number of rows in a scrolling list.

select   §3.12.9

> `public abstract void select(int index)`

>> Selects the item at the specified index.

> **PARAMETERS:**

> `index`: the position of the item to select.

> **SEE ALSO:**

> `deselect` (**II-§3.12.4**).

setMultipleSelections   §3.12.10

> `public abstract void setMultipleSelections(boolean v)`

>> Sets whether this scolling list allows multiple selections.

> **PARAMETERS:**

> `v`: if `true`, then multiple selections are allowed; otherwise, only one item can be selected at a time.

3.13 Interface MenuBarPeer

```
public interface java.awt.peer.MenuBarPeer
    extends java.awt.peer.MenuComponentPeer (II-§3.14)
{
    // Methods
    public abstract void addHelpMenu(Menu m);            §3.13.1
    public abstract void addMenu(Menu m);                §3.13.2
    public abstract void delMenu(int index);             §3.13.3
}
```

The menu bar peer interface specifies the methods that all implementations of Abstract Window Toolkit menu bars must define.

Methods

addHelpMenu §3.13.1

```
public abstract void addHelpMenu(Menu m)
```

Sets the help menu on the menu bar to be the specified menu.

PARAMETERS:

m: the help menu.

addMenu §3.13.2

```
public abstract void addMenu(Menu m)
```

Adds the specified menu to the menu bar.

PARAMETERS:

m: the menu to be added.

delMenu §3.13.3

```
public abstract void delMenu(int index)
```

Removes the menu located at the specified index from the menu bar.

PARAMETERS:

index: the position of the menu to be removed.

3.14 Interface MenuComponentPeer

```
public interface java.awt.peer.MenuComponentPeer
{
    // Methods
    public abstract void dispose();                §3.14.1
}
```

The menu component peer interface specifies the methods that all implementations of Abstract Window Toolkit menu components must define.

Methods

dispose §3.14.1

```
public abstract void dispose()
```

Disposes of the menu component peer and any resources used by it.

3.15 Interface MenuItemPeer

```
public interface java.awt.peer.MenuItemPeer
    extends java.awt.peer.MenuComponentPeer (II-§3.14)
{
    // Methods
    public abstract void disable();                          §3.15.1
    public abstract void enable();                           §3.15.2
    public abstract void setLabel(String label);            §3.15.3
}
```

The menu item peer interface specifies the methods that all implementations of Abstract Window Toolkit menu items must define.

Methods

disable   §3.15.1

```
public abstract void disable()
```
Disables this menu item. It can no longer be selected by the user.

enable   §3.15.2

```
public abstract void enable()
```
Enables this menu item. It can be selected by the user.

setLabel   §3.15.3

```
public abstract void setLabel(String label)
```
Changes the menu item's label to be the specified string.

PARAMETERS:
label: the new label, or null for no label.

3.16 Interface MenuPeer

```
public interface java.awt.peer.MenuPeer
    extends java.awt.peer.MenuItemPeer (II-§3.15)
{
    // Methods
    public abstract void addItem(MenuItem item);            §3.16.1
    public abstract void addSeparator();                    §3.16.2
    public abstract void delItem(int index);                §3.16.3
}
```

The menu peer interface specifies the methods that all implementations of Abstract Window Toolkit menus must define.

Methods

---

addItem §3.16.1

    `public abstract void addItem(MenuItem item)`

      Adds the specified menu item to this menu.

    PARAMETERS:

    `item`: the menu item to be added.

addSeparator §3.16.2

    `public abstract void addSeparator()`

      Adds a separator line to this menu.

delItem §3.16.3

    `public abstract void delItem(int index)`

      Deletes the item at the specified index from this menu.

    PARAMETERS:

    `index`: an index in the menu.

3.17 Interface PanelPeer

```
public interface java.awt.peer.PanelPeer
    extends java.awt.peer.ContainerPeer (II-§3.7)
{
}
```

The panel peer interface specifies the methods that all implementations of Abstract Window Toolkit panels must define.

3.18 Interface ScrollbarPeer

```
public interface java.awt.peer.ScrollbarPeer
    extends java.awt.peer.ComponentPeer (II-§3.6)
{
    // Methods
    public abstract void setLineIncrement(int l);       §3.18.1
    public abstract void setPageIncrement(int l);       §3.18.2
    public abstract void setValue(int value);           §3.18.3
    public abstract void setValues(int value, int visible  §3.18.4
                                   int minimum,
                                   int maximum);
}
```

The scroll bar peer interface specifies the methods that all implementations of Abstract Window Toolkit scroll bars must define.

Methods

setLineIncrement   §3.18.1

```
public abstract void setLineIncrement(int l)
```

Sets the line increment of the scroll bar.

The line increment is the value that is added to or subtracted from the value of the scroll bar when the user hits the line down or line up gadget.

PARAMETERS:

l: the new line increment.

setPageIncrement   §3.18.2

```
public abstract void setPageIncrement(int l)
```

Sets the page increment of the scroll bar.

The page increment is the value that is added to or subtracted from the value of the scroll bar when the user hits the page down or page up gadget.

PARAMETERS:

l: the new page increment.

setValue   §3.18.3

```
public abstract void setValue(int value)
```

Sets the value of the scroll bar to the specified value.

PARAMETERS:

value: the new value of the scroll bar.

setValues   §3.18.4

```
public abstract void setValues(int value, int visible,
                               int minimum, int maximum)
```

Sets several parameters of the scroll bar simultaneously.

PARAMETERS:

value: the value of the scroll bar.
visible: the amount visible per page.
minimum: the minimum value of the scroll bar.
maximum: the maximum value of the scroll bar.

3.19 Interface TextAreaPeer

```
public interface java.awt.peer.TextAreaPeer
    extends java.awt.peer.TextComponentPeer (II-§3.20)
{
    // Methods
    public abstract void insertText(String txt, int pos);   §3.19.1
    public abstract Dimension                               §3.19.2
        minimumSize(int rows, int cols);
    public abstract Dimension                               §3.19.3
        preferredSize(int rows, int cols);
    public abstract void replaceText(String txt,            §3.19.4
                                     int start, int end);
}
```

The text area peer interface specifies the methods that all implementations of Abstract Window Toolkit text areas must define.

Methods

insertText   §3.19.1

> public abstract void insertText(String txt, int pos)

> Inserts the specified text at the specified position.

PARAMETERS:

str: the text to insert.
pos: the position at which to insert the text.

minimumSize   §3.19.2

> public abstract Dimension minimumSize(int rows, int cols)

> **RETURNS:**

the minimum dimensions needed for the text area.

preferredSize   §3.19.3

> public abstract Dimension preferredSize(int rows, int cols)

> **RETURNS:**

the preferred dimensions needed for the text area.

replaceText   §3.19.4

```
public abstract void
replaceText(String txt, int start, int end)
```

Replaces the text from the start (inclusive) index to the end (exclusive) index with the new text specified.

PARAMETERS:

str: the replacement text.
start: the start position.
end: the end position.

SEE ALSO:

insertText (II-§3.19.1).

3.20 Interface TextComponentPeer

```
public interface java.awt.peer.TextComponentPeer
    extends java.awt.peer.ComponentPeer (II-§3.6)
{
    // Methods
    public abstract int getSelectionEnd();                §3.20.1
    public abstract int getSelectionStart();              §3.20.2
    public abstract String getText();                     §3.20.3
    public abstract void select(int selStart, int selEnd); §3.20.4
    public abstract void setEditable(boolean editable)    §3.20.5
    public abstract void setText(String l);               §3.20.6
}
```

The text component peer interface specifies the methods that all implementations of Abstract Window Toolkit text components must define.

Methods

getSelectionEnd   §3.20.1

```
public abstract int getSelectionEnd()
```
RETURNS:

selected text's end position.

getSelectionStart   §3.20.2

```
public abstract int getSelectionStart()
```
RETURNS:

selected text's start position.

getText §3.20.3

    public abstract String getText()

RETURNS:

the text of this text component.

select §3.20.4

    public abstract void select(int selStart, int selEnd)

Selects the text in the text component from the start (inclusive) index to the end (exclusive) index.

PARAMETERS:

selStart: the start position of the text to select.
selEnd: the end position of the text to select.

setEditable §3.20.5

    public abstract void setEditable(boolean editable)

Sets the text component to be user editable if the boolean argument is true. If the flag is false, sets the text component so that the user cannot change its contents.

PARAMETERS:

editable: a flag indicating whether the text component should become user editable.

setText §3.20.6

    public abstract void setText(String l)

Sets the text of this text component to the specified text.

PARAMETERS:

l: the new text.

3.21 Interface TextFieldPeer

```
public interface java.awt.peer.TextFieldPeer
    extends java.awt.peer.TextComponentPeer (II-§3.20)
{
    // Methods
    public abstract Dimension minimumSize(int cols);       §3.21.1
    public abstract Dimension preferredSize(int cols);     §3.21.2
    public abstract void setEchoCharacter(char c);         §3.21.3
}
```

The text field peer interface specifies the methods that all implementations of Abstract Window Toolkit text fields must define.

Methods

---

minimumSize   §3.21.1

```
public abstract Dimension minimumSize(int cols)
```

PARAMETERS:

cols: the number of columns.

RETURNS:

the minimum dimensions needed to display the text field with the specified
number of columns.

preferredSize   §3.21.2

```
public abstract Dimension preferredSize(int cols)
```

PARAMETERS:

cols: the number of columns.

RETURNS:

the preferred dimensions needed to display the text field with the specified
number of columns.

setEchoCharacter   §3.21.3

```
public abstract void setEchoCharacter(char c)
```

Sets the echo character for this text field. Any character that the user types
in the text field is echoed in the text field as the echo character.

An echo character is useful for fields where the user input shouldn't be
echoed to the screen, such as in the case of a text field for typing in a password.

PARAMETERS:

c: the echo character for this text field.

3.22 Interface WindowPeer

```
public interface java.awt.peer.WindowPeer
    extends java.awt.peer.ContainerPeer (II-§3.7)
{
    // Methods
    public abstract void toBack();                      §3.22.1
    public abstract void toFront();                     §3.22.2
}
```

The window peer interface specifies the methods that all implementations of Abstract Window Toolkit windows must define.

Methods

toBack   §3.22.1

```
    public abstract void toBack()
```
Sends this window to the back.

toFront   §3.22.2

```
    public abstract void toFront()
```
Brings this window to the front.

CHAPTER 4

Package java.applet

THIS package contains the `Applet` class and several interfaces used by this class.

- The `Applet` class (**II-§4.1**) is the base class of all applets; an application must subclass the `Applet` class if it is an applet. Applets are applications intended to be embedded in HTML pages or otherwise transported across a network.

- The interface `AppletContext` (**II-§4.2**) gives an applet information about the document containing the applet, and information about the other applets on the same document.

- The interface `AppletStub` (**II-§4.3**) is an internal hook between the applet and the browser or applet viewer displaying the applet.

- The interface `AudioClip` (**II-§4.4**) provides a simple abstraction for applets that want to include sound clips or background music.

4.1 Class Applet

```
public class java.applet.Applet
    extends java.awt.Panel (II-§1.33)
{
    // Constructors
    public Applet();                                                    §4.1.1

    // Methods
    public void destroy();                                             §4.1.2
    public AppletContext getAppletContext();                          §4.1.3
    public String getAppletInfo();                                    §4.1.4
    public AudioClip getAudioClip(URL url);                          §4.1.5
    public AudioClip getAudioClip(URL url, String name);           §4.1.6
    public URL getCodeBase();                                         §4.1.7
    public URL getDocumentBase();                                     §4.1.8
    public Image getImage(URL url);                                   §4.1.9
    public Image getImage(URL url, String name);                    §4.1.10
    public String getParameter(String name);                         §4.1.11
    public String[][] getParameterInfo();                            §4.1.12
    public void init();                                               §4.1.13
    public boolean isActive();                                        §4.1.14
    public void play(URL url);                                        §4.1.15
    public void play(URL url, String name);                         §4.1.16
    public void resize(Dimension d);                                 §4.1.17
    public void resize(int width, int height);                      §4.1.18
    public final void setStub(AppletStub stub);                     §4.1.19
    public void showStatus(String msg);                             §4.1.20
    public void start();                                              §4.1.21
    public void stop();                                               §4.1.22
}
```

An applet is a small program that is intended not to be run on its own, but ratther to be embedded inside another application.

The Applet class must be the superclass of any applet that is to be embedded in a Web page or viewed by the Java Applet Viewer. The Applet class provides a standard interface between applets and their environment.

Constructors

Applet   §4.1.1

```
public Applet()
```

The default constructor for an applet.

Methods

destroy §4.1.2

```
public void destroy()
```

This method is called by the browser or applet viewer to inform this applet that it is being reclaimed and that it should destroy any resources that it has allocated. The stop (II-§4.1.22) method will always be called before destroy.

A subclass of Applet should override this method if it has any operation that it wants to perform before it is destroyed. For example, an applet with threads would use the init (II-§4.1.13) method to create the threads and the destroy method to kill them.

The implementation of this method provided by the Applet class does nothing.

SEE ALSO:

start (II-§4.1.21).

getAppletContext §4.1.3

```
public AppletContext getAppletContext()
```

Determines this applet's context, which allows the applet to query and affect the environment in which it runs.

This environment of an applet represents the document that contains the applet.

RETURNS:

the applet's context.

getAppletInfo §4.1.4

```
public String getAppletInfo()
```

Returns information about this applet. An applet should override this method to return a String containing information about the author, version, and copyright of the applet.

The implementation of this method provided by the Applet class returns null.

RETURNS:

a string containing information about the author, version and copyright of the applet.

getAudioClip   §4.1.5

    `public AudioClip getAudioClip(URL url):`

      Returns the `AudioClip` object (**II-§4.4**) specified by the URL argument.

      This method always returns immediately, whether or not the audio clip exists. When this applet attempts to play the audio clip, the data will be loaded.

      PARAMETERS:

      `url`: an absolute URL giving the location of the audio clip.

      RETURNS:

      the audio clip at the specified URL.

getAudioClip   §4.1.6

    `public AudioClip getAudioClip(URL url, String name)`

      Returns the `AudioClip` object (**II-§4.4**) specified by the URL and name arguments.

      This method always returns immediately, whether or not the audio clip exists. When this applet attempts to play the audio clip, the data will be loaded.

      PARAMETERS:

      `url`: an absolute URL giving the base location of the audio clip.
      `name`: the location of the audio clip, relative to the `url` argument.

      RETURNS:

      the audio clip at the specified URL.

getCodeBase   §4.1.7

    `public URL getCodeBase()`

      RETURNS:

      the URL (**I-§4.8**) of this applet.

      SEE ALSO:

      `getDocumentBase` (**II-§4.1.8**).

getDocumentBase   §4.1.8

    `public URL getDocumentBase()`

      RETURNS:

      the URL (**I-§4.8**) of the document that contains this applet.

      SEE ALSO:

      `getCodeBase` (**II-§4.1.7**).

getImage §4.1.9

```
public Image getImage(URL url)
```

Returns an Image object (**II-§1.24**) that can then be painted on the screen. The url that is passed as an argument must specify an absolute URL.

This method always returns immediately, whether or not the image exists. When this applet attempts to draw the image on the screen, the data will be loaded. The graphics primitives that draw the image will incrementally paint on the screen.

PARAMETERS:

url: an absolute URL giving the location of the image.

RETURNS:

the image at the specified URL.

getImage §4.1.10

```
public Image getImage(URL url, String name)
```

Returns an Image object (**II-§1.24**) that can then be painted on the screen. The url argument must specify an absolute URL. The name argument is a specifier that is relative to the url argument.

This method always returns immediately, whether or not the image exists. When this applet attempts to draw the image on the screen, the data will be loaded. The graphics primitives that draw the image will incrementally paint on the screen.

PARAMETERS:

url: an absolute URL giving the base location of the image.
name: the location of the image, relative to the url argument.

RETURNS:

the image at the specified URL.

getParameter   §4.1.11

```
public String getParameter(String name)
```

Returns the value of the named parameter in the HTML tag. For example, if this applet is specified as

```
<applet code="Clock" width=50 height=50>
<param name=Color value="blue">
</applet>
```

then a call to getParameter("Color") returns the value "blue".
The name argument is case insensitive.

PARAMETERS:

name: a parameter name.

RETURNS:

the value of the named parameter.

getParameterInfo   §4.1.12

```
public String[][] getParameterInfo()
```

Returns information about the parameters than are understood by this applet. An applet should override this method to return an array of Strings describing these parameters.

Each element of the array should be a set of three Strings containing the name, the type, and a description. For example:

```
String pinfo[][] = {
   {"fps",    "1-10",    "frames per second"},
   {"repeat", "boolean", "repeat image loop"},
   {"imgs",   "url",     "images directory"}
};
```

The implementation of this method provided by the Applet class returns null.

RETURNS:

An array describing the parameters this applet looks for.

init §4.1.13

```
public void init()
```

This method is called by the browser or applet viewer to inform this applet that it has been loaded into the system. It is always called before the first time that the start method (**II-§4.1.21**) is called.

A subclass of Applet should override this method if it has initialization to perform. For example, an applet with threads would use the init method to create the threads and the destroy (**II-§4.1.2**) method to kill them.

The implementation of this method provided by the Applet class does nothing.

SEE ALSO:

stop (**II-§4.1.22**).

isActive §4.1.14

```
public boolean isActive()
```

Determines if this applet is active. An applet is marked active just before its start method (**II-§4.1.21**) is called. It becomes inactive immediately after its stop (**II-§4.1.22**) method is called.

RETURNS:

true if the applet is active; false otherwise.

SEE ALSO:

start (**II-§4.1.21**).

play §4.1.15

```
public void play(URL url)
```

Plays the audio clip at the specified absolute URL. Nothing happens if the audio clip cannot be found.

PARAMETERS:

url: an absolute URL giving the location of the audio clip.

play §4.1.16

```
public void play(URL url, String name)
```

Plays the audio clip given the URL and a specifier that is relative to it. Nothing happens if the audio clip cannot be found.

PARAMETERS:

url: an absolute URL giving the base location of the audio clip.
name: the location of the audio clip, relative to the url argument.

resize   **§4.1.17**

```
public void resize(Dimension d)
```
Requests that this applet be resized.

PARAMETERS:

d: An object giving the new width and height.

OVERRIDES:

resize in class Component (**II-§1.10.65**).

resize   **§4.1.18**

```
public void resize(int width, int height)
```
Requests that this applet be resized.

PARAMETERS:

width: the new requested width for the applet.
height: the new requested height for the applet.

OVERRIDES:

resize in class Component (**II-§1.10.66**).

setStub   **§4.1.19**

```
public final void setStub(AppletStub stub)
```
Sets this applet's stub. This is done automatically by the system.

PARAMETERS:

stub: the new stub.

showStatus   **§4.1.20**

```
public void showStatus(String msg)
```
Requests that the argument string be displayed in the "status window." Many browsers and applet viewers provide such a window, where the application can inform users of its current state.

PARAMETERS:

msg: a string to display in the status window.

start §4.1.21

```
public void start()
```

This method is called by the browser or applet viewer to inform this applet that it should start its execution. It is called after the `init` method and each time the applet is revisited in a Web page.

A subclass of `Applet` should override this method if it has any operation that it wants to perform each time the Web page containing it is visited. For example, an applet with animation might want to use the `start` method to resume animation, and the `stop` method (**II-§4.1.22**) to suspend the animation.

The implementation of this method provided by the `Applet` class does nothing.

SEE ALSO:

`init` (**II-§4.1.13**).

`destroy` (**II-§4.1.2**).

stop §4.1.22

```
public void stop()
```

This method is called by the browser or applet viewer to inform this applet that it should stop its execution. It is called when the Web page that contains this applet has been replaced by another page, and also just before the applet is to be destroyed.

A subclass of `Applet` should override this method if it has any operation that it wants to perform each time the Web page containing it is no longer visible. For example, an applet with animation might want to use the `start` (**II-§4.1.21**) method to resume animation, and the `stop` method to suspend the animation.

The implementation of this method provided by the `Applet` class does nothing.

SEE ALSO:

`init` (**II-§4.1.13**).

`destroy` (**II-§4.1.2**).

4.2 Interface AppletContext

```
public interface java.applet.AppletContext
{
    // Methods
    public abstract Applet getApplet(String name);          §4.2.1
    public abstract Enumeration getApplets();                §4.2.2
    public abstract AudioClip getAudioClip(URL url);        §4.2.3
    public abstract Image getImage(URL url);                §4.2.4
    public abstract void showDocument(URL url);             §4.2.5
    public abstract void                                    §4.2.6
        showDocument(URL url, String target);
    public abstract void showStatus(String status);        §4.2.7
}
```

This interface corresponds to an applet's environment: the document containing the applet and the other applets in the same document.

The methods in this interface can be used by an applet to obtain information about its environment.

Methods

getApplet   §4.2.1

```
public abstract Applet getApplet(String name)
```

Finds and returns the applet in the document represented by this applet context with the given name. The name can be set in the HTML tag by setting the name attribute.

PARAMETERS:

name: an applet name.

RETURNS:

the applet with the given name, or null if not found.

getApplets   §4.2.2

```
public abstract Enumeration getApplets()
```

Finds all the applets in the document represented by this applet context.

RETURNS:

an enumeration of all applets in the document represented by this applet context.

getAudioClip §4.2.3

```
public abstract AudioClip getAudioClip(URL url)
```

Creates an audio clip.

PARAMETERS:

url: an absolute URL giving the location of the audio clip.

RETURNS:

the audio clip at the specified URL.

getImage §4.2.4

```
public abstract Image getImage(URL url)
```

Returns an Image object (**II-§1.24**) that can then be painted on the screen. The url argument that is passed as an argument must specify an absolute URL.

This method always returns immediately, whether or not the image exists. When the applet attempts to draw the image on the screen, the data will be loaded. The graphics primitives that draw the image will incrementally paint on the screen.

PARAMETERS:

url: an absolute URL giving the location of the image.

RETURNS:

the image at the specified URL.

showDocument §4.2.5

```
public abstract void showDocument(URL url)
```

Replaces the Web page currently being viewed with the given URL. This method may be ignored by applet contexts that are not browsers.

PARAMETERS:

url: an absolute URL giving the location of the document.

showDocument §4.2.6

```
public abstract void showDocument(URL url, String target)
```

Requests that the browser or applet viewer show the Web page indicated by the url argument. The target argument indicates where to display the frame. The target argument is interpreted as follows:

"_self"	show in the current frame
"_parent"	show in the parent frame
"_top"	show in the topmost frame
"_blank"	show in a new unnamed top-level window
name	show in a new top-level window named *name*

An applet viewer or browser is free to ignore showDocument.

PARAMETERS:

url: an absolute URL giving the location of the document.
target: a String indicating where to display the page.

showStatus §4.2.7

```
public abstract void showStatus(String status)
```

Requests that the argument string be displayed in the "status window." Many browsers and applet viewers provide such a window, where the application can inform users of its current state.

PARAMETERS:

status: a string to display in the status window.

4.3 Interface AppletStub

```
public interface java.applet.AppletStub
{
    // Methods
    public abstract void appletResize(int width,          §4.3.1
                                      int height);
    public abstract AppletContext getAppletContext();     §4.3.2
    public abstract URL getCodeBase();                    §4.3.3
    public abstract URL getDocumentBase();                §4.3.4
    public abstract String getParameter(String name);     §4.3.5
    public abstract boolean isActive();                   §4.3.6
}
```

When an applet is first created, an applet stub is attached to it using the applet's setStub method (**II-§4.1.19**). This stub serves as the interface between the applet and the browser environment or applet viewer environment in which the application is running.

Methods

appletResize   §4.3.1

    public abstract void appletResize(int width, int height)

Called when the applet wants to be resized.

PARAMETERS:

width: the new requested width for the applet.
height: the new requested height for the applet.

getAppletContext   §4.3.2

    public abstract AppletContext getAppletContext()

RETURNS:

the applet's context.

getCodeBase   §4.3.3

    public abstract URL getCodeBase()

RETURNS:

the URL of the applet.

getDocumentBase   §4.3.4

    public abstract URL getDocumentBase()

RETURNS:

the URL of the document containing the applet.

getParameter   §4.3.5

    public abstract String getParameter(String name)

Returns the value of the named parameter in the HTML tag. For example, if an applet is specified as

```
<applet code="Clock" width=50 height=50>
<param name=Color value="blue">
</applet>
```

then a call to getParameter("Color") returns the value "blue".

PARAMETERS:

name: a parameter name.

RETURNS:

the value of the named parameter.

isActive   §4.3.6

```
public abstract boolean isActive()
```

Determines if the applet is active. An applet is active just before its start method (II-§4.1.21) is called. It becomes inactive immediately after its stop method (II-§4.1.22) is called.

RETURNS:

true if the applet is active; false otherwise.

4.4 Interface AudioClip

```
public interface java.applet.AudioClip
{
    // Methods
    public abstract void loop();                              §4.4.1
    public abstract void play();                              §4.4.2
    public abstract void stop();                              §4.4.3
}
```

The AudioClip interface is a simple abstraction for playing a sound clip. Multiple AudioClip items can be playing at the same time, and the resulting sound is mixed together to produce a composite.

Methods

loop   §4.4.1

```
public abstract void loop()
```

Starts playing this audio clip in a loop.

play   §4.4.2

> `public abstract void play()`
>
> Starts playing this audio clip. Each time this method is called, the clip is restarted from the beginning.

stop   §4.4.3

> `public abstract void stop()`
>
> Stops playing this audio clip.

Index